MOTHERING AT THE MARGINS

Claire Malcolm and Melissa Green

MOTHERING AT THE MARGINS

Black Mothers Raising Autistic Children in the UK

Foreword by

Jason Arday

Gender Studies

Collection Editors

Jan Etienne & Reham ElMorally

LPP

First published in 2025 by Lived Places Publishing

British Library Cataloguing in Publication Data
A CIP record for this book is available from the British Library.

ISBN: 9781916985001 (pbk)
ISBN: 9781916985025 (ePDF)
ISBN: 9781916985018 (ePUB)

Cover design by Fiachra McCarthy
Book design by Rachel Trolove of Twin Trail Design
Typeset by Newgen Publishing, UK

Lived Places Publishing
P.O. Box 1845
47 Echo Avenue
Miller Place, NY 11764

www.livedplacespublishing.com

Abstract

Mothering at the Margins combines collective autoethnography with rigorous participant research, creating an authentic, deeply moving narrative grounded in both lived experience and scholarly inquiry. In so doing, it amplifies the voices of an overlooked community: Black mothers raising autistic children in the UK. This project surfaces common experiences of women whose lives sit at the complex intersection of race, gender, and disability – termed by the authors as the 'triad of oppression'. These experiences include those of both co-authors, 26 survey respondents, and 9 participants. Through semi-structured interviews and focus groups, the authors empowered participants to share their journeys in accessing support for, and advocating on behalf of, their autistic children. Research findings revealed patterns of marginalisation and oppression, which the authors distilled into the 'multiplicity of burdens' model. The research highlights the challenges Black mothers of autistic children face, including underdiagnosis, referral bias, deficit-based assumptions of neglect and parental blame, and the impact of systemic racism and discrimination. It informs ongoing debates concerning the importance of cultural competence and anti-racism in autism research and the need for greater equity in access to crucial frontline services for racially minoritised individuals and communities. The book posits changes to both policy and practice in the fields of healthcare, education and social care. Since the researchers are themselves Black mothers of autistic children, this project is uniquely placed to address the paucity of studies that centre the lived experiences of this demographic. As a consequence, *Mothering at the Margins* respects and enhances the agency of those whom it seeks to support and offers a pioneering framework for the development of specific recommendations that will engender meaningful societal change.

Key words

Blackness, Motherhood, Autism, Neurodiversity, Intersectionality, Marginalisation, Critical Race Theory, Education, Health and Social Care, Policy and Practice

Acknowledgements

Claire

Deepest thanks go from the bottom of my heart straight to the following precious souls:

My husband, Leigh, for being my best friend and my partner in all things. Thank you for giving me a new reason to choose you every day for the last 20 years, and for being a fantastic dad to our babies.

My parents, my brother, my sister-in-law, and my 'first babies' (my wonderful nephews).

My found family (Catherine, the SWGS and Senghennydd Ladies, and Sarah).

So many kind and supportive colleagues at The Open University.

Mel, who came into my life late and instantly made sense of it, in ways I could never have anticipated and for which I'll always be grateful.

And, of course, to my children, with whom the sun rises and sets. This book exists in service of my boundless love for you. I may have brought you into the world, but it's you who gave me life. Thank you beyond words for the privilege of being your Mama.

Finally, to our research participants – our fellow 'mothers at the margins' – whose voices, generosity and trust made this project possible. We owe you everything.

Mel

My deepest gratitude is held for Jan Etienne, one of our collection's editors, for keeping me in mind for writing this book after our meeting years ago. Thank you, Jan, for reaching out and believing I could do this topic justice.

Thank you, Claire, for sharing the load and writing this book with me.

To my husband – your role as my rock has helped me become the mother I am today. There is no one I would rather live my life with. Thank you for being the best father to our children.

To my OU mentors, Mimi and Alison, and my sisters from other misters, Suddie and Ann, thank you for your support and unwavering belief in my abilities.

To my beautiful children, thank you for being the source of endless joy and learning, and for teaching me who I am and who I can be. Being your Mummy is an honour and blessing that I hope to always do justice to.

And my final thanks to the 'othered' mothers in this book. I was humbled by you sharing your stories with us and helping us to shine a much-needed light on the experiences of Black mothers raising autistic children.

Claire and Mel

Heartfelt thanks go to Sonah (Black Mothers Matter) and to Michelle and Reyss (Global Child and Maternal Health) for your time and for your wisdom.

Foreword

In the quiet corners of society, where voices too often go unheard, this book—*Mothering at the Margins: Black Mothers Raising Autistic Children in the UK*—amplifies the lived realities of Black women whose daily labour, love, and resistance defy both systemic neglect and social invisibility. These are the stories of Black mothers navigating the intersecting terrains of race, disability, gender, and class in a society that has historically overlooked or misunderstood their unique plight. Their experiences are not just personal; they are political. And this work rightly insists we listen.

Autism in the UK is most frequently represented through a singular often white, middle-class lens—a narrative that flattens the complexity of neurodivergence whilst erasing the unique challenges faced by those on the periphery of mainstream visibility. For Black mothers, parenting an autistic child involves far more than access to care or securing a diagnosis. It demands constant advocacy in schools, battles with healthcare systems, and the emotional toll of combating societal assumptions that either criminalize their children or dismiss their mothering as inadequate. Their love, patience, and strategic resilience are acts of radical care in a world that too often denies their full humanity.

This book does not offer easy answers or heroic tropes. Instead, it provides space for nuance, for contradiction, for truth. The exceptional mothers here speak in their own voices, revealing the complexity of their parenting journeys—at times marked by joy, cultural pride, and deep connections, and at other times shaped by exhaustion, bureaucratic obstacles, and racialized disbelief. The intersections of their identities mean they are forced to mother both visibly and invisibly—pushed into hypervigilance while simultaneously being rendered unseen by the very institutions designed to support them.

What is profoundly powerful about *Mothering at the Margins* is that it disrupts the narrative that Black motherhood is singular or monolithic. It resists both deficit-based portrayals and simplistic celebrations. Instead, it invites us to witness mothering as a dynamic, context-bound, and deeply social practice—one that is deeply impacted by structural inequalities yet always striving for dignity and justice.

This work is also a call to action. For policymakers, educators, health professionals, and scholars, it challenges us to reconsider what inclusive support truly means. It urges us to centre Black voices in conversations about neurodiversity and care. And most importantly, it reminds us that knowledge does not only reside in institutions—it lives in the hearts, kitchens, waiting rooms, and WhatsApp chats of Black mothers who have always known how to navigate the margins.

In reading this book, we are offered not just insight, but responsibility. To honour these stories is to commit to transformation. To read closely is to begin listening differently. And to understand these mothers' struggles and triumphs is to glimpse the future of a more just, more caring society. Society at large is eternally indebted to the strength, brilliance, fortitude and advocacy of Claire and Mel. Thank you for this most empowering treatise.

Jason Arday, Professor of Sociology of Education, University of Cambridge, UK

I dream of never being called 'resilient' again in my life. I'm exhausted by strength. I want support. I want softness. I want ease. I want to be amongst kin. Not patted on the back for how well I take a hit. Or for how many…

– US writer and director, Zandashé Brown (2021)

Contents

Figures

Learning objectives

1. To **demonstrate** how Intersectionality, Critical Race Theory and Critical Disability Studies illuminate and centre the experiences of marginalised communities.

2. To **amplify** the voices of Black women whose experiences of motherhood sit at the intersection of gender, race, and disability.

3. To **encourage** students to interrogate their own biases in light of these counter-narratives and consider the implications for their professional practice.

4. To **evaluate** how the lived experiences of Black mothers of autistic children inform calls for meaningful reform in education, healthcare, and social care systems.

5. To **provide** students with critical tools to analyse and propose improvements to policies and practices affecting Black mothers and autistic children.

Introduction

Our story

Meet Claire

"My name's Claire", I began, before racing through my various roles and credentials to a Teams Meeting full of strangers. This was something I was so accustomed to having to do that it almost felt like muscle memory but, today, I decided that I wanted to include one additional detail.

"At the moment, I'm working part-time because I have complex caring responsibilities".

"Should I stop there?", I wondered to myself, in the pregnant pause that followed. Do I really want to give these people – whom I'm meeting for the first time – a glimpse into the delicate balancing act that almost caused me to be late for this meeting? Do they need to know that, just off-camera, bruises are starting to appear on my forearms from the meltdown my daughter had, only minutes earlier, before she left for school? Can they tell that my eyes are pricking with tears and my forced smile is making my face hurt?

Maybe it was something about the almost unprecedented feeling of being in an online space that was exclusively occupied by fellow Black women academics. Maybe it was the sight of the welts and scratches, and the intrusive thoughts about the little girl who had given them to me. Maybe it was the guilt of not being able to abandon my professional responsibilities and keep her at home with me where, between us, we could have found ways to manage her anxiety and give her the reassurance she desperately needed. Maybe it was just the exhaustion of masking and the unwillingness to force myself to do so for a moment longer.

"My daughter is autistic", I added, as nonchalantly as the morning's traumas would allow.

There was no real response. Why would there be? My circumstances at home had no bearing on these women and their pursuit of career development – and neither should they. But, nonetheless, I was pleased to have heard myself say it. Glad that I had named my experience as a Black woman raising a disabled child, while trying to progress in a competitive and unforgiving sector. Proud of myself for shaking off my perception that giving an honest appraisal of the challenges I was facing amounted to making excuses for myself and failing in my duty to live up to the 'Strong Black Woman' trope that usually prevented me from speaking out.

Then, in the bottom left-hand corner of the screen, another woman began to introduce herself to the group. "I'm Mel", she said, before detailing her own thoroughly impressive laundry list of academic achievements. "And it's funny you should say that Claire, because I also have an autistic child".

Within a few short minutes, and by way of coincidence, we found ourselves in a breakout room for a brief 'icebreaker'. By the end of that five-minute session, I had found in Mel a fellow 'othered mother' – a friend and collaborator who instinctively understood what it was to mother at the margins and who, like me wanted to give voice to that experience on behalf of those who could not.

Meet Mel

I couldn't contain my excitement. It's always a boon when you meet another mother – perhaps their kids are the same age as yours, or they live in the same area and are up for regular playdates or they just give off the same parenting-style vibes. Whatever the advantage, I had no expectations of ever meeting a colleague, who was Black, a mother and a fellow mother of an autistic child. For me, this was the equivalent of finding a unicorn. She was funny too. I'd hit the jackpot! I had no shame and asked Claire for her number in the same MS Teams meeting in which we had met.

It didn't seem too strange a thing to do as I was conducting a research project at the time, and I knew she would make a perfect candidate for it – so I asked if I could give her a call to discuss what the study entailed. I was comforted immediately as I heard her daughter's echolalic scripting in the background; my own son was also making high-pitched vocalisations as I attempted to introduce myself properly.

The conversation swiftly progressed to us talking about our everyday lives and our children. I distinctly remember pacing my bedroom, nodding furiously as Claire described her daughter, the process of gaining a diagnosis for her, and the challenges of finding and registering in an appropriate specialist school. The similarities were so uncanny, I was thrown by them. "This woman is living my life", I thought.

I soon found myself telling her about incidents I hadn't told my own family. I confessed my vulnerability in ways I hadn't ever expected to with a work colleague. It was both liberating and scary. Throughout the rest of 2023, Claire and I advanced from colleagues who had worked in the same university for six years without being aware of each other's existence to friends who sent multiple daily voice notes to each other on WhatsApp.

By the end of the year, we had completed several internal and external research projects together despite only having met face-to-face a total of twice. On 21st November, during Claire's annual Christmas family trip to London, our families met. I felt giddy waiting, standing by my front window looking out for their car. Once we had greeted each other like old friends reunited after years apart, our two autistic children, Sam and Mae, took each other into the garden and swung on swings next to each other, giving each other eye contact and smiles, while their little brothers gleefully tore open their early Christmas presents.

The highlight of the evening had to be watching Sam and Mae on the video monitor in my son's room, snuggled up next to each other on his bed like they had known each other from birth rather than a couple of hours. They didn't know that their mothers were sitting close to each other on the sofa downstairs, sobbing as they watched them.

It is our babies who have inspired us to translate this personal and professional partnership into a book which can offer support for women whose circumstances reflect our own.

Our goals

This book is for Black women and our children. This is not part of the acknowledgements page but is an acknowledgement of the significance of the writing you are about to read. This book is the work of two Black mothers joined together by our careers in academia, bound by our shared motherhood experience – a relationship solidified by the writing of this book.

We contend that a Black woman's experience of mothering is always political. The experiences of Black women, particularly in motherhood, have been and continue to be shaped by a history of slavery, colonialism, and racial oppression. Black women have never been able to own their bodies without the gaze of the policy-making and legal communities undermining their agency (Collins et al., 2021).

In a contemporary context, Black mothers who have autistic children have no choice but to navigate myriad obstacles surrounding disability such as accessing funding, securing support, and managing multiple forms of bureaucracy. While aiming to develop the advocacy strategies needed to fight for their children's rights, these mothers are forced to negotiate barriers generated by intersecting oppressions of race, gender, and (proximity to) disability. It is the aim of this book to highlight and problematise those struggles, and the injustices that perpetuate them.

Social construction

The language we use throughout this volume requires definition and delineation precisely because the concepts under discussion are **social constructions**. By this we mean that many aspects described in this book are the lived experiences of Black women and are rooted in the multiple, intersecting identities that are imposed on us on the basis of our perceived member-ship in a socially defined group (Geronimus, 2023).

As noted by Geronimus (2023, p. 129):

> *social identity categories can correspond to society's con-structs of race, class, ethnicity, gender, religion, ancestry, language, sexual orientation, immigrant documentation status, place of residence, and other currently or historically salient nodes of racialisation and social classification.*

So it is that the experiences of Black women are not inherent or natural but instead are shaped by the society and cultures in which those women participate. All too often, they are defined *in opposition* to a perceived 'norm', based on the needs, preferences, and experiences of social groups to which Black women do not belong. From the prevalence of certain illnesses to the effects of given medications, to the aims, objectives, and parameters of support services, the experiential baseline embedded into professional training in the fields of healthcare, education, and social care is almost always derived from stories which actively exclude Black women. This is notably the case with respect to the discourse of 'motherhood', in which the experiences of Black women are often either falsely conflated with those of White women or viewed through the prism of negative stereotypes regarding Black women and their family relationships.

Thus, as one of our research participants so powerfully observed:

> *No one tells [our stories]... No one wants to hear our sto-ries... They're not ready to hear our stories. Our voices are so invisible in this space, and that bothers me so much. Because how can we change things if we don't know?*

And I want people to genuinely want to know – Survey Respondent, anonymous

Counternarrative

In conducting this research, we have been struck by the frequency with which we have been asked, in relation to our chosen participants for the study "Why not White mothers?". This inherent suspicion and hostility toward our conscious decision to amplify the voices of Black women is indicative of a broader issue which frequently derails discussions foregrounding race and racism; specifically, **'colour evasiveness'**. This term refers to behaviours and ideologies which underestimate, or even refuse to acknowledge the impact of race and racism, particularly within educational contexts. We employ it in lieu of the more commonly used term 'colour-blindness' since, as Annamma, Jackson, and Morrison (2016) demonstrate, the metaphor of 'colour-blindness' inadvertently reinforces ableist assumptions by equating visual impairment with ignorance or deficit, when blindness actually provides unique and valuable ways of understanding the world. Not only is such imprecise language at odds with our commitment to inclusion and intersectional awareness, it also obscures the extent to which 'colour evasiveness' is an active choice, rather than a passive state. Denial and obfuscation, particularly in response to attempts by those who are racially minoritised to share their lived experience of discrimination, function to silence marginalised voices and to maintain and reinforce existing power structures. In contrast, acknowledging the impact of racism and sitting in the discomfort that this acknowledgement gives rise to, facilitates empathy, growth and transformation.

As such, throughout this book, we have exposed the problematic nature of the question 'Why not White women?' (or, by implication, 'Why only Black women?') by reclaiming readings of social identity through the use of **counternarrative**, affording the stories of Black women the prominence and respect that they so richly deserve. Our goal is to make a significant contribution to the political, social and structural emancipation of Black women who are raising autistic children, by, not just liberating ourselves through our storytelling but by liberating our communities and our communities' children.

Our shared meanings

Throughout this book, we use certain turns of phrase, or embed certain perspectives into our commentary. Since virtually every facet of our identities and experiences as Black mothers of autistic children is contested, we wish to briefly explain some of those choices before sharing our journeys and the journeys of the incredible women who joined us as research participants.

Being autistic

In the first instance, in discussing our children, we elect to use 'identity-first' rather than 'person-first' language. That is to say that we describe our children as **'being autistic'**, rather than as 'having autism'. We respectfully acknowledge that there are people, both within and beyond the autistic community who may be uncomfortable with this expression. In fact, the book contains some direct quotes from research participants for whom 'person-first' language is a preference. However, we explain, at length, why in the case of our eldest children in particular, we feel that it is disingenuous and misleading to separate their autism presentations from their identities and lived experiences. Our children are, of course, more than their autism but their lives are, nonetheless, dictated in large part by their limited capacity for verbal and social communication, their extremely complex sensory challenges, and the struggles they face in navigating their immediate and wider environments. We believe that describing them as 'being autistic' illustrates this reality more accurately than any other alternative turn of phrase.

Further in our bid to use neuro-affirming language, we choose not to use terms such as ASD ('Autism Spectrum Disorder'), ASC ('Autism Spectrum Condition'), or Asperger's, which are either outmoded or which, in our view, place excessive emphasis on perceived deficits.

We use the term **neurodiversity** to describe the broader range of developmental issues which can often affect autistic people (for example, Attention Deficit Hyperactivity Disorder [ADHD] and dyslexia).

We state that we each have two children: one autistic and one **'awaiting assessment'.** We use this language to denote that, while our younger children have not yet been formally diagnosed, this is due in part to the protracted nature of the diagnostic process. The estimated waiting time for the completion of an autism assessment in the UK varies greatly but, on average, it is approximately 2–3 years and is now almost always undertaken in conjunction with education professionals. This ensures that it is rare for a diagnosis to be issued (via the NHS) before a child is already attending school on a full-time basis. At the time of writing, Claire's younger child, Joshua, is not yet old enough to be in full-time education, whereas Mel began the process of engaging staff in her son Daniel's school in 2024, just as he started Reception, in a bid to begin the assessment process. As addressed in the first substantive chapter, the specifics of Daniel's presentation, which Mel suspects is a profile of Pathological Demand Avoidance, further complicate this journey.

Furthermore, to date, our younger children present very differently from their siblings. Specifically, our eldest children have **'high support'** needs, whereas their younger brothers currently have relatively **'low support'** presentations.

The American Psychiatric Association's Diagnostic and Statistical Manual (DSM-5) offers a definition of autism relating to an individual's need for support, as identified during the diagnostic process (American Psychiatric Association, 2013). It is outlined as follows:

Level 1: Requires support
Level 2: Requires substantial support
Level 3: Requires very substantial support

However, to better articulate our children's needs and those of the participants' children, we expand and clarify these definitions. We characterise 'high support' needs as those which result in a complex autism presentation generating some or all of the following issues:

- Significantly reduced capacity for (social) communication, impacting the child's ability to express their needs, or to use spontaneous or purposive language that could be easily recognised by a third party.
- Significant impact on learning, resulting in the need for specialist educational provision.

- Significant behavioural challenges (e.g. frequent meltdowns which cause physical harm to the child and/or their caregivers and peers; lack of awareness of danger necessitating constant supervision, etc.)
- Significantly reduced capacity for self-care (e.g. difficulties with toileting, etc.) which renders the prospect of the child living independently in adulthood, extremely unlikely.

We characterise 'low support' needs as those which may require life-long support and intervention, but which can potentially be met, or at least mitigated, by changes to the individual's environment. This is not intended to underestimate the impact of a low support presentation, but rather to illustrate the breadth of diagnoses to which the word 'autism' can refer.

Our definition of 'low support' applies to presentations in which a child has some, or all, of the following:

- (Relatively) effective expressive, receptive, and mixed language abilities.
- A degree of awareness of, and ability to express and understand, their own identity as an autistic person.
- The capacity to access (and, with appropriate support, to function and flourish in) a mainstream educational environment.
- An awareness of danger and a capacity for self-care, underscoring the potential ability to live independently in adulthood.

While we acknowledge that such a gradation is crude at best, our decision to make use of these descriptive categories (in lieu of outdated or inappropriate expressions such as 'high' or 'low functioning') has been a source of extensive reflection in writing this book. As will be demonstrated in Chapters 3 and

4, several of the women who have shared their experiences with us are raising children who, according to the metrics we deploy above, would be considered to have 'low support' presentations but, as we will go on to demonstrate, this does not diminish the challenges faced by those children, or by their caregivers.

Models of disability

The use of such gradations also relates to our discussions on the differences between, and respective strengths and limitations of, the medical and social models of disability. The **medical model** is often deficit-focused, defining autism in line with perceptions of what an autistic person *cannot* do and, by implication, positioning 'autistic traits' as a 'failed' or 'deviant' version of a non-disabled 'norm'. In contrast, the **social model** emphasises 'disability' as a social construction. In other words, as an identity category which is the product of mutually agreed upon meanings which are subject to interpretation and change, and which – crucially – should not be dismissed as a 'lesser' version of a non-disabled identity. Disabled people are acknowledged as individuals with a range of capacities, characteristics, aspirations, and experiences that are valid in their own right.

Furthermore, on this interpretation, it is often societal structures that are 'disabling'. To take a simple example, a wheelchair user accessing a public space need not be 'impaired' by their ambulatory disability, provided that the environment has been adapted to guarantee ease of access, by means of ramps, automatic doors, lowered pavements, and other similar adaptations.

It is the failure to put such adjustments in place that needlessly transforms an otherwise neutral difference into a disabling inequality.

Little wonder then, that many members of, and advocates for, the autistic community roundly reject the medical model in favour of the social model, arguing that the 'impairments' that result from autism are the consequence of a lack of awareness and acceptance of autistic traits and experiences, rather than being the by-product of autism itself.

We will illustrate, however, why we subscribe to neither extreme, believing that neither accurately captures the reality of living with autism, particularly in the context of a high support presentation. Instead, we will define our relationship with our children's autism as one which foregrounds **normalisation** and adaptation, reframing the environment to support their needs where possible, while also striving to avail them of whatever tools we can to enable them to develop and improve their 'life skills'.

This focus on normalisation also informs the terms in which we describe our children's learning differences. While we acknowledge that our children are categorised within the UK's Special Educational Needs and Disability (SEND) framework, we consciously choose not to adopt the term 'Special Educational Needs, or SEN. This terminology, though well-intentioned and legally enshrined, carries implicit assumptions that position our children's learning differences as deficits requiring correction rather than natural variations in human cognition that merit accommodation and celebration. The framing of 'special needs' inadvertently perpetuates a medical model perspective that views autism through a lens of inadequacy, suggesting that our children require something beyond the 'normal' provision of education. In contrast, we prefer language that recognises our children's educational requirements as legitimate and necessary accommodations within an inclusive system, rather than exceptional provisions for those deemed to have 'special' requirements. We believe this approach better reflects our understanding of autism as neurological difference rather than deficit and avoids the subtle othering that occurs when children are consistently described as having needs that are inherently 'special' or separate from those of their peers. Our preference for more neuro-affirming language aligns with our broader commitment to challenging deficit-based narratives while advocating for educational environments that truly embrace neurodiversity.

The reason that we have chosen to place such emphasis on the terminology we deploy relates to our belief that the language in which autism is framed has a significant influence over how autistic people are perceived and treated. In embracing an understanding of both the power, and the stigma, associated with social labelling, we have also reflected carefully on the language used to describe ourselves and our research participants.

Othered vs other-mothers

Throughout the book, we refer to ourselves as **'othered mothers'.** This concept builds on, but is distinct from, the work of Patricia Hill Collins and her definition of 'othermothering' (2022), which defines 'motherwork' as a community-wide endeavour rooted in the virtues of caring, ethics, teaching and community service. Collins positions 'othermothers' – usually sisters, aunts, grandmothers, or even neighbours – as central pillars within the Black community, supporting those women who are raising children of their own, and epitomising selflessness and dedication by contributing extensively, and often beyond their means, to the welfare of the community. She explains that these women provide a specific form of nurturing which she refers to as 'mothering the mind' (2022) and she speaks of the potential for this to create a sense of shared sisterhood and solidarity, which in turn provides the foundations for activism and the pursuit of social justice.

We reconceptualise this notion to argue that Black mothers of autistic children experience a form of marginalised motherhood which is unique to them and are, therefore, able to provide one another with a form of community support that cannot be replicated in other spaces. Unlike Collins' othermothers, 'othered mothers' are those whose experiences of motherhood are shaped by their intersectional oppressions that push them to the margins of dominant motherhood narratives, even within Black communities. In bringing together these mothers, we sought to create a **'community of resistance'** among those whose motherhood stories had been rendered invisible, enabling them to share their experiences both with us, and with one another. It was our hope that these 'othered mothers' would find solace, catharsis, and inspiration in one another, and that their combined insight and expertise would inform recommendations for change in policy and practice.

The term 'othered mothers' captures the extent to which women like us are excluded from dominant motherhood discourses. This exclusion and othering occur not only in wider society but sometimes even within other marginalised communities, making this definition a product of the social identity that has been imposed upon us, rather than a matter of choice.

Being an 'othered mother' also precludes acts of meaningful **self-care**, such as rest, recuperation, and opportunities to withdraw and recover from a relentless roster of emotionally triggering, and physically demanding tasks. This is why, as we will illustrate throughout the book, our experience of 'mothering' is often both too broad and too narrow to be seen, or understood, by the **culturally incompetent** services upon which we are forced to rely.

This uncomfortable balance between invisibility and hyper-visibility contributes to what we have termed the **'triad of oppression'** facing Black women raising autistic children. We will illustrate how the combination of racism, misogyny, and ableism that women in this position have to negotiate in order to meet their children's needs, often at the expense of their own, echoes through encounters in both the public and private spheres, underpinning what we refer to as the **'multiplicity of burdens'** to which 'othered mothers' are constantly subjected.

Our frequent use of the term 'burden' is one which we wish to foreground and contextualise immediately, since it is such a value-laden expression which could easily be misinterpreted.

In what follows, we draw on Black Feminist discourse to define 'burden' in light of the complex relationship between **productive** and **reproductive labour**. While it has been well established that women, in general, face a 'double-burden' of undertaking both paid work outside the home, and domestic labour within it, and that Black women's caring responsibilities tend to be proportionally higher, even than those of White women (Fyre, 2020; Adkins, 2022; TUC, 2023), we argue that there is a sense in which the labour entailed in raising racially minoritised disabled children is characterised by society as being *lesser* still. Hence, Black mothers of autistic children face the 'burdens' associated with what is all too often perceived to be the **'unproductive labour'** of raising children whose societal value is marked as minimal, owing both to their race and to their inability (real or perceived) to contribute to capitalist society. In other words, othered mothers are judged by their children's limited capacity to function within the neoliberal economic model of individualism, self-sufficiency, and privatisation.

For over 50 years, neoliberalism has been the dominant socio-political ideology in British society, and the prevailing consensus within global economic institutions. This, despite the fact that, as we have argued elsewhere:

> *[m]any of the neoliberal assumptions regarding the nature of meritocracy, and the capacity of competition and privatisation to improve standards and services, are intrinsically*

problematic and demonstrably false. (Green and Malcolm, 2023, p. 2)

Furthermore, neoliberalism is also deeply implicated in multiple overlapping forms of oppression because, as Hamilton (2020, p. 25) states:

With its emphasis on individual choice and freedom, neoliberalism rejects the notion that social class, race, and gender present structural constraints that limit life chances. […] Race is recast in terms of 'cultural difference' rather than as a structural and political obstacle to racial-ised people's ability to meet the standards of neoliberal citizenship.

The additional dimension of disability further consolidates these constraints. Therefore, while our children themselves are by no means a burden and having them in our lives is a source of boundless joy, the structural and political disadvantage gen-erated by their, and our, intersectional identities creates insur-mountable barriers to their participation in a society constructed to reflect neoliberal ideals.

As Dillon (2012) states:

Recognition of interlocking forms of oppression and articu-lation of the precise and complex ways in which the inter-relationships between race, gender, and social class among others shape policy and lived experience, is a crucial aspect of understanding and undermining the effects of neoliberal projects.

Therefore, in sharing our stories and those of the women who took this journey with us, we do not shy away from providing honest and unflinching accounts of the realities of our day-to-day lives and the ways in which the challenges we face are exacerbated by a lack of effective services and support. We do so from a perspective which is both personal and political, and which is explicitly concerned with dismantling the institutional racism underpinning those experiences.

To ensure that such experiences are conveyed with the greatest possible degree of authenticity, we based the initial phase of our research in **collective autoethnography**, a methodology in which two or more researchers co-construct narratives by sharing their stories with one another and situating them within broader socio-cultural trends, debates, and calls for change. To this end, our own experiences are detailed throughout the book in the form of collective autoethnographic **vignettes**, which are used to illuminate key concepts such as 'blackness' and 'motherhood', and to exemplify the individual components of the multiplicity of burdens. These vignettes are interspersed among the accounts provided by our research participants.

Thus our work is consciously presented in a manner which differs from the (already minimal) literature and training resources, pertaining to Blackness and disability in the fields of health-care, education, and social care. Since we are among the first researchers to combine this intersectional focus with the theme of motherhood, we have chosen to do so by means that honour and elevate the lives of our own children, and which create a platform enabling other women like us to do the same. In this respect, we are proud to stand apart from more 'conventional' forms of research, since we believe that such arbitrary academic parameters have long functioned to silence precisely the voices that we are choosing to amplify, through our **participant research**.

A final consideration, in respect of **positionality**, is the fact that we are both cisgender, heterosexual, women who are married to the fathers of our children. Although we did not intend for the study to be explicitly heteronormative in its focus, none of our participants identified as trans, or were in same-sex relationships. Furthermore, none of the mothers who participated in our research had adopted their children. As such, we are aware that there are intersectional dimensions of the experience of Black motherhood to which our research cannot speak. While these perspectives would certainly be fruitful areas for further exploration, they are beyond the purview of our own findings, at this time.

Similarly, we elected to base our research exclusively on the stories of women who are Black, or of dual heritage (defined throughout this book as those who have parents with differing racial identities, including one parent who is Black) rather than to take into account the views and experiences of non-Black women who are raising Black children, or non-Black women raising children of dual heritage. This was a deliberate choice on our part because we felt that centring **'Blackness'**, a concept defined in further detail in the forthcoming chapters, was a crucial component of the social mission informing our research. While some participants in the study, including Claire who is of dual heritage, may have increased **'proximity to whiteness'** relative to others, they all shared a recognisably Black identity which proved to be a definitive factor in their interactions with healthcare, education, and social care professionals.

Chapter breakdown

The remainder of this book is structured as follows. In the first substantive chapter, we outline our conceptual framework, which combines elements of Black Feminist Thought, Critical Race Theory, and Critical Disability Studies, and use it as a basis for a model which encapsulates the experiences of Black mothers of autistic children.

Chapter 2 details the hybridised methodology deployed in pursuit of our research. It provides a rationale for the decision to combine collective autoethnography with quantitative and qualitative participant research and elucidates both the obstacles and opportunities generated by this approach.

Chapters 3 and 4 present the key findings of the research study and systematise them in light of the multiplicity of burdens model that we have created. They each synthesise autoethnographic vignettes with accounts drawn from our quantitative survey, participant interviews, and focus groups. In so doing, they offer an intimate and emotive account which lays bare both the joys and the challenges of raising autistic children and highlights the ways in which more effective support services could significantly improve the lives of these children and those of their primary caregivers. Chapter 3 does this through a focus on the physical and psychological burdens, and Chapter 4 foregrounds the cultural, practical and temporal burdens.

In Chapter 5, we draw out the lessons of this research to outline recommendations for policymakers and for healthcare, education, and social care professionals, suggesting ways that practice can be improved and modified in line with increased cultural competence, anti-racism, and efficacy.

Chapter 6 provides answers to our initial research questions and identifies areas for future research to further embed and extend these practices, with a view to creating optimal support services for Black mothers of autistic children and their families.

1
Black motherhood and autism: Theory and reality

What do we mean by autism?
Claire's story

The diagnostic process for Mae was frustrating and protracted. It also served as an early indicator of how gender would factor into perceptions of her autism presentation. Her development had been entirely typical until the age of approximately two and a half and, owing to a lack of family history and an extremely limited understanding of neurodiversity on our part, the possibility that changes in her behaviour, including an apparent regression in her use of language, a tendency not to respond to her own name, and signs of inattentiveness and hyperactivity, could be linked with autism, was not something we really considered, even after her Health Visitor initially flagged it.

However, out of an abundance of caution, we nonetheless began to pursue a diagnosis, first unilaterally and then later in conjunction with teaching staff in Mae's preschool setting. The waiting list was interminable, and as time passed her atypical behaviours seemed to be rapidly increasing in severity. So we arranged a private appointment with a paediatrician. He dismissed our concerns based on his (false) belief that Mae was exhibiting signs of 'imaginative play'. A second male paediatrician, whom we were eventually able to see through the NHS, affirmed his colleague's position by effectively (and erroneously) stating that autism was something that rarely, if ever, affects women and girls.

Finally, a third Paediatrician (a woman) spent five minutes in Mae's company and immediately referred her to a diagnostic panel, consisting of doctors, educators, and child psychologists. Our parental views and those of her teachers were also taken into account. The diagnosis was formally issued within the month, and we were immediately able to transfer her into specialist educational provision.

By then, she was four years old, and her long-sought diagnosis felt like a potent cocktail of devastation and vindication, bringing with it both a fresh start and an uncertain future.

Mel's story

Sam's diagnosis was a relief. I had known for some time that he was 'different'. Little things like him not looking at where I was pointing. His speech, when it came, was the repetition of phrases he had learned from CBeebies or his electronic toys, and he seemed physically uncomfortable when children took an interest in him. I began noting this when he was around 18 months old and shared my concerns with my husband and family members. However, the fact that he had age-appropriate speech, took an interest in his adult family members, and demonstrated high levels of cognitive ability for his age led them to ignore my apprehensions. What I apparently had was intuition, not fact.

He had begun crawling at five months, walking at 10 months and was reciting the whole alphabet by 16 months. My family were amazed at his intelligence and my concerns made it seem that I was not. I began to keep my concerns to myself. As a former primary school teacher who had specialised in working with autistic children, I was accused of seeing things that were not there. Yet, in those early years, I only worked a few hours a week, meaning that I spent all my time with Sam and saw what I think others did not want to.

For my husband, it took me being pregnant with our second child and a visit to a potential preschool for Sam for him to see exactly what I had been seeing at the many playgroups and parks I had attended with our son. That visit to a local Montessori school in which Sam actively avoided and became distressed by the closeness of other children who kindly offered to show him around, and which ended in one of the first sensory meltdowns he ever had, enabled my husband to join me in my conclusion that Sam was different. My husband cried at the genuine discomfort Sam had experienced from being approached by his peers who had only wanted to welcome him. He cried because the headteacher who had shown us around used the word 'autism' too.

The journey to diagnosis was long and protracted, not unrelated to the sudden presence of COVID-19 around six months into it. We were initially told it would be 18 months until we would receive our first appointment but we received letters every three months extending this by at least five more. By this time, Sam was two and a half years old. I had been told various things, like that he was too young to receive a diagnosis, or that we should wait until he was in school to start the process. As a former teacher, I knew that he would not be comfortable in a mainstream setting and that once he was in school, the assessment process would take longer. We decided to go for a private diagnosis, and for this, we borrowed money from my in-laws. We chose to go with the Lorna Wing Centre, a reputable and well-known assessment centre, due to the potential for local councils not to authorise private diagnoses. After receiving the final report and diagnosis, I felt validated that I did indeed know my child and now I could begin to support him better.

Autism is a heavily contested diagnosis in society's current health and social care landscape. According to the fifth edition of the DSM (American Psychiatric Association, 2022), Autism Spectrum Disorders (ASD) are lifelong neuropsychological conditions severely impairing social skills and autonomy. Conditions that may be familiar, such as Asperger's Disorder and Pervasive Developmental Disorder (PDD), have been abolished from the most recent DSM.

When we discuss autism in this book, we are describing a lifelong developmental disability affecting how someone communicates and interacts with other people. Within medical definitions of autism, it is expected that there is a 'triad of impairment' demonstrated in communication/language (expressive, receptive, and mixed), behavioural challenges (stereotypical motor behaviour; restrictive, repetitive), and social interaction (Ennis-Cole, 2019). This plotting of 'impairments' (ibid.) aligns well with a medical approach to viewing autism, as it defines the person as needing medical intervention. As we have already intimated, this model has been criticised for over-focusing on what the person *cannot* do instead of what they can do.

In opposition, there have been decades-long calls for the adoption of the 'social model', which would view autism as a different 'way-of-being' that results in autistic persons being unnecessarily and unfairly excluded from society because they often behave differently from the 'norm' (Anderson-Chavarria, 2021, p. 1321).

We recognise that the medical model is not without its strengths. For our children, and many other autistic people, medical labels and interventions have been lifesaving (Anderson-Chavarria, 2021). Without the medical label and diagnostic reports of Paediatricians and Psychiatrists to confirm that our children were indeed autistic, we would not have been able to enrol them in specialist schools. Further, we would not have been able to provide them with the various medical interventions that have resulted in the reduction of sensory meltdowns or the increased ability to survive in certain contexts. We often discuss how horrific it feels to describe your child in purely deficit-based terms, in order to obtain Disability Living Allowance (DLA) or educational support. Yet do it we must, to secure access to finances and resources which make our children's lives more joyful and less restricting.

However, this reliance on medical labelling and professional validation is fraught with risks for parents of autistic children, who may face heightened discrimination when seeking help for their child(ren). Ferguson and Hollingsworth (2024) conducted a study of parents, carers and/or guardians living in

England who had approached health, education, and social care services for an assessment and/or support for their autistic child and found that these parents are more likely to be misunderstood or unfairly judged by professionals unfamiliar with autistic communication styles and presentations. Eighty-six per cent of parents in this study who experienced parent blame reported that it occurred prior to their child's autism assessment and diagnosis.

Parents described experiencing blame in various ways, including:

- Professionals, such as healthcare, education, and social care providers, questioning, criticising, or making judgemental comments about their parenting.
- Professionals doubting parents' accounts of their child's behavioural symptoms or the need for an autism assessment.
- Professionals accusing parents of causing their child's behaviour.

These findings expose a critical flaw in the medical model's reliance on professional gatekeeping and deficit-focused narratives. While medical validation provides access to essential resources and interventions, it also entrenches a culture of parental scrutiny and blame, particularly for those already navigating systemic biases. As noted in the commonalities of our experiences described later in the book, parent blame is something we have both experienced and did indeed delay the diagnoses of both our children.

The challenges presented by the medical model also highlight the importance of using language that accurately reflects the lived experiences of autistic children and their families, ensuring that discussions around disability remain grounded in their realities and not diluted by misconceptions.

For instance, we are entirely comfortable with the use of the term 'disabled', rather than alternatives such as 'differently abled' which do not describe the reality of our children's lived experiences. For Joon, Kumar, and Parle (2021):

> *a developmental disability means a severe, chronic disability of an individual attributable to a mental or physical impairment alone or in combination, which begins during the developmental period and is likely to continue indefinitely resulting in substantial limitations in social, occupational, and day-to-day functioning.*

We describe our (eldest) children as disabled because we know that if they were expected to participate in mainstream schooling and follow standard trajectories of school, university, and employment, they would be, at best, hugely disadvantaged and, at worst, severely harmed. Based on their high support presentations, we do not expect our children to live independently or to be financially stable once they leave compulsory education. The term, 'disabled', allows us to acknowledge the limitations and implications of this reality.

This is also the rationale behind our use of identity-first language (i.e. autistic person) rather than person-first language (i.e. person with autism). We concur with Vivanti (2020) who claims that the universal adoption of identity-first language is premature because there is no consensus in the autistic community, and with Tepest (2021) who argues that this should be a matter of individual choice. Yet, in the same way that we do not consider ourselves as 'people with Blackness' or as 'people with mother-hood', we believe our children are partly who they are *because* of their autism not *despite* it. We acknowledge autism as being within the whole identity of our children in the same way as their other social identities. Therefore, while we do not make use of all the terminology associated with the medical model (e.g. ASD or ASC), neither do we jettison all forms of language and labelling associated with it.

That being said, we do acknowledge that the medical approach to viewing autism lacks consideration of the impact that society and environments have on our children. This means that we also seek an alternative approach to viewing autism, whereby our children are seen as 'different' but neutral in society, and in which their differences are not *automatically* assumed to be deficits (Kapp, 2019).

Kintzinger (2021) suggests a social model in which we acknowledge society's success and/or failure to accommodate autistic people as disabling or enabling (Berghs et al., 2016). This model emphasises that autism is not just a matter of individual impairment, but is also shaped by societal attitudes, structures, and barriers that can disable those with impairments. This aligns with the imperative to 'see the person, not the disability' and it has become something of a rallying cry for some members of the autistic community, particularly those with low support presentations, who find that they are able to flourish when their environment can be flexed to meet their needs.

However, this purely social constructivist approach to viewing autism does not accord with the lived experiences of our eldest children, in that it fails to reflect that significant elements of their autism presentations result from endogenous, as well as exogenous, factors. In other words, even in the face of extensive societal accommodations, our children would still have to contend with very real and tangible 'impairments' that directly result from their disability.

As Reeve (2008, p. 30) notes, the social model of disability has been criticised for its focus on "structural disabling barriers" at the expense of "experience and cultural aspects of disability" (Cooper, 2020). This critique raises an important question: how do we account for the embodied and lived experiences of disabled individuals alongside societal barriers? In contrast to the social model, the tensional model addresses this gap by emphasising the materiality of the body and the physical realities of living with a disability. As Williams (2021) argues, the tensional model prioritises the material and emotional dimensions of disabled experiences, which are inseparable from the complexities of day-to-day life. This approach provides a more holistic understanding of disabled embodiment and its interplay with broader societal contexts.

While there are many alternative models, such as the tensional model, that go beyond the medical and social approaches, the experiences of our children resonate most clearly with the work of Lennard Davis (1995), which asks us to focus our gaze on normalcy rather than disability. Within Davis's approach to viewing disability, "the 'problem' is not the person with disabilities; the problem is the way that normalcy is constructed to create the 'problem' of the disabled person" (1995, p. 24). This model also accounts for the material and lived experiences of those living with disability.

For instance, Mae is what is known as a 'Gestalt Language Processor' which, in her case, essentially means that she communicates predominantly through repetitive chunks of 'script', rather than through more purposive or spontaneous language. The meanings that she attaches to these 'gestalts' will often bear no direct connection to the words themselves, and this can make it very difficult for even her closest caregivers, to decipher what she is trying to say. Unfortunately, when Mae is not understood she will often become intensely frustrated, and this can result in prolonged episodes of screaming and acts of self-harm. An additional challenge lies in disaggregating those gestalts which *do* carry a specific meaning (albeit one which may not be immediately apparent) from those which are simply verbal 'tics' or stims from which Mae derives sensory feedback and comfort.

An intervention based purely on the medical model would take as its key priority the need to 'mitigate' her gestalts in such a way as to align her mode of speech as closely as possible with that of her neurotypical peers. There is a chance that such strategies may eventually enable her to make herself understood more effectively, but the interventions themselves are predicated on the assumption that there is something inherently 'deficient' in the way that Mae naturally communicates, and that this needs to be remedied even if doing so causes her distress, or risks denying her agency and individuality. Equally, though, the social model with its emphasis on celebrating Mae's difference, and encouraging those around her to modify their own communication style accordingly, risks underestimating the degree to which she is genuinely 'impaired' by the high anxiety levels that feed into her echolalia and potentially overlooks the practical challenges of her moving through the world without the ability to effectively express her needs and feelings.

The response in Claire's household is one which is rooted in the normalisation of Mae's speech pattern. Claire and her husband work hard to recognise when Mae needs space to repeat herself (sometimes dozens of times in a row), and they happily play their own part in mirroring or responding to 'scripts' in ways which Mae finds predictable and reassuring. Where appropriate, this is combined with gentle forms of distraction, using visuals, games, and activities that help her to refocus and ensure that repetition does not give way to forms of overstimulation which may harm her. When she is relatively emotionally regulated, Mae is given every opportunity to develop her capacity to use more spontaneous communication, since this is a crucial component of the development of her life skills, but her caregivers are always at pains to ensure that she knows there is nothing 'wrong' in her need to share her scripts and that, if anything, those close to her are appreciative of her attempts to invite them into her world.

Similarly, Sam's sensory needs are deeply embedded in his everyday routines and are fully normalised within Mel's home. Sam has a high need for vestibular and proprioceptive input, which he seeks out through spinning, jumping, climbing, and crashing. These are fundamental to his ability to regulate his emotions and remain connected to his environment. He will often be found climbing on furniture, climbing frames or bannisters. When he is not climbing, he is jumping from heights, flinging himself onto crash mats, beanbags, or spinning in circles in the middle of the room or on a spinning chair. Mel and her family do not view repetitive movements as behaviours to be managed or redirected, but as expressions of his sensory self.

Rather than pathologising these movements or seeking to eliminate them, Mel and her husband respond by curating sensory experiences that align with Sam's needs. They are lucky to have a play space that is adapted accordingly, with soft play, climbing equipment, crash mats, and open floor areas that allow for safe movement. Even though Sam is now 8, his sensory play at home mirrors the kinds of sensory tables often found in early years settings: taste-safe paint, sand trays, and jelly play to provide Sam with rich tactile and oral sensory input. When he mouths non-food items or explores textures with his hands, these actions are not discouraged but understood as part of how Sam experiences and makes sense of the world.

From a medical model perspective, Sam's needs might be interpreted as behaviours requiring a carefully controlled 'sensory diet', where scheduled interventions (such as time on a spinning seat) are prescribed throughout the day to help maintain regulation. While such strategies can be helpful, they risk reducing Sam's sensory experiences to tools of compliance, rather than recognising their expressive, joyful, and self-regulatory purposes. Through the lens of the social model, however, Sam's movement and sensory play can pose challenges in public settings, where space, noise, and others' expectations can make inclusion difficult. Mel's family has often had to avoid public spaces, activities and environments that may be either overstimulating or that cannot accommodate Sam's need to move freely without judgment or danger.

Both the medical and social models offer partial insights, but they are not enough on their own. Mel's family's approach is centred on acceptance and attunement with Sam, understanding that his sensory needs are not obstacles to be overcome, but integral to his identity. Normalising Sam's needs enables him to be seen as a whole person whose needs are valid rather than as a disruption or problem to be solved. In this space, he is not reduced to a collection of behaviours. He is, simply, Sam.

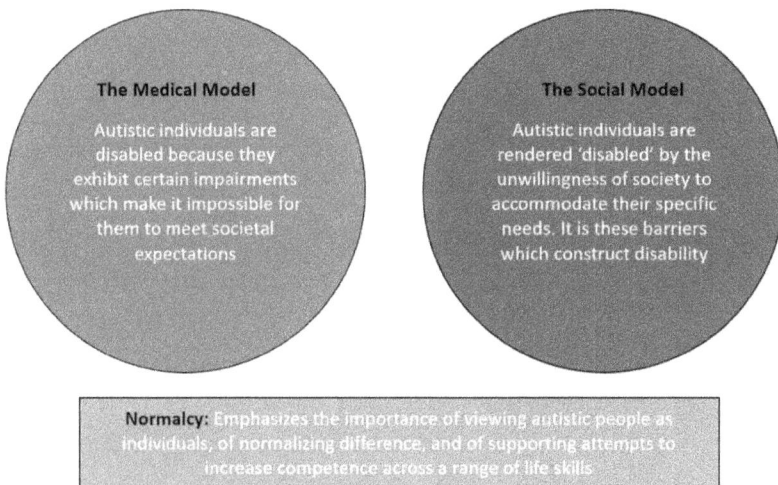

The Medical Model

Autistic individuals are disabled because they exhibit certain impairments which make it impossible for them to meet societal expectations

The Social Model

Autistic individuals are rendered 'disabled' by the unwillingness of society to accommodate their specific needs. It is these barriers which construct disability

Normalcy: Emphasizes the importance of viewing autistic people as individuals, of normalizing difference, and of supporting attempts to increase competence across a range of life skills

Figure 1: A middle ground between the medical and social models of understanding autism

As the term 'spectrum' implies, autism is highly heterogeneous, meaning that it manifests in a wide variety of forms, and affects individuals in many ways. Autism is often 'comorbid', meaning that many autistic individuals have co-occurring conditions, such as intellectual disabilities, sensory sensitivities, epilepsy, or mental health issues like anxiety and depression. For example, Claire's daughter, Mae, has a diagnosis of autism AND ADHD AND learning disabilities, while Sam has been diagnosed as autistic AND as having Sensory Processing Disorder (SPD). The presence and intensity of these comorbidities can greatly affect an individual's experience of autism, meaning no two people experience autism in exactly the same way. For us, as mothers of autistic children, it means that while our parenting experiences are much more similar to one another's than they are to those of mothers of neurotypical children, the differences are nonetheless numerous and far-ranging.

What 'counts' as autism remains a contested aspect of diagnosis, largely due to the continued framing of autism through 'cognitivist/functionalist/behaviourist' perspectives (Milton, 2018). These approaches adopt exterior rather than interior standpoints, interpreting autistic behaviour from an outsider's perspective and often attributing it to assumed 'deficits' or 'impairments' associated with autism. This framing shapes how autism is understood, diagnosed, and supported.

Mel believes her youngest son, Daniel, is autistic but recognises that his hyper-verbal, high-anxiety, high-masking, and socially 'able' presentation aligns with a profile of Pathological Demand Avoidance (PDA) and for this reason will struggle to receive a diagnosis. Coined in 1983 (Moore, 2020), PDA is described as a behaviour profile within the autism spectrum. However, a literature review by Kildahl et al., (2021), highlights significant issues with the definition and measurement of PDA, limiting conclusions about the stability of the behaviours it describes or the characteristics of individuals who exhibit them. This lack of diagnostic clarity is part of what leaves Mel sceptical that Daniel will ever receive a formal autism diagnosis, particularly as long as he performs well in school.

While the National Autistic Society recognises PDA as part of the autism spectrum, researchers like Moore (2020) argue that there is nothing inherently pathological about the behaviours classified under this label, characterising them instead as an extension of high anxiety or other behavioural issues. Similarly, debates around Sensory Processing Disorder (SPD) raise questions about whether that too should be recognised as part of an autism diagnosis or treated as an independent condition.

These ongoing uncertainties reveal the complexities and limitations of current diagnostic frameworks, which risk excluding or misinterpreting individuals whose experiences fall outside traditional categories. They also highlight a broader critique of the medical model for its prioritisation of rigid classifications and deficit-based understandings over a nuanced appreciation of individual experiences and strengths.

There is extensive variability in the traits and behaviours of autistic people. Some may have significant challenges with social communication and interactions, while others might have minimal difficulties in this area. This is often linked to why autism has historically been identified in girls and women at a substantially lower rate than in boys and men, as female autistic people are usually more likely to be able to "camouflage" their social impairments (Lai et al., 2016). Underdiagnosis in women and girls is, of course, also the product of patriarchal influences and pressures that impact behaviours and perceptions among healthcare, education, and social care professionals with the damaging myth that 'girls aren't autistic' having persisted until very recently, even in the face of mounting evidence to the contrary.

Furthermore, the developmental pathways of autistic people can also be highly variable. While people love to share with us anecdotes like "I met an autistic person who didn't speak as a child and now they're a doctor!", we became comfortable, very early into our parenting journeys, with acknowledging the fact that our children will reach different 'milestones' at different times, and sometimes not at all. For us, 'autism success stories' of this kind are something of a double-edged sword which, while ostensibly intended to inspire autistic people and their caregivers, can sometimes function to undermine and misrepresent the reality of living with a high support autism presentation, leading to feelings of failure or anxiety on the part of caregivers whose children do not go on to exceed initial developmental expectations.

In this respect, the overrepresentation of 'late bloomer' narratives can be as unhelpful as the assumption that all autistic people share common interests and hyper-fixations. Claire's daughter responds positively to swimming, while Mel's son prefers music therapy. Neither of them is interested in, for example, memorising train timetables and yet this is an assumption that we, as their parents, have both had to rebuff on their behalf, on multiple occasions. Similarly, savantism (a particular aptitude for a specific task or type of activity, such as mathematics or music) is also a relative rarity among those with an autism diagnosis, and yet the legacy of the 1988 Academy Award-winning film *Rain Man* still figures large in the public consciousness when it comes to an understanding of the 'super' abilities of autistic people.

The reality is that the autism spectrum contains richness and diversity which extends far beyond any of these monolithic conceptions, hence the adage that "If you've met one autistic person, you've met one autistic person". While it is often mistakenly perceived as something that is linear, progressing from 'not very autistic' to 'very autistic', the autism spectrum is, in fact, much more nuanced than a simplistic gradation might imply, with some individuals having 'high support needs' in certain areas, and 'low support needs' in others. In this respect, it is most effectively represented through graphics such as this:

What it actually looks like:

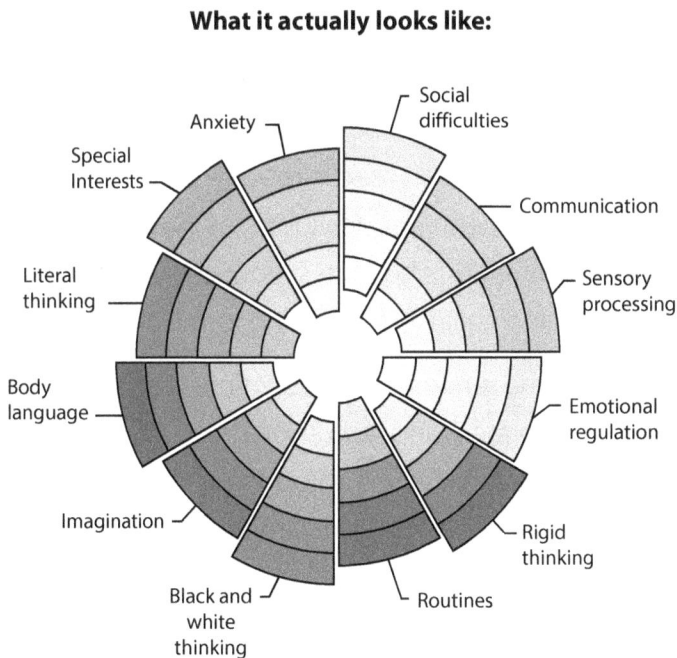

Figure 2: The linear spectrum vs. the multidimensional spectrum (Enna Global, 2022)

The heterogeneity of developmental disorders has been explored through Judy Singer's philosophies and writings, which emphasise the diversity and spectrum of neurological experiences, particularly in the context of the neurodiversity movement. Singer (1999) coined the term 'neurodiversity' in her thesis and other writing, arguing that neurological differences should be recognised and respected as a social category, similar to ethnicity, sexual orientation, or disability status (Singer, 1999).

While initially closely associated with autism, neurodiversity advocates adapted this principle to argue that society would benefit from recognising and developing the strengths of other neurological differences such as ADHD, dyslexia, and Tourette's syndrome instead of pathologising their 'weaknesses'. Singer proposed the concept of neurodiversity as an additional dimension of intersectionality, a concept closely associated with Black Feminist Thought and discussed in more detail later in this book. This latter theory identifies individuals as possessing multiple marginalised identities and notes how these individuals are often unprotected against overlapping forms of discrimination.

We welcome and endorse the assertion that neurodiversity should be celebrated and accommodated, in line with the social model of disability, and throughout this book we highlight the immense joy associated with raising our children in all their beauty and uniqueness. We also placed no restrictions on the 'type' of autism presentation that would be the focus of our research. It was the choice of our participants to share their stories, irrespective of the particular ways in which autism impacted their children, and we made clear that we had no 'threshold' or pre-defined expectations in mind when we invited them to do so.

We acknowledge that the terms in which we choose to identify our children are contested but we affirm that they are also the product of extensive reflection on our part because we take very seriously the responsibility of giving voice to our (largely) non-speaking children, while still respecting the mantra of the wider disability community: 'Nothing about us, without us'. In other words, while the linguistic choices made throughout this book reflect *our* preferences, these preferences are derived from what we genuinely believe to be best for our children.

What do we mean by Blackness?
Mel's story

I attended a majority-White secondary school in a majority-White town. It was at this school that I learnt to hate my Blackness. At primary school, there were many other children who looked like me, had families like me. At my secondary school, I was one of a few dotted across the school. I quickly learned that my Blackness was unattractive to boys and girls alike. I survived by creating a bubbly, fun-loving personality that succeeded in helping me to secure the role of the 'funny Black sidekick'. I stupidly developed a crush on one of the most popular boys in the school, only for him to tell me, politely enough, that he only liked girls with White skin. I remember being angry at myself for not being desirable, for having this Black, unattractive skin.

Conversations about Blackness in my home revolved around our presentation, our speech and our general existen ce. "You can't be seen out of the house playing on the streets all the time, people will think you are in a gang" or "You need to speak properly, people will think you weren't raised right". The need to assimilate taught me that who we were wasn't right. We needed to be something else, something other than Black, to be the right sort of person. Yet, I thought racism was something that you only saw in movies because no one had called me the n-word (though this would come) and because I was getting to go to school with wealthy White children.

I learnt to internalise shame in Blackness and parts of my upbringing because I was being brought up by a single Black woman and I didn't know my father, slotting right into the clichés and stereotypes associated with Black children and their families. My mum survived by working two jobs and receiving welfare benefits. My father, absent. I knew what I was the day I got into an argument with a friend in my last year of primary school and they retaliated from an insult I had thrown by calling me a 'bastard'. They described, in detail, how I met the definition.

I distinctly remember reading a statistic in my Sociology class that said something like Black children who grow up in a single-parent household are more likely to end up as criminals and/or social deviants. Without the critical reading skills I was to develop as an academic, I took this at face-value and failing to identify the experience of internalised racism, I decided that this statistic wasn't going to be me.

It was my husband who taught me to love the physical parts of my Blackness. My full lips and behind were attractive to him, and I began to see what he saw when I looked in the mirror. But it was becoming a mother that rid me of my self-hating. Through my children's eyes, I have been able to see my own worth with them teaching me to love the parts of me that others made me feel were unlovable.

Claire's story

I take an immense amount of pride in my Blackness but, in many ways, I feel that this is a consciousness that came to me later in life. Growing up in a household with a Black father and a White mother, in a predominantly White community and attending a school in which I was one of very few Black pupils initially imbued me with a conception of 'dual heritage' as being somewhat separate from 'Blackness' – a distinction which I now roundly reject.

My 'proximity to Whiteness', via my mother, my marriage, and the fact that my children are light-skinned to the point where their ethnicity is not necessarily immediately apparent, ensures that my experience of Black motherhood is characterised by a version of privilege which is not available to darker-skinned Black women and their children. Nonetheless, observing the ways in which my own children can move through the world differently depending upon which parent they are in company with, has reinforced for me the sense in which 'Blackness' is more than just a way in which I identify myself, it is also a lens through which I am viewed by others, often in terms which result in me being underestimated, maligned, or mistreated.

Becoming a mother ignited in me a determination to connect with myself and to connect my children to their heritage. It also forced me to confront some of the tropes and stereotypes that I had unwittingly absorbed about my own identity, not least the image of the 'Strong Black Woman' who manages trauma through 'resilience' and internalisation.

I know now that every element of my lived experience is impacted by my Blackness and this is something that I embrace as a source of strength and as an inspiration to effect social change for my community and for my children.

Just as the theme of social construction is key to an understanding of autism, 'Blackness' is also a product of shared meaning-making and unequal power dynamics. When we define Black people in this book, we are describing those who have been *racialised* as Black with 'racialise' very much being a verb, the act of 'putting race upon a person'.

The belief that humans can be categorised into distinct biological races, characterised by unique and hierarchical traits and attributes, emerged through the commodification of Black people through enslavement and the growth of capitalist systems (Kinouani, 2021). In 2020, Guilaine Kinouani conducted an online survey of those racialised as Black and found that of the 725 respondents, 94% identified as Black yet 59% believed Blackness was an identity imposed on them by society, indicating that opposition to the term was based on its homogenising nature (Kinouani, 2021). Like autism, Blackness is something that is felt internally but defined externally. Also, like autism, Blackness is heterogeneous, no two people with a Black identity are the same.

So, if no two Black people are the same, why conduct a study into the impact of Blackness on the experiences of mothers of autistic children? In Kinouani's study 78% of the participants agreed that Blackness was a marker of African ancestry. The authors of this book use this idea of the 'African diaspora' to refer to the global communities of people descended from native Africans, primarily due to historical mass movements that occurred through the forced displacement of enslavement. As Kinouani notes, Blackness covers a "huge range of ethnic and cultural groups that are heterogeneous and have various histories, ethnicities and geopolitical positioning" (2021, p. 8). Blackness for us incorporates individuals with two Black parents as well as those with one Black parent, herein described as 'dual heritage' and we refuse to engage in questions of 'dilution'.

Individuals who possess more of the features related to their social group are often more explicitly denigrated through stereotypes about that group (Blair et al., 2022; Walker and Wänke, 2017). This can be seen in how research exploring stereotypes frequently centres on physical traits. As Kinouani (2021) states it is the melanin in our skin, the shape of our bodies, the breadth of our noses, the thickness of our lips, the kinkiness of our hair that is often used to racialise us. Therefore, individuals possessing features such as fuller lips or broader noses are often perceived as having a more prototypical Black appearance (Blair et al., 2002; Hagiwara et al., 2012). These features, characteristic of African ancestry, may be considered individually or alongside skin colour to influence judgements of racial typicality (Stepanova and Strube, 2009; Dunham et al., 2015). This focus on physical features as markers of Blackness underscores and perpetuates narrow and monolithic views of what Black individuals should look like and be like.

On an individual level, Blackness has multi-layered meaning and significance. In terms of physicality, Mel, who has darker skin than Claire and dreadlocked Afro hair is immediately recognisable as physically belonging to a community sorted by its melanated skin. However, beyond these factors, it is our commonalities in experiences and shared fate that create an understanding of Blackness which transcends physicality. This commonality is rooted in our experiences of anti-Blackness.

Anti-Blackness casts those who are perceived as Black as being irreducibly different and excluded from the concept of human (Wynter, 2002, p. 152). Blackness is punished through systemic racism, which refers to the policies and practices entrenched in institutions that disproportionately harm Black people. This can be seen in various sectors such as the criminal justice system, where Black individuals are more likely to be stopped, searched, arrested, and sentenced harshly compared to their White counterparts. In education, systemic racism can manifest in lower expectations for Black students, disproportionate disciplinary actions, and under-resourced schools predominantly attended by Black children.

It is important to note that anti-Blackness does not perfectly equate with class oppression. Although we certainly do not deny that the intersectional identity of being Black and working class often further exacerbates the experience of oppression and discrimination, we wish to guard against the tendency to subsume issues of race into an account of class which underestimates the degree to which discrimination on the basis of the former can be, and often is, distinct from the latter.

Anti-Blackness manifests through stereotypes, systemic discrimination, media representation, and everyday social interactions. There are many prevailing stereotypes about Black individuals that perpetuate negative and harmful perceptions. These include, but are not limited to, stereotypes that portray Black people as inherently criminal, less intelligent, or aggressive. Such stereotypes can lead to biased attitudes and unjust treatment in various social settings, including workplaces, schools, and public spaces. For example, Black individuals are more likely to be associated with crime or a criminal label by both members of the general public and police officers (Eberhardt et al., 2004; Kleider et al., 2012); Black people are more likely to be detained in psychiatric hospitals against our will (Nazroo, Bhui and Rhodes, 2019); and Black Caribbean and Mixed White and Black Caribbean children are more likely to be excluded from school than White British children (GOV.UK, 2024).

All of this speaks to the pressure for Black people to develop alternative forms of 'cultural capital' (Bourdieu, 1973), relative to White people, in order to ensure our survival in societies which are inherently hostile toward our needs and identities. Cultural capital was originally defined as "a person's social assets, such as their education, style of speech, and intellect," (Bourdieu, 1973 in Morgan and Stahmer, 2020, p. 3). However, we concur with Yosso's (2005) contention that in order to be a meaningful category for racially minoritised people, 'cultural capital' must be reframed in terms of the 'Community Cultural Wealth Model' which is subdivided into:

1. Aspirational: the ability to maintain hopes and dreams in oppressive environments.
2. Linguistic: the intellectual and social skills attained through communication experiences in more than one language and/or style.

3.   Familial: the cultural knowledge from family or kin that carries a sense of community, memory, and cultural intuition.

4.   Social: the networks of people and community resources.

5.   Navigational: the ability to navigate systems not built with a marginalised population of people in mind.

6.   Resistant: the ability to oppose and challenge inequality.

Morgan and Stahmer (2020, p. 5) elaborate on this formulation, arguing that Black mothers have no choice but to develop an advocacy strategy "based on the specific tasks and skills needed" to engage with professionals. In part, this takes the form of "Black cultural capital" (Carter, 2003), which relates to the ability to occupy more than one cultural space (dominant and non-dominant) simultaneously, as well as the ability and necessity to 'code switch' (linguistically and stylistically) between each.

As details of our participant research will illustrate, all the mothers featured in this study (including the co-researchers) possess high levels of aspirational, linguistic, and navigational capital, with varying degrees of familial capital, as well as Black cultural capital. The recommendations that we outline in Chapter 5 are intended, in part, to create the conditions for increased social capital and resistant capital.

One final form of capital, identified by Morgan and Stahmer (2020, p. 5), is 'Motherhood capital' which refers to how mothers "use their influence" in healthcare, education, and social care settings "to be mother advocates for their children". In order to appreciate the nature and functions of "Motherhood capital", it is necessary to explore our understandings of motherhood itself.

What do we mean by mother?
Claire's story

*My father recently asked me why I use the word 'parent**ing**', as opposed to 'parent**hood**', when discussing my children. I answered his question by posing another, why should that matter when they mean the same thing? I found his response to be enormously thought-provoking. He explained that 'parenthood' struck him as a state of being that remains constant, a status at once secured and maintained by simply having a child. In contrast 'parenting' conveys an active process, an ongoing challenge that necessitates near constant 'proof' of achievement. "It seems like a lot of pressure to put yourself under", he observed with a wry smile and a degree of serenity that only a grandparent can possess.*

*I always wanted to be a mother to at least two children, and I am perennially grateful (particularly following the experience of two successive pregnancy losses) to have my daughter and son in my life. They're everything to me and being around them brings me a sense of fulfilment unlike anything else I've ever known. But I could never have anticipated the intensity and anxiety associated with keeping them happy and safe, the elusive work-life balance which so often really just translates to feeling as if I'm simultaneously failing on both fronts, the fear that my 'parent**ing**' is somehow being judged as inadequate, or that I might inadvertently cause harm to the most important people in my world.*

For me, to be a mother is to be a vessel for other people's needs, to be your own harshest critic, and to exist in a world of total vulnerability because so much of your heart lives outside your body.

Mel's story

As an only child whose cousins were born nine years after I was, I spent a lot of time by myself wishing for a big family. I imagined large family gatherings, intergenerational meetings of minds, kids playing with kids. My own childhood was often very quiet and, a lot of the time, very lonely. I knew I was going to be a mother who played with her children and gave them worldly-wise advice.

Before I became a mother publicly, I lost a baby at 10 weeks pregnant. It was a painful miscarriage, both physically and emotionally, as I bled and cramped heavily for seven days. It was this loss that taught me my first lesson of motherhood – a lesson that has stayed with me throughout my motherhood journey: motherhood is guilt.

When I lost my first child, I felt guilty, like there was something wrong with my body and that's why we lost them. When my eldest was born, I felt a visceral need to protect him, never to let anything harm him. Yet, when I realised there would be times when he was hurt or sad, I felt guilt. I've spent an inordinate amount of time feeling guilty as a mother so I now associate it as being part of the role.

Yet, in motherhood, I am privy to the growth and development of two human beings. I get to watch my children develop personalities, navigate the twists and turns of life, and decide what paths they want to take. Everything about this is an honour to me, a gift. It is just that the gift is accompanied by guilt and fear: fear about something happening to them, fear of something happening to me or their father.

The simplest definition of a mother is a 'woman who is a parent' but, as in discussions of both autism and Blackness, there is much in this social construction which requires interrogation.

The social category of 'mother' is often defined in relation to, and in opposition to, the category of 'father' and predicated on the assumption that children of the mother are created in her womb. However, we do not subscribe to the Western "bio-logic" (i.e. the use of biology as an ideology for organising the social world) (Oyěwùmí, 1997, p.IX) nor do we claim that all mothers experience motherhood in the same way. The scope of our research has been limited by the identities of the members of our participant study which, in turn, has restricted our evidential findings to those based on a heteronormative experience of motherhood. However, we do not personally define motherhood in these narrow terms, with trans women, co-mothers (i.e. mothers in same-sex relationships), stepmothers, and adoptive mothers all experiencing mothering journeys which are valid and worthy of extensive research in their own right.

Nonetheless, it is also vitally important not to underestimate the long- and short-term effects (physiological and psychological) of pregnancy and childbirth. For those mothers who give birth to their children, the effects of a birth experience can be positive and empowering, or negative and traumatising, or all of these at once.

As Galea, Qui, and Duarte-Guterman (2018) state:

> *Pregnancy is associated with dramatic changes in physiology (cardiac, pulmonary, immune, and metabolic) and endocrinology (steroids and peptide hormones, many of which are unique to pregnancy). [...] These hormones are*

needed to ensure successful gestation; however, the long-term consequences of exposure to these hormones to the host mother have not been frequently addressed in the literature. This is an important consideration as maternal physiology is altered for decades after giving birth [...]. These changes in physiology likely affect drug efficacy, disease susceptibility, outcome, and manifestation, and yet reproductive experience is not often considered in women's health research. [...] [R]eproductive experience is a critical determinant of female physiology that has been grossly overlooked in the health and wellbeing of women.

Thus, as well as immediate postpartum effects which can run the gamut of: exhaustion, afterpains, perineal injury, incontinence, potential guilt at the 'failure' to have a vaginal delivery or to establish breastfeeding, and depression, birthing mothers face multiple, longer-term consequences. These can include bodily changes, sleep deprivation, loss of sexual appetite and identity disruption. For women, these pressures are felt at an almost cellular level, and this is rarely true of their male partners. This is because fatherhood is subjected to far less scrutiny and standardisation than motherhood. The responsibility for a child's wellbeing is frequently individualised and placed predominantly on mothers. This perspective suggests that the measure of a mother's effectiveness is gauged by the extent of energy, resources, and attention she dedicates to fostering her child's optimal development.

In addition to the stressors encountered in the private sphere comes the expectation that mothers ought also to be wage-earners. In many societies, it is now common for women with children of school age (and younger) to work both within and beyond the household. Yet this is rarely reflected in the division of labour within the home, with time-use surveys revealing that across the full range of OECD countries, women undertake an average of 12 hours more domestic and child-rearing responsibilities per week, than men (OECD.Stat, 2020).

Alongside this existing 'double burden' come the pressures associated with the 'professionalisation of parenting' and the role of social media in pushing narratives about the lengths to which mothers must go to be seen to meet their children's needs. The projection of ideal versions of motherhood underscores perceptions of what it means to be 'a good mother', further reinforcing culturally specific demarcations of what motherhood should look like.

The authors of this book are, ostensibly, 'good mothers' in that society would deem us being degree educated, employed in a university, long-term married and speaking mostly in accents of received pronunciation as indicative of this. We are not too old or too young. We have the ideal heterosexual 'nuclear' family structure, we have an acceptable socio-economic status, and our parenting follows the currently trendy 'authoritative' and 'conscious' parenting styles.

However, existing literature highlights how working mothers such as ourselves might experience vilification in societies where there is a strong belief in the mother's role being primarily at home. Confusingly, in these same societies, non-working and even part-time working mothers can be criticised for being a drain on society and *only* being 'stay-at-home mums'. In late

2024, Mel temporarily reduced her full-time hours to manage Sam's increased needs but due to financial reasons, later returned to full-time work and to navigating the loaded comments from her children's teachers about 'Daddy' being the one doing the school run. Claire, on the other hand, works part-time and has to contend with her colleagues' potential lack of understanding when managing her workload.

Thus, those mothers who do return to the workforce (on either a part, or full-time basis) must contend with the so-called 'Motherhood Penalty' (Carr, 2023), a toxic blend of exorbitantly high childcare costs, a potential lag in career progression, and a likely reduction in earning capacity.

Little wonder, then, that the impossible and often contradictory expectations attached to 'mothering' can have such significant psychological and social impacts on mothers, including feelings of shame, isolation, and increased stress, since the experience of motherhood (like that of disability and Blackness) is one which is frequently characterised by stigmatisation.

Stigma and stigmatisation

So far it has been demonstrated that all three components of the identity of Black mothers of autistic children are subject to varying types and degrees of stigma.

By 'stigma', we mean the culturally specific, social constructions that identify certain attributes, behaviours, or conditions as undesirable or discrediting, resulting in reduced status and discrimination for those associated with the stigma (Link and Phelan, 2001). Grinker (2020) also notes how stigma has "come to connote a flawed psychological or physical state" with stigmatised people "often seen as incompetent, blamed for their suffering, and socially marginalised".

As we have demonstrated, autistic people themselves face stigma, with a number of negative stereotypes associated with both low and high support autism presentations and with the nature and effects of autism being widely misunderstood and underestimated. Furthermore, in a neoliberal society in which a person's 'worth' is inextricably linked with their capacity to contribute to capital accumulation, a high support autism presentation immediately marks an individual as being 'unproductive', in that they are more likely to 'cost' money than to generate it. Even an autistic individual with relatively low support needs may also require adaptations and reasonable adjustments in order to fulfil their wage-earning potential and, again, this can contribute to perceptions of them as being a 'drain' on public resources. So it is that often the 'D' in 'ASD' refers to the 'disordered' ability to meet the expectations of the capitalist system.

By extension, the 'reproductive labour' of child-rearing which is inadequately remunerated and disproportionately undertaken by women is further maligned when it does not result in the maturation of an employable adult. By this measure, a woman who is raising an autistic child is engaged in 'unproductive' labour which may hinder her own ability to function as a wage labourer even as she supports a child who may themselves never be able to take her place in the workforce. Thus, mothers of disabled children are, by definition, a highly stigmatised group, with Davis and Manago (2016) noting that this group experiences blame and shame through their connection to a stigmatised child. This significantly exacerbates the physiological, psychosocial, and practical consequences that all women weather when they become mothers, an impact which is then further consolidated by the stigma attached to Blackness.

Blackness is stigmatised in a variety of ways across different societies and cultures. In the context of Black motherhood, anti-Blackness has surfaced multiple stereotypes. Collins (2022) refers to these as "controlling images" which lead to the dehumanisation and exploitation of Black women. These images include:

- The 'Mammy' figure, an asexual, usually overweight caricature of a Black woman whose only purpose is to care for children. For this woman, motherhood is a responsibility that transcends her family unit, making her a surrogate mother for White families. The 'Mammy' image has its roots in US cultural touchstones, such as Hattie McDaniel's role in *Gone with the Wind*. A version of this trope more culturally specific to the UK is what we have chosen to term the 'Community mother', a Black woman whose maternal role extends into spaces beyond her own household. She frequently endures caring responsibilities for relatives (real and surrogate) but also finds herself being called upon to provide unreciprocated practical and emotional support to friends, colleagues, and members of the wider community, even as her own well-being is continually compromised.
- The 'Welfare Queen', or – in UK parlance, the 'Benefit Scrounger' – is a sexually promiscuous, impoverished, morally bankrupt Black woman whose many children all have different absentee fathers. For this woman, motherhood is a means through which to access handouts from the state.

In the context of Black mothers of autistic children in the UK, this links with 'anti-parent narratives' predicated on the belief that an autism diagnosis amounts to a 'Golden Ticket' for a mother who is seeking to secure benefits in her child's name, which might then fuel her own lazy and ineffectual lifestyle. Parenting deficits are also assumed to be responsible for the behaviours exhibited by the autistic child themselves.

- The Matriarch, an unmarried, overly aggressive Black woman who falls short of standards of 'femininity'. The Matriarch emasculates (Black) men by rejecting the 'passivity' of the Mammy. For this woman, motherhood necessitates an unsustainable degree of strength and resilience and is usually undertaken alone.

As our findings will demonstrate, the tendency to praise Black women for silently exceeding their capacity, rather than to provide them with support and the tools for self-care, can result in significant physiological and psychological harms.

In effect then, Black women are defined in terms of three tropes: the 'Lazy Black Woman', the 'Angry Black Woman', or the 'Strong Black Woman'. For Black mothers of autistic children, these stereotypes are particularly damaging because of their insidious influence on healthcare, education, and social care professionals who gatekeep the support and resources we need to access on behalf of our children.

Since the identity of the 'Black woman raising one or more autistic children' is one associated "with intersecting oppressions of race, class, gender […]" and disability (Collins, 2022), this experience of stigma is felt even more acutely and is the reason that such mothers find themselves marginalised and 'othered' by the very services and support mechanisms that they are forced to rely on for their children's well-being.

So it is that the discrimination faced by othered mothers takes the form of a triad of oppression in which the three key elements of their identities are all subject to forms of stigmatisation:

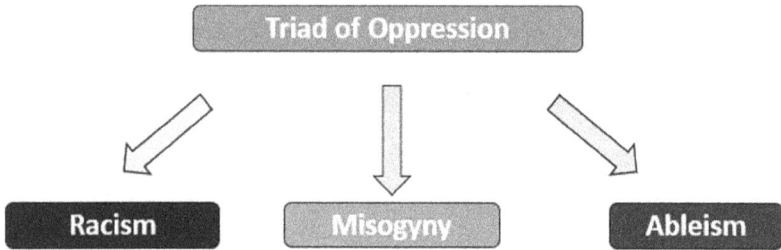

Figure 3: The triad of oppression

Outlining our conceptual framework

In exploring the journeys and experiences of 'othered mothers', we have developed and reconceptualised multiple concepts, drawn from several different schools and traditions. In particular, we have been influenced by the tenets underpinning the following theoretical approaches:

- Black Feminist Thought (BFT): Black Feminism, in its various forms, seeks to highlight the experiences of women, who are adversely affected not just by patriarchy (essentially, 'rule by men') but also by White supremacy and systemic racism. It is a storied and multi-dimensional tradition which is consciously inter and multi-disciplinary in its focus and which treats as its ultimate goal the emancipation of Black women from the systems and structures that oppress them. Black Feminists demonstrate the many ways in which the advancement of White women often relies upon the continued marginalisation and exploitation of their Black counterparts and demonstrate how misogynoir causes Black women to be doubly disadvantaged by the intersection of race and gender (Collins, 2000).

- Critical Race Theory (CRT): CRT affirms that racism, race, and its intersections (with gender, class, etc.) are an endemic part of society. It challenges dominant frameworks and ideologies that are White-centred or White supremacist in origin. Scholarship based in CRT works toward social justice, including the empowerment of oppressed groups and the elimination of racism and poverty. It values, above all else, the experiential knowledge of people of colour, asserting that these perspectives offer a legitimate way of understanding the world. Like Black Feminism, CRT is interdisciplinary in its focus. (Yosso, Parker, Solórzano and Lynn, 2004)

- Critical Disability Studies (CDS): "Critical disability studies seek to change conventional notions of disabled people as pitiable, tragic victims who should adjust to the world around them" (Reaume, 2014, p. 1248). CDS pushes back against the pathologising of 'difference' and against the medical model of defining disability, in deficit-based terms. Although, as we have observed elsewhere, the social model of disability also requires some degree of critical scrutiny, the fundamental assertion of CDS scholars that disability should be viewed "as both a lived reality in which the experiences of people with disabilities are central to interpreting

their place in the world, and as a social and political definition based on societal power relations" (ibid.) is one which
has framed the understanding of autism upon which this
book is based.

All three approaches converge around the amplification of
underrepresented voices, and all contend that experiential
accounts from the 'margins' of society are a crucial component
of fostering and embedding social change. All illustrate that to
truly appreciate the nature, and consequences, of oppression –
and, by extension, to overcome it – we must take direct account
of the viewpoints of those who are subjected to it. Finally, all
three theoretical schools take what might be considered to be
an 'unconventional' approach to academic enquiry, highlighting
the value of creativity and authenticity, as well as the power of
storytelling.

As such, in creating an academic model to reflect the experiences of Black mothers of autistic children, we have sought to
incorporate and hybridise elements of BFT, CRT, and CDS, and to
embrace what Evans-Winters (2019, p. 14) identifies as a choice,
among Black women scholars, to "'borrow' different language
and/or frames to accentuate and forefront our memories and
lived realities".

We have demonstrated this 'borrowing' in our adaptation of
the concept of the 'othermother' (into our image of the 'othered
mother'), and the Feminist delineation of productive and reproductive labour (into our discussions in respect of 'unproductive
labour'), and now we further extend it to develop our conception of the 'triad of oppression', a reworking of the 'triad of
impairments' associated with autism, and in our overview of the

'multiplicity of burdens' developed from Guy-Sheftall's concept of (1995) 'triple jeopardy'.

The triad of oppression and the multiplicity of burdens

It has been comprehensively demonstrated that Black mothers of autistic children exist at the intersection of discrimination and stigmatisation, based on overlapping identities of race, gender, and (proximity to) disability. In what follows, we turn our attention to the implications of this by exploring the consequences that the triad of oppression generates for those who are mothering at the margins.

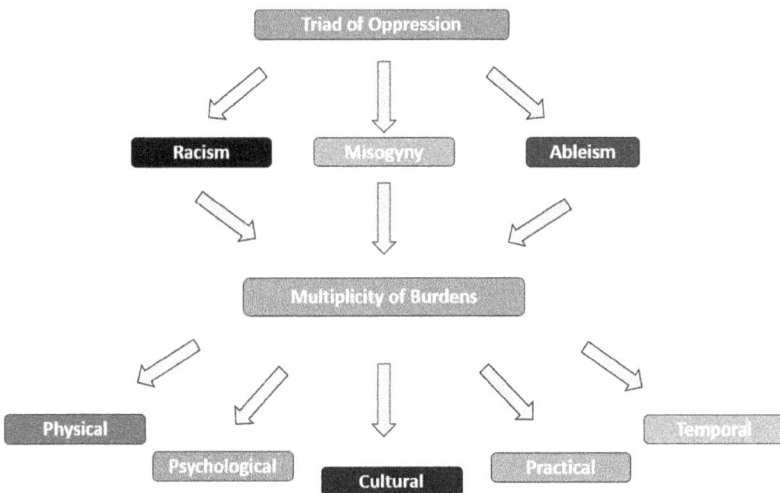

Figure 4: Model of how the triad of oppression leads to the multiplicity of burdens

The above diagram outlines the ways in which stereotypes pertaining to Blackness, motherhood, and autism combine to create negative perceptions of Black mothers of autistic children, including among the very service providers and healthcare, education, and social care professionals upon whom we have no choice but to rely.

The findings of our participant research illustrate that, as Black women, our race defines us as either incompetent and blameworthy, or 'strong' to the point of requiring only the most limited support. Our status as mothers is undervalued, unremunerated, and underestimated, and our proximity to stigmatised children, whose potential to become wage-earners in the capitalist system is likely to be limited, underscores the assumption that we are raising 'the *wrong* children in the *wrong* ways'.

This, in turn, as noted in chapters 3 and 4 generates a range of 'burdens' which may take some, or all, of the following forms:

Physical	• Exhaustion
	• Increased susceptibility to chronic illness
	• Poor sleep
	• Physical harm resulting from displays of aggression from an autistic child
	• Physical symptoms associated with psychological challenges (e.g. heightened cortisol levels resulting from anxiety)
Psychological	• Self-doubt
	• Self-recrimination
	• Fear of failure
	• Depression
	• High levels of anxiety
	• Internalised racism

	• Internalised misogyny • Psychological impacts of physical exhaustion
Cultural	• The challenge of contending with misconceptions of autism which can be common among Black families, and the wider Black community • Challenge of balancing multiple, sometimes conflicting, cultural expectations regarding parenting • Failure of service providers to demonstrate cultural competence in engaging with Black mothers • Racist stereotypes and (micro)aggressions influencing the quality of service provision that is made available to Black mothers • Cultures of systemic racism, neglect, and parent blame
Practical	• The additional pre-planning, and contingency planning, needed to navigate even relatively basic family tasks • Managing relationships with a partner • Managing relationship(s) between an autistic child and their sibling(s) • The demands of regular meetings with healthcare, education, and social care professionals • The need to complete dense and complex paperwork in order to access resources

	• Increased costs (e.g. specialised childcare, private healthcare, etc.) • Decreased earning capacity, owing to the impact of caring responsibilities on career progression
Temporal	• Time poverty • The lack of standard 'parental progression', typically experienced by a parent as their child develops toward independence in adulthood • Constant fears for the child's future • Concerns over who else can provide care for the child, once their mother is no longer able to do so

It bears repeating that since no two autistic children are alike, no two parenting journeys for Black mothers of autistic children will be entirely interchangeable. There may be, for example, those whose children have a relatively low support presentation, meaning that the prospect of them living independently, as adults, is a realistic aspiration. There may be those whose financial circumstances are sufficiently comfortable to absorb the so-called 'Autism Tax' associated with meeting their child's (expensive) needs. There may be those who find that small changes to their household, such as the use of visual timetables or planning apps, are enough to offset some of the requirements of 'autism parenting'. However, what is common to almost all Black mothers of autistic children is the societal expectation that whatever trauma may result from raising an atypical child, is to be borne privately by that mother.

This expectation gives rise to the final element of the multiplicity of burdens framework, in which Black mothers, who are routinely failed by services and systems across healthcare, education, and social care adapt to a lack of professional support by developing coping strategies rooted in isolation and internalisation. We term this process the 'privatisation of trauma':

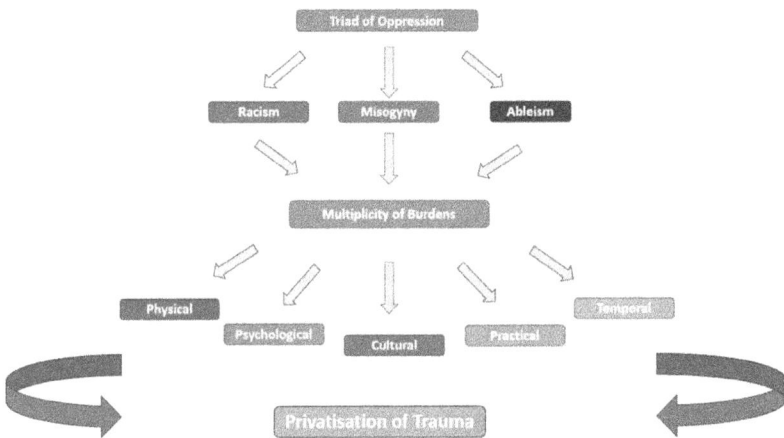

Figure 5: Model of how the triad of oppression and the multiplicity of burdens give rise to the privatisation of trauma

As our findings in subsequent chapters will illustrate, in the absence of culturally competent services that recognise the unique and multi-layered challenges facing 'othered mothers', Black women often have nowhere to turn to secure the resources we need to support our autistic children. Both within and beyond our own communities, there is an unspoken assumption that we can, and should, internalise the effects of the multiplicity of burdens and there is extremely limited understanding of, or regard for, the harm this is likely to cause.

2

Constructing a view from the margins: Hybridising collective autoethnography and participant research

In what follows, the research design and methodology that generated the findings of this project will be outlined. This entails an overview of the nature and purposes of collective autoethnography and an account of how this approach was embedded in a framework of participant research, which included elements of both quantitative and qualitative data collection. The chapter also elucidates our rationale for these choices, along with a detailed explanation of why we believe our research design is essential to achieving the transformative outcomes we aim to realise.

As has been established, this book foregrounds the lived experience of the triad of oppression and of the multiplicity of burdens to which Black mothers of autistic children are subjected. It seeks to empower, amplify, and validate the women who have lent their voices to it and to create a blueprint for the kind of support that they need and deserve. It is for this reason that the choice of methodology is one which consciously creates permeability in the line between participant and (co)researcher.

Just as the theoretical and conceptual approaches we have taken combine the analytical power of BFT, CRT, and CDS to illuminate the particular lived experiences of women who are mothering at the intersection of race and disability, the methodology that underpins our research also fuses two distinct traditions: collective autoethnography (hereafter CoAE) and participant research.

To understand why a hybridisation of CoAE and participant research is the most effective mechanism for situating and developing our perspectives, it is necessary to outline exactly what each of these research methods entails and to unpack some of the practical and ethical dilemmas associated with them. In so doing, we draw out the tenets of each approach and explore the ways in which they differ from and complement one another, and we illustrate the rationale behind distilling their respective strengths into a multifaceted research design that maximises insight and authenticity.

Moreover, we detail the various 'phases' of the research, and the iterative and reflexive processes through which findings were surfaced and analysed. We outline the relationship between our own collective autoethnographic vignettes (featured throughout this book), the quantitative survey that helped to inform the rest of our research design, the semi-structured interviews that were conducted with a sample of survey respondents, and the focus groups that enabled further exploration of the themes that the previous research instruments had served to identify.

We provide this information to demonstrate the rigour of our own research, to enable the core elements of the study to be adapted, or replicated, by other researchers, and to generate guidelines for policymakers and service providers seeking to reach and support Black mothers of autistic children in the UK.

The research design

As outlined in Chapter 1, the development of our research questions is rooted in the intersectional frameworks of Black Feminist Thought (BFT), Critical Disability Studies (CDS), and Critical Race Theory (CRT). These theoretical lenses provided the foundation for exploring the multilayered experiences of Black mothers raising autistic children in the UK, recognising the complex interplay of race, gender, and disability in shaping their lives.

The four research questions upon which this project is based are as follows:

1. What are the common experiences of Black mothers in the UK raising autistic children?
2. How do Black mothers perceive and navigate UK healthcare, education and social care services for their autistic children?
3. How do Black mothers perceive the role of 'their' racial and/ or gender identity in their experiences?

4. What specific recommendations do Black mothers have for improving healthcare, education, and social care services for their autistic children?

These questions were designed to draw out a unique, and hitherto unresearched area of inquiry, focused specifically on the lived experiences of Black mothers of autistic children. Together, the theoretical and conceptual frameworks shaped our research questions by directing our attention to key dimensions of Black mothers' experiences. Question 1 emerges from our commitment to documenting shared experiences as a means of amplifying collective voice. Question 2 reflects our interest in understanding how structural and systemic inequities manifest in healthcare, education, and social care services, while Question 3 examines the role of social identity in shaping these interactions. Finally, Question 4 seeks to centre Black mothers as 'agents of change', whose insights are essential for informing more equitable and inclusive practices across these sectors.

In reviewing extant literature, we had been disappointed to note how few research projects had taken account of the challenges facing Black mothers in the UK who are raising children with disabilities. Even where research has highlighted the support needs of mothers who are raising autistic children (Bromley et al., 2004), findings have not been sufficiently disaggregated to assess the impact of intersectional factors linked with race.

Literature from the United States paints a clear picture of delays in autism referrals and diagnoses, and of increased instances of misdiagnosis, for Black children relative to their White counterparts (Dababnah et al., 2018; Angell, Empey, and Zuckerman,

2018). A quantitative study undertaken in the Netherlands suggests that this is an issue which transcends borders, with clear evidence emerging of "underdiagnosis and referral bias of autism in ethnic communities" (Begeer et al., 2009). However, at the time of writing, no equivalent UK study has been undertaken.

Dababnah, Kim, and Shaia (2018, p. 1) have attempted to quantify the stress levels of caregivers of Black autistic children in the US, using their findings as a basis for "recommendations for family-centred and culturally relevant efforts to assess and address parenting stress in this population". Again, while many of the insights offered are pertinent to our own recommendations (outlined in Chapter 5), no UK-based equivalent study exists at this time.

There have been a small number of studies assessing the impact of autism on minoritised groups in the UK. For instance, Heer, Rose, and Larkin (2012, p. 949) framed their analysis of the "experiences and needs of South Asian families caring for a child with learning disabilities in the United Kingdom" in light of what they termed "an experiential-contextual framework" which took account of "interpretations and understanding of learning disabilities; interactions with healthcare systems; minority group pressures; and the influence of acculturation and diversity within ethnic groups".

Similarly, Fox et al. (2017) explored the experiences that members of a UK Somali migrant community had faced in managing perceptions of autism and accessing services and support.

Akbar and Woods (2020) focused their analysis on how Pakistani parents in England experienced the adjustment to raising a child with special educational needs, and ethnographic studies have been undertaken to improve understanding of the interplay between religious beliefs and raising autistic children, in Muslim families (Jegatheesan, Miller, and Fowler, 2010: Jegatheesan and Witz, 2013).

Furthermore, Munroe, Hammond, and Cole (2016) concluded that there were conflicts between African cultural beliefs and a Western, medical understanding of autism which created a feeling of cognitive dissonance for the participants in their study of six African immigrant mothers living in the UK.

As explored in Chapter 5, we echo some of the recommendations regarding the need to "[understand] cultural views of autism and the need to raise awareness, reduce stigma and provide support to encourage families not to delay seeking help for their children" that have emerged from such studies (Fox et al., 2017, p. 305). However, we contend that this 'cultural dimension' is only one among many 'burdens' facing Black mothers of autistic children.

A doctoral thesis (Gemegah, 2022) shed light on the fact that "Black parents experienced distinct and nuanced difficulties associated with race, culture, gender, and socio-economic status", while navigating the challenges of raising an autistic child. Many of the insights presented in this study are of vital importance. However, its principal contention is not one which accords entirely with our own research. Specifically, Gemegah asserts:

> *Whilst this study recognises the multiple structural factors that may contribute to delay in diagnosis and treatment, its main emphasis is on the importance of culture and the cultural lens that limits parents' awareness and understanding,*

which ultimately shapes their attitude to autism and marginal experiences in their community.

Our own stories, and those of our participants reflect the impact of some of the cultural factors that Gemegah outlines, but – on balance – our research has demonstrated that this is one among many factors, with structural racism (rather than cultural barriers within the Black community) acting as the keystone to the multiplicity of burdens.

Of course, we do not deny that the internalisation of such racism further consolidates the struggles of Black mothers of autistic children; neither do we underestimate the psychological toll of balancing multiple cultural influences in our child-rearing, nor diminish the importance of recognising that disability is understood differently in different cultural contexts. After all, disability, as Goodley (2014) and others in CDS emphasise, is not a universal experience but one shaped by sociocultural, economic, and political contexts. Nonetheless, we maintain that 'cultural burdens' are one of several elements of a parenting journey rendered infinitely more challenging by the insidious influence of patriarchy and White supremacy. These systemic forces exacerbate the challenges of parenting, particularly for Black mothers raising autistic children, by embedding inequities into healthcare, education, and social care services (Crenshaw, 1989; Hill Collins, 2000).

To explore these intersecting dynamics comprehensively, we designed a multi-phase research process that integrated qualitative and quantitative methodologies. Our design reflects a commitment to intersectional analysis, guided by the principles of BFT (Collins, 2000), CRT (Delgado & Stefancic, 2017), and CDS (Goodley,

2014; Cooper, 2020). These frameworks stress the importance of centring marginalised voices, challenging dominant narratives, and capturing the complexity of lived experiences.

Table 1: Phases of research design

Phase 1 – Building our collective autoethnographic account
o An initial series of collective autoethnographic vignettes, created through recorded Microsoft Teams meetings and transcribed voice notes.
o Aligns with Chang et al.'s (2013) assertion that CoAE allows researchers to co-construct narratives that merge personal experience with critical analysis.
o Enabled us to identify common experiences and points of departure between the co-researchers.

Phase 2 – Quantitative survey
o The creation of a short quantitative survey (with some qualitative elements) to capture a broader spectrum of experiences.
o Scholars like Ladson-Billings and Tate (1995) advocate for mixed-methods approaches within CRT to bridge individual narratives with structural trends.
o Demographic questions were used to ensure that all respondents met the research criteria (i.e. were Black mothers raising autistic children in the UK).
o A combination of closed, semi-structured, and Likert scale questions was used to solicit responses regarding how Black mothers of autistic children have experienced engaging with healthcare, education, and social care professionals.

(continued)

Table 1: Phases of research design (continued)

o A combination of closed and semi-structured questions was used to solicit responses regarding the physical, psychological, social, and financial impact that Black mothers of autistic children have experienced throughout their parenting journeys.
o Open-ended questions were included to invite respondents to suggest potential improvements to the services they access on behalf of their children.
Midway between Phases 2 and 3, we conducted the second phase of collective autoethnographic research and reflection, in which the co-researchers synthesised survey findings with their own initial vignettes and reviewed key themes, with a view to designing research questions for semi-structured interviews.
Phase 3 – Semi-structured interviews
o Nine survey respondents who had self-selected were invited to participate in online, 90-minute, recorded semi-structured interviews with one or other of the two co-researchers. o These interviews, as Kvale and Brinkmann (2009) suggest, allowed for in-depth exploration of participants' perspectives while maintaining flexibility to address emergent themes. o Participants were provided with transcripts, which they could use to request amendments, additions, or redactions, with a view to ensuring that the accounts they had provided reflected their experiences and viewpoints as accurately as possible.
A third phase of collective autoethnographic research, conducted via reflexive journals and recorded and transcribed Microsoft Teams meetings, resulted in the creation of 'prompts' for the focus groups.

Table 1: Phases of research design (continued)

Phase 4 – Focus groups
o Focus groups, which are widely used in intersectional research (Hankivsky & Grace, 2015), provided a collaborative setting to explore collective themes.
o Six of the participants who had taken part in the semi-structured interviews, self-selected to join one of the two focus groups.
o Each focus group included three participants and both of the two co-researchers.
o Focus groups were conducted online, for approximately 90 minutes, and were recorded and transcribed.
o As above, participants were provided with transcripts, which they could use to request that their contributions be edited as they saw fit.
o Co-researchers then conducted a bilateral focus group where they addressed the prompts in conversation with one another, recording, transcribing, and analysing the findings as a final phase of collective autoethnographic research, leading to the editing and completion of the initial vignettes.
At this point, it was agreed that data saturation had been reached for the collective autoethnography stage of the research, and a synthesis of the vignettes, survey responses, interviews and focus group transcripts was used to devise the multiplicity of burdens framework, based on the challenges and experiences that all respondents (including the co-researchers) had identified.

(continued)

Table 1: Phases of research design (continued)

Phase 5 – Practitioner interviews
• Drawing on Lipsky's (1980) theory of street-level bureaucracy and Evans's (2015) expansion of this within a UK-context, this phase sought to uncover how frontline professionals perceive and respond to the needs of Black mothers raising autistic children.
• The co-researchers interviewed representatives of civil society groups and organisations, which already take as their focus dimensions of Black maternal health. • These groups were invited to share their own best practices and recommendations for identifying and supporting the needs of Black mothers. • The co-researchers reviewed and reflected on these recommendations and considered how they could be adapted to alleviate the burdens facing Black mothers of autistic children in the UK.

Why collective autoethnography?
Autoethnography

> Autoethnography (AE) is an approach to qualitative inquiry in which a researcher recounts a story of his or her own personal experience, coupled with an ethnographic analysis of the cultural context and implications of that experience. (Lapadat, 2017, p. 589)

In deploying CoAE, we recognise it as an extension of ethnography. Ethnography itself entails researchers observing and documenting aspects of a given culture, society, or community and situating the subsequent findings in light of broader socio-cultural analysis. The limitations of a traditional ethnographic approach, particularly from the perspective of race, have been well-documented (Autry, 2020; Adhikari, 2023; Brown, 2023); in essence, a significant risk associated with it is the potential for the researcher to co-opt, appropriate, misrepresent, exploit, or fetishise the experiences of a group to which they do not belong. We also note the potential for the research to be compromised, or rendered unethical, by an intrinsically unbalanced power dynamic between the observed and the observer, with the former encouraged to share aspects of themselves and their lives, in ways which can be challenging or triggering, while the latter is able to maintain a 'safe distance' from that process.

In contrast, AE sees the researcher turn the 'lens' on themselves, by recounting their own stories and embracing the vulnerability and honesty that this necessitates. The value of this form of research is grounded in the fact that "[o]ur autoethnographic experiences are not isolated from larger historical-sociocultural norms and issues of power, privilege and difference" (Hernández-Saca and Cannon, 2019, p. 243), and, as such, surfacing those personal accounts highlights the fact that these societal forces have "been structured in reference to non-disabled/able bodied and minded, male, White, upper class, Judeo-Christian and heterosexual norms" (Tyack, 1974). This is why AE has been characterised "as a radical democratic politics – a politics committed to creating space for dialogue and debate that instigates and shapes social change" (Holman Jones, 2005, p. 763).

Furthermore, AE is also thought to resolve some of the ethical quandaries linked with ethnography, in that it ensures that there is no disjuncture between the voice of the researcher and that of the research subject. Crucially, AE "capitalizes on the power of the story as a way of knowing and teaching" (Bruner, 1986; Frank, 2016; King, 2003) and helps to break down some of the arbitrary disciplinary and methodological barriers that have tended to gatekeep conceptions of what constitutes 'legitimate' academic knowledge.

In the specific context of our research, AE is also well-placed to provide an outlet for some of the more traumatic or emotionally jarring elements of our parenting journeys. This is not only because it "recognizes self-experience as a social phenomenon valuable and worthy of examination" (Edwards, 2021, p. 1) but also because "[t]roubling experience is often the focus of autoethnographic study, such as the personal experience of loss through bereavement" (ibid.). Of course, we do not intend to implicitly conflate the experience of raising an autistic child with that of losing a loved one but rather to point out that AE, as a methodology, has been employed in a great many studies as a means for the researcher to grapple with emotive issues, and to extrapolate from them culturally and socially relevant insights which can serve to effect change.

The counterweight to this, however, is that the sharing of such an intense and personal account carries with it a number of challenges. The first concern is the potential ethical implication of the researcher being unable to prioritise and maintain their own self-care. This is summarised by Tolich (2010, p. 1605), who cautions autoethnographers to "treat all the persons mentioned in the text as vulnerable, *including the researcher*" (emphasis added), and by Lapadat (2017, p. 594) who persuasively claims that AE "can affect the researcher in unforeseen ways. The evocative power of a personal narrative that makes it so compelling and able to shift readers' perspectives rests in narrators offering themselves up for public scrutiny by an audience or readership". In simple terms, a researcher sitting alone in their recollections can inadvertently put themselves at risk of considerable harm, of the type they would otherwise be at pains to avoid on the part of others whom they had recruited for participant research.

The second concern is that a lack of 'distance' between topic, subject, and researcher can result in a 'self-indulgent' account which is closer to autobiography than it is to rigorous academic inquiry. The somewhat alarmist suggestion is that:

> *[l]egitimizing AE could lead to a generation of researchers focused on self-absorption and self-celebration rather than using their research skills to examine global social issues. From this perspective, autoethnographers have reneged on the social expectation that researchers will use their privileged positions in universities and their theoretical and professional knowledge and research training to make a real and positive difference to the world. (Lapadat 2017, p. 596)*

In our view, this accusation is most commonly levelled by those who wish to gatekeep definitions of 'real research' and, as our hybridised conceptual framework has already illustrated, it is deftly rebuffed by scholars of BFT, CRT, and CDS who have all demonstrated the value of 'bottom-up' research methods in problematising and dismantling dominant and discriminatory "cultural-historical master narratives" (Hernández-Saca and Cannon, 2019, p. 248) that perpetuate violence against marginalised groups. Nonetheless, there is scope for conceding that "AE *can* fall short of its ideological promise due to a lack of distance that results from the subject and the researcher being the same person, and because it can be challenging to translate personal experience into sociocultural and political action" (Lapadat, 2017, p. 589, emphasis added).

As such, we knew that capturing our stories (and, crucially, the stories of our children) needed to be more than an autobiographical undertaking. It needed to combine, as AE research methods have always sought to "the value of the researcher's personal experience and subjectivity" with a reading of "cultural context, exploring the link between the individual and society" (Karalis Noel, Minematsu, and Bosca, 2023, p. 2).

A promising solution to some of these challenges was to move beyond AE into CoAE, in which the risk of harm, accusations of 'self-indulgence' and the "scope constraints" (ibid.) of single-authored autoethnographic accounts could be mitigated through collaboration between two or more researchers.

Collective autoethnography

Collective Autoethnography [is] a participatory and democratic research methodology distinct from other autoethnographic methodologies in its emphasis on co-constructing narratives […]. Owing to its focus on shared meaning-making and mutual respect, CoAE is well-suited to anyone aiming to examine shared experiences within a community or group setting in a qualitative research context. (Karalis Noel, Minematsu, and Bosca, 2023, p. 1)

The decision to ground our research in CoAE was both a simplistic and a complex one. The intuitive appeal of situating our work in the broader tradition of AE lay in its ability to enable us to platform and explore our own journeys as Black mothers raising autistic children in the UK. The catharsis we had enjoyed as we had come to know one another socially – and see in one another both the challenges and the triumphs of our respective experiences – was something that we instinctively knew would not be a comfortable fit with more 'conventional' forms of research, in which the writer (falsely) situates herself as an objective or neutral observer, equipped with an emotionless and contextless 'view from nowhere'. If our experiences were to be shared, they needed to reflect our own authenticity and positionality, and to convey the relief we had felt in being 'seen' by each other in such raw and unapologetic terms. They would also benefit from the increased academic rigour resulting from a co-constructed narrative in which we each called upon our distinct disciplinary backgrounds (Politics and Education, respectively) to "contribute to data generation, analysis, and writing/performing" since "CoAE is strengthened by the contribution of multidimensional perspectives on the research" (Chang et al., 2013).

We also came to realise, early into our collaboration, that we were already 'doing' CoAE in some form. Our (sometimes daily) WhatsApp voice notes were organically forming a rich archive of shared experiences, reflections, and critical analysis, shaped by the ebb and flow of our daily lives as Black mothers navigating the UK healthcare, education, and social care systems for our children. These voice notes, which began as informal exchanges of support, validation, and solidarity, gradually evolved into a foundational element of our research process.

While there were numerous opportunities afforded by the scope of our research, not least the chance to address the alarming paucity of pre-existing literature that foregrounds the lives of Black mothers, (let alone those of Black mothers raising autistic children), embracing CoAE also presented a number of considerations that we knew we would have to pre-emptively build into our research design. As well as the imperative to implement strategies for the co-researchers' self-care (such as reflexive journalling, and regular breaks from engagement with emotionally challenging research materials), we were also committed to what Ellis (2007) describes as "relational ethics" in autoethnographic research – essentially the cautionary note that the 'self' does not exist in isolation and that, as a consequence, telling one's own story necessarily entails telling the stories of others. As Bishop (2020, p. 6) asserts:

> [...] my knowledge is not just coming from me, or from the books and articles accessed because of my exclusive university library membership. My knowledge primarily comes from my family, my communities, my connections. My 'self' belongs to them. Therefore, I must constantly be reflecting on 'Who do I speak for?', 'Whose stories and knowledge am I able to share?' alongside 'What am I speaking for?' and 'Who am I speaking to?'

One obvious implication of this is that standard processes for seeking consent from research subjects cannot be straight-forwardly applied to autoethnographic research. For us, this challenge was twofold because we needed to consider that, at times, we would be retelling the story of a 'relational other' from a perspective that they may not necessarily be inclined to endorse.

For this reason, it was important for us to protect the identities of those featured in our accounts. We achieved this through the careful use of anonymisation and pseudonymisation, which enabled us to withhold information which we did not believe could, or should, be shared within the parameters of ethical research. We replicated such methods in attending to ethical considerations in the participant research phases of the project.

The second issue related to the most important subjects of our research, our own children, all of whom are minors who cannot provide informed consent. Reconciling this fact with our commitment to 'relational ethics' was a matter of extensive reflection for us, especially in light of our views in respect of 'sharenting' on social media platforms such as Instagram and TikTok. In recent years, the proliferation of accounts, linked with self-described 'Autism Moms' primarily in the States, has given rise to the monetisation of home life 'content' derived from the experiences and behaviours of autistic children. While some of these accounts could arguably be viewed as support resources for struggling parents, or as attempts to increase autism awareness and acceptance, a great many can reasonably be described as problematic and exploitative in character. Referring to the general phenomenon of 'Sharenting', Steinberg (2017, p. 839) summarised some of the unintended consequences of parents choosing to publish online content on behalf of, or featuring, their minor children:

When parents share information about their children online, they do so without their children's consent. These parents act as both gatekeepers of their children's personal information and as narrators of their children's personal stories. This dual role of parents in their children's online identity gives children little protection as their online identity evolves. A conflict of interests exists as children might one day resent the disclosures made years earlier by their parents.

As has been detailed elsewhere, each of us is a mother to two young children, one of whom has a diagnosis of autism, and one of whom is awaiting assessment. None of these children is in a position to actively consent to the account we have chosen to provide of our experiences of raising them. In the case of our younger children, it remains unclear what level of comprehension and self-awareness they may ultimately develop but, at the ages of 5 and 3, respectively, they will hold a limited understanding of what it means to be included in this research. In the case of our older children, Claire's 13-year-old daughter and Mel's 8-year-old son, the high support needs associated with their autism presentations ensure that it is extremely unlikely that they will ever be able to access the research or even be aware that their stories have been embedded into it. Mindful of these uncertainties, and cognisant of the implications of them for our children's future relationship with this research, we have taken all possible steps to protect their identity, including pseudonymisation. However, we have elected to stop short of disguising our own names, by means of nom de plume, since we feel that to do so is to fundamentally undermine the authenticity that is so crucial to the purposes of our research.

The intersections of our children's identities subject them to a potent cocktail of discrimination and diminished life chances, from diagnosis to educational opportunities, to the ways they will be perceived and treated in all areas of their lives. This is why we consider it our duty, not just as academics but also as parents, to expose the limitations of the models and services (healthcare, education and social care) upon which our children have no choice but to rely, both now and into the future. Our stories are their stories and, we centre and prioritise their needs in everything we undertake. CoAE provided us with the means to do this in a manner which was as safe and supportive as possible. It also served to generate a model for the second phase of our research, the participant study in which we would invite other Black mothers of autistic children to join us in exploring their journeys as othered mothers.

Phase 1: Building our collective autoethnographic account

The research questions upon which the project is based were the product of 'Phase 1' of our research, in which we constructed our initial collective autoethnographic account of our children's respective complex needs, and of our experiences with the various healthcare, education, and social care professionals whom we had encountered before, during, and after our children's diagnoses. The discussions in which we engaged were deliberately informal and open-ended, designed, in as far as possible, to inform a timeline of our journeys, and that of our children, from initial developmental concerns, to and through the diagnostic process, and subsequent decisions surrounding educational provision and engagement with additional services and resources.

In our early voice notes, we were immediately struck by the degree of commonality in these experiences. Our eldest children's presentations are markedly different from one another. In fact, they are similar only inasmuch as both children are profoundly affected by their autism and by their comorbid diagnoses (of ADHD and learning disabilities in Mae's case, and SPD in Sam's). However, our experiences of attempting to secure support for them were, in many respects, largely indistinguishable from one another.

As we began sharing these experiences, via a number of WhatsApp voice notes, recorded meetings in Microsoft Teams, and in a series of autoethnographic vignettes, we noted that we had both:

Table 2: Commonalities in Claire and Mel's parenting experiences

• Had our parental concerns regarding our children's developmental delays dismissed by healthcare professionals, for some considerable time after we had broached them.
• Experienced racist (micro)aggressions in encounters with healthcare, education and social care professionals.
• Been made to feel as if our parenting was being called into question by these same professionals (with multiple, baseless, implied suggestions of neglect, incompetence, or parental irresponsibility).
• Felt compelled to 'deputise' our husbands, both of whom are White, to represent our families in meetings and discussions, despite us being objectively better qualified to do so.

Table 2: Commonalities in Claire and Mel's parenting experiences (continued)

- Learned to 'credentialise' in predominantly White spaces, by establishing ourselves as education professionals, in hopes of being taken more seriously in such appointments.
- Been accused of being 'angry' or 'aggressive' in our encounters with professionals, despite not having comported ourselves in a way which would support such a suggestion.
- Been faced with no choice (partly due to the issues outlined above) but to seek out expensive private healthcare for our children…
- … thereby increasing a financial burden already generated by our caring responsibilities and their impact on our careers.
- Experienced 'weathering' (Geronimus, 2023), in the sense that our own physical and mental health had been adversely affected by the demands placed upon us in supporting our children.
- Found that our children's behaviours had been labelled in much more negative terms than those of the non-Black children in their cohorts.

Although we were conscious that coincidence is not causation and that our shared experiences were not necessarily common to others in comparable circumstances, we nonetheless hypothesised that they may well resonate with fellow 'othered mothers'.

Given the value that CoAE places on lived experience, we wished to create a platform where other Black mothers of autistic children could share theirs. Even armed with the "navigational capital" (Morgan and Stahmer, 2020, p. 25) that we as academics, in what societal standards would judge to be 'stable, middle-class', homes, might be said to command, we had felt the impact of racial stigma and discrimination in advocating for our children. This led us to consider what others, both in similar and in less privileged circumstances, might have endured.

In order to further explore this in as academically rigorous a manner as possible, we sought to supplement and critique our own collective autoethnographic vignettes against findings generated via participant research.

Animated by our belief that "a feminist cannot claim to possess the theory and the method; she seeks to be multidimensional and intersecting" (Vergès, 2019), we have included the voices of mothers with similar lived experiences to ourselves, thereby enabling us to see what we do not see and to deconstruct our understanding of our own experiences.

Participant research

We believe, as emphasised by Toliver (2022, p. 183), that as researchers, we must "engage with the stories of our research partners by becoming story listeners", interpreting their accounts for ourselves and finding synergy between the stories they tell and our own personal stories. This approach acknowledges the inherent impossibility of true objectivity and the need to consider both the personal and the external. We knew we needed to include stories beyond our own in this research, but we also recognised that the choices we made during the recruitment process might expose us to accusations of subjectivity and 'confirmation bias' (Nickerson, 1998), commonly levelled by those in Westernised, non-feminist focused research environments, who are inclined to criticise research that is based on narrative accounts. However, we embraced those choices precisely because this misogynist and White supremacist paradigm is something which we explicitly reject.

Recruitment

Throughout our recruitment process, we maintained a Black Feminist lens, which prioritised the lived experiences of Black women and their children, by ensuring that our materials and strategies were both respectful and reflective of their realities (Collins, 2000). For instance, we devoted considerable time to the design of our recruitment poster, understanding that within BFT, aesthetics, beauty, and representation hold significant cultural and political weight (Nash, 2019), particularly in representations of Black women. We aimed to create a poster that was not only visually appealing but also inclusive, ensuring that it accurately represented the diversity of our intended participants. This included the careful selection of imagery and colour schemes that resonate with the communities we sought to engage, as well as the correct usage of logos to signify relation to the autism community. This meant actively choosing the infinity logo rather than the puzzle piece, which is disliked by many members of the autistic community, due in part to its association with problematic organisations such as 'Autism Speaks'. We were conscious of the potentially alienating impact of our choice to make use of 'identity-first' language in our recruitment materials, and we engaged with two potential respondents who took umbrage with it. Our explanation (as outlined in the previous chapter) proved sufficient to assuage their concerns.

Peterson-Salahuddin (2022) asserts that Twitter (now referred to as X) and Instagram serve as spaces for Black Feminist discourse, allowing researchers to connect with individuals who are already engaged in these conversations. As such, we employed social media platforms as recruitment tools, recognising their potential to reach broader audiences and foster community engagement. We included a QR code and a bit.ly link on our poster and shared our creation on X (formerly Twitter), Instagram, Facebook and LinkedIn. However, conscious of the importance of bridging any potential 'digital divide', we also undertook 'offline' recruitment by distributing posters and flyers in accessible locations such as doctors' surgeries, libraries, community centres, and schools within our local communities in England and Wales. We also posted hard copies of our recruitment poster to Black community centres and social groups across the UK, and to further extend our reach, we contacted organisations and community networks, such as Black SEN Mamas and Global Child and Maternal Health to cascade our information.

Phase 2: The quantitative survey

'Phase 2' of our research design led us to create and disseminate a brief quantitative survey (containing qualitative elements), the purpose of which was twofold. In the first instance, the objective was to capture a larger number of responses than could realistically be reached through exclusively qualitative methods. Secondly, the survey was intended as a 'recruitment tool' to invite respondents to participate in 'Phase 3' and 'Phase 4' of the research: a semi-structured interview and a focus group, respectively.

The survey consisted of demographic questions, which enabled us to establish key facts about the gender, age range, ethnicity, location, and relationship status of our respondents, as well as the number and age of autistic children that they were raising.

Crucially, we did not stipulate that the children needed to have been formally diagnosed with autism. This decision was informed by our own experience of the attenuated and inconsistent nature of the diagnostic process and the way in which this, in and of itself, can exacerbate the burdens facing parents with children who have additional needs. We aimed to include the voices of those still seeking recognition for their child's presentation, accepting that any challenges with verifying diagnoses were a necessary trade-off for prioritising inclusion.

Similarly, we did not place any restrictions on the age of the children under discussion, instead encouraging responses from mothers who had parental responsibilities for (vulnerable) adults, as well as those with children of school age and younger. This reflected our own discussions, during 'Phase 1' of the research, concerning the 'temporal burden' associated with supporting a child who may not be positioned to develop the requisite 'life skills' to leave home or live independently in adulthood. Autism is a lifelong neurological condition meaning that the complex needs associated with it continue to impact the life of an autistic person, and their caregivers, long after the child themselves has 'aged out' of the services and resources that are linked with full-time education. Again, we wished to acknowledge and amplify the experiences of those mothers for whom managing such challenges, on behalf of their children, was a commitment that endured far beyond that of parents of neurotypical children.

With a view to exploring the 'weathering' impact (Geronimus, 2023) of this long-term and complex caregiving, we invited respondents to share with us whether they were contending with any physical and mental health conditions of their own (again, diagnosed or undiagnosed). As well as an indicative list of conditions associated with neurodiversity (autism, ADHD, PDA, etc.) and mental health challenges (depression, anxiety, OCD, etc.), there was a free-text option to enable respondents to provide details of any other health problems. Here, the purpose was to establish whether any respondents faced the dual burden of managing their own poor health, while also supporting an autistic child.

Respondents were also invited to reflect on their level of pre-existing knowledge of autism (prior to their child presenting with autism symptomatology), as well as the degree of support that they felt able to secure from their partner, family, friends, and wider community. The data gleaned from this response spoke to issues of potential isolation and the impact of being the primary caregiver in a household that included one or more autistic children, as well as highlighting the likely challenge of having to become an 'expert' in a condition that had perhaps previously been unfamiliar.

Closed questions and Likert scales were deployed to enable respondents to rate their experiences of engaging with healthcare, education and social care professionals. However, free text boxes were also included as addenda to these questions, in order to ensure that fuller explanations could be provided. This introduced a qualitative component to the survey and began the process of constructing 'narrative' accounts of respondents' experiences. Furthermore, statements, both positive and negative, were provided in respect of each of the different services (healthcare, education, and social care), with respondents invited to use a Likert scale to indicate the extent to which they agreed or disagreed. The purpose of these questions was to inform an 'at-a-glance' insight into the extent to which respondents had found the professionals they encountered to be respectful, informative, supportive, inclusive, effective, and culturally competent. Specifically, it was an opportunity to begin to assess whether respondents felt that there were any particular challenges they had faced as Black women navigating these services on behalf of their children.

The final question, which again took the form of a free-text box, provided an opportunity to share any recommendations for how healthcare, education, and social care services might have engaged more effectively with the respondents, and to offer any additional information which might be deemed relevant to the research. This was a further attempt to weave qualitative elements into the survey while still ensuring that it remained manageable in terms of scope and completion time.

The findings of the survey are explored in detail in Chapter 3. However, it suffices to say at this juncture that while the number of viable responses was relatively low (26 in total), some indicative patterns and trends could be said to have emerged from this second phase of the research, with many of the experiences described by the co-researchers in their autoethnographic vignettes being echoed by the survey respondents. The qualitative component of the survey provided some extremely useful insights (a number of which are quoted verbatim in Chapters 3, 4 and 5), and the invitation to participate in subsequent semi-structured interviews ultimately resulted in 9 participants choosing to do so, 6 of whom also joined one of the focus groups conducted by the researchers.

Phase 3: Semi-structured interviews

As promising as this initial phase of the research proved to be, it had always been our intention to move beyond simply collating and analysing quantitative data. Those whom we had hoped to reach and represent with this project are effectively a minoritised group, within a minoritised group, and one which – by dint of their circumstances – tends to be time poor and (as later findings will illustrate) understandably suspicious of organisations seeking their participation in research. Despite engaging community groups such as 'Black SEN Mamas' and 'Black Mothers Matter' in our use of 'convenience' and 'snowball' sampling, and making use of social media platforms such as Facebook and Instagram, we were aware that our sample size was liable to be limited and that quantitative methods alone would not be sufficient to capture the voices of othered mothers.

Unlike a traditional participant study, for us 'Phase 3' of the research represented an extension of CoAE practices and principles. Our watchword throughout the discussions was 'amplification', in that we were motivated by the ambition to disseminate and validate the voices of one of the most marginalised groups in UK society: Black women raising children who have disabilities. In this respect, the ethos of 'co-constructed narratives' that is so central to CoAE was further embodied in the approach taken to 'Phase 3' and 'Phase 4'.

A crucial step toward achieving this was to draw out the links between our CoAE account and the lived experiences of our participants through "a focus on relationship building, flattening hierarchies, and establishing trust. Collaborators who trust each other begin to see themselves as members of a democratic community and make the shift from individual to collective agency" (Lapadat, 2017, p. 600). Building on Lapadat (ibid.), we embraced the belief that working alongside "co-researchers from communities beyond the university" and focusing on "issues and experiences of social concern" would set us on "a path toward personally engaging, non-exploitative, accessible research that makes a difference".

It was this conviction which informed the approach we took to the semi-structured interviews and focus groups which constituted Phases 3 and 4 of the research. The use of these qualitative instruments was vital in gaining insight into the "lived experiences of service users, carers and practitioners" and in developing "in depth understanding of how policies and practices are played out in situated contexts" (Sharland, 2013, p. 14).

Participants were invited to:

1.   discuss their pre-existing knowledge of autism
2.   explain what had prompted their suspicion that their child(ren) might be autistic
3.   detail their journey to and through the diagnostic process (where this was complete or ongoing)
4.   reflect on any and all support systems that they drew upon to manage their caring responsibilities
5.   consider the impact that supporting their children had on their own health, career, and social lives
6.   recall their encounters (positive, negative, or both) with healthcare, education, and social care professionals

7.   recommend any changes that could be made to such services with a view to improving engagement with, and outcomes for, Black mothers and their autistic children.

Although this was the approximate format of every discussion, the researchers felt that only a semi-structured interview, in which participants were encouraged to share their own accounts could hope to do justice to the specificity and complexity of the experience of 'mothering' at the intersection of race and disability. We recognised the individuality and heterogeneity of our participants, and their children, and we felt strongly that each one of them would have a perspective that would greatly enrich the research. Therefore, we did not wish to restrict this contribution through the use of needlessly inflexible research instruments. Instead, we sought to enable our participants to reshape, or redirect, discussions to reflect their own personal and authentic experiences, so as to ensure that they felt represented by, and invested in, a project designed to empower and uplift them.

Each interview was analysed multiple times by both co-researchers, who each reviewed the transcripts independently of one another to identify key words, common experiences, and recurrent trends. Then followed a joint discussion in which preliminary findings and reflexive journals were compared, with co-researchers recording and transcribing this analytical process.

Participant interviews are quoted verbatim throughout Chapters 3 and 4, in which we illustrate how the multiplicity of burdens was borne out through the accounts that were provided, and in Chapter 5 which details participant recommendations for improved professional practice. Furthermore, in those instances where themes resonated and recurred across multiple interviews (and were common to experiences already featured in the initial collective autoethnographic vignettes), they were also used as the basis for the 'prompts' around which the subsequent focus groups were designed.

Phase 4: Focus groups

The themes that functioned as focus group prompts included: **guilt**, **gaslighting**, **racial profiling and the negative impact of the tropes of Black womanhood**, **fears for the future**, and – perhaps most significantly – the sense that all interview participants had characterised their experiences in terms of a **'constant fight'** with the service providers who were ostensibly tasked with helping them to meet their children's needs.

A free-flowing discussion was encouraged, and barely any facilitation proved necessary, with participants welcomed to reflect on the prompts in their own terms, and in conversation with one another, absent any specific questions of the sort posed in the interviews.

The themes were revisited in a 'bilateral focus group' (i.e. a semi-structured discussion between the co-researchers), the transcription and analysis of which provided the basis for the completion of the collective autoethnographic vignettes. We felt that it was important that the final phase of our collective autoethnography should fully reflect the journey that our participants had taken. As such, we reviewed our vignettes through the lens of the same key themes on which the participant focus groups had been based. This process further illustrated the extensive commonality of experience between the participants and the co-researchers.

The fact that participants and co-researchers, of varying ages, from a diversity of geographical and socio-economic backgrounds, with a range of different domestic circumstances, expressed such a confluence of concerns and frustrations illustrates that "individual experiences of racism, cultural stigma, [and] gender stereotypes from a patriarchal [and White supremacist] society become part of Black mothers' collective experiences" (Gemegah, 2022, p. 86).

These 'collective experiences' are most effectively summarised by means of the multiplicity of burdens, a framework we deploy throughout Chapters 3 and 4 to analyse and systematise the narratives which our participants shared with us through their survey, interview, and focus group responses. They were also key to the composition of the interview questions for Phase 5 of the research, the discussions undertaken with representatives from 'Black Mothers Matter' and 'Global Child and Maternal Health' (which are detailed in Chapter 5).

The overarching theme of **'collective experience'** has also guided us in synthesising our own stories with those shared by our participants, enabling us to extend and embed the initial phases of our collective autoethnography into a broader account of the impact of mothering at the margins. We have done so to honour the fellow othered mothers who were gracious enough to participate in our research. It is our hope that highlighting the nature and impact of the triad of oppression and its associated multiplicity of burdens on the lived experiences of these mothers, and their children, will demonstrate the urgent need for culturally competent and anti-racist services to support Black mothers raising autistic children.

3
The multiplicity of burdens: Physical and psychological

This chapter presents findings derived from the first four phases of the research project: the collective autoethnographic accounts, the survey, the semi-structured interviews, and the focus groups. These research outcomes are themed in accordance with the multiplicity of burdens framework and subdivided into five categories: physical, psychological, cultural, practical, and temporal.

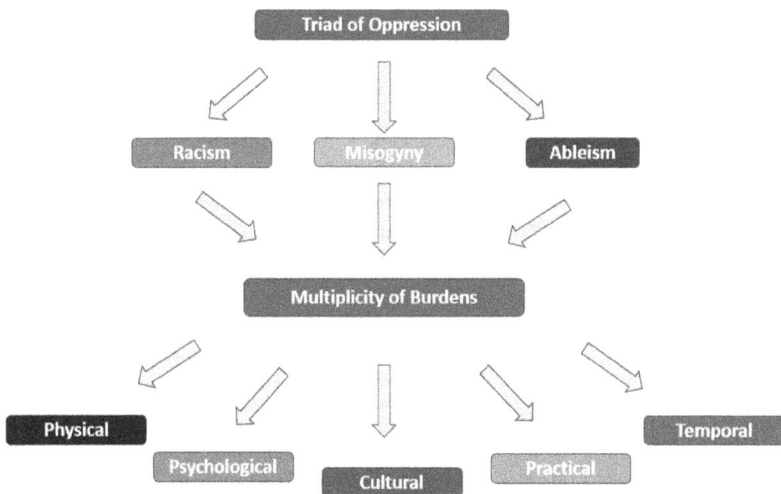

Figure 6: Revisiting the multiplicity of burdens model

The first two burdens are expounded below, with the latter three categories unpacked in Chapter 4.

Each of the 'burdens' identified from the testimonials of the participants (including those of the co-researchers) is explored separately, albeit with the caveat that they cannot be entirely disaggregated from one another. The effects of psychological trauma frequently manifest in physical forms of ill-health, the cultural specificity of Black women's experiences will often have practical implications for their parenting journey, fears for the future (associated with the temporal burden) generate their own psychological struggles, and so the list goes on.

Nonetheless, in order to capture the richness of the lived experience of our participants, each category has been deemed worthy of consideration on its own terms, since each contributes to the trauma which is internalised by Black mothers when they are not provided with effective support in advocating for their autistic children.

Crucially, however, our stories and the stories of our participants are not simply tales of struggle. There is immeasurable joy in raising our children and the most noteworthy collective experience of all is the immense and unconditional love and gratitude that each mother expressed towards her incredible children. Honouring that provides vital context for some of the more distressing insights that must necessarily form part of our account.

As such, the chapter begins with the co-researchers and participants celebrating the gift of motherhood and paying tribute to their children.

Claire's story

Mae is one of my two favourite people in the world. (I know my husband won't be offended to hear that he now only makes the top three.) She is warm, kind, and cheeky and she makes me laugh like a drain. All bias aside, Mae is utterly gorgeous – with huge Bambi-esque brown eyes, soft natural ringlets, and a starlight smile that (as clichéd as this might sound) genuinely lights up the room. She has a giggle that is as contagious as it is filthy and, although as an academic I usually try to avoid making unsupported statements, I'm reasonably sure she gives the best hugs on the planet.

Mae has made the seemingly unlikely transition to big sister with a grace and patience that I could not have imagined, even in my wildest dreams. And while much of the time she only appears to tolerate the tiny human being who turned up out of nowhere and wrestled away her only child status, she also regularly catches us off-guard with how protective and tender she can be toward him. In particular, she shares with Joshua, uncomplainingly and without prompting, in a way which she would not be inclined to do with anyone else.

Mae loves to sing and dance, often to the same songs on a seemingly endless loop, but the joy this brings her means that listening to Clean Bandit (feat. Jess Glynne) 'Rather Be' dozens of times a day is a small price to pay. Watching her showing off these performance skills during a solo of 'The Bare Necessities' at a recent end of term show at her school made me fear that my heart might just burst with pride.

Mae is at her happiest when she is physically active – especially in water. My husband and I often joke that she must secretly have gills because, given the chance, she would spend no time at all on dry land. Watching her at peace, and in her element, nourishes my soul like almost nothing else.

She is brave and adventurous and, as much as I treat the word 'resilient' with great suspicion (because, as we explore throughout this book, it is so commonly weaponised against Black women), she deserves endless credit for how hard she works to navigate the challenges that her autism presents for her, and for how unapologetically authentic she is in all aspects of her life.

I adore her creativity, her enthusiasm, and her energy (boundless as it may be), and I treasure the time we spend together, baking cupcakes, snuggling up in an all-but-empty cinema watching special screenings of films we've already seen a hundred times, spinning around on fairground rides which she embraces with glorious sensory abandon but that make me feel like I'm going to lose my lunch, and reading (well, reciting, because Mae isn't able to read) many of the books I first shared with her when she was still in utero.

I'm thankful every day for my beautiful (not-so-)little Bestie and for the enormous privilege of getting to be her mother. For everything else I might go on to detail about my parenting experiences, what matters most is that Mae is the person who made me a mother, and that's the most precious gift I could ever have hoped for. She, and her brother, are everything to me. The sun rises and sets with them, and they are my inspiration in all things. Whatever else this life might throw at us, that will never change.

Mel's story

I always say Sam made me a mother and the person I am today. After the painful and stressful birthing experience of bringing him into the *world, one of the first things I said was, "I did it! I'm Superwoman!" and that has been a theme of my relationship with him. The lessons he has taught me and continues to teach me about myself encourage me to look at myself through lenses of self-worth and self-belief that I simply did not possess before he was born.*

As mentioned before, I knew that he was autistic early in his life, primarily from observing his interactions with others. Sam is interested in you until he is not.

At my father-in-law's funeral wake, Sam, who was two years old at the time, was faced with meeting family members and friends he had never encountered before. He handled that in typical Sam fashion: he set himself on a path throughout the venue (a local pub) and walked laps of it for over an hour, pausing only to pick crumbs off the floor or nibble on bits of the lunch we had prepared for him. When an overzealous and inquisitive family friend stopped Sam in his tracks, bent down to his level, and leaned in to say hello and hold a conversation, Sam placed his small hand over her face and gently, but firmly, pushed her away. When she stepped back, he cast her a disapproving look for a few seconds before resuming his journey.

The family laughed, of course. What a precocious action from such a cute little boy! Yet, it was in that moment that I gained a profound respect for Sam, a respect that has stayed with me throughout his life. He has an innate ability to create boundaries based on his needs and assert them without hesitation. He has not absorbed the people-pleasing tendencies of his mother or the stoic avoidance of his father; he will, without reservation, make it known if someone has crossed a line.

I also love the way he sees the world, or rather, the way I perceive him seeing the world. When we play music he enjoys, the way his eyes dart and dance across the room makes me feel as if he can see the music itself—a beautiful, vivid visual experience that only he has access to.

When he spins on our kitchen rug (one of his favourite forms of stimming) at a speed that would leave me dizzy and nauseous, I am captivated by the precision of his movements, how his eyes track a fixed point even as his body embodies wild, joyous abandon. It is awe-inspiring to witness that perfect balance of freedom and control. And then there is the joy on his face as he swings in the garden, so high that he nearly peers over the rooftop, with his grin broadening as the wind whips across his face.

When Sam was two, I was told by a psychologist that he would not be capable of love, or empathy and to get comfortable with the fact he would never say I love you. The words 'I love you' are the only full sentence with multiple words Sam has ever said. He shows me he loves me in ways that that psychologist never even considered – involving me in his stimming through deep pressure cuddles, rubbing his fingers over the tips of my locs, staring into my eyes for three minutes at a time. He loves me and I love him.

Sam's lessons have taught me to find beauty in the parts of myself that do not seek validation from others. He has shown me the value of moving beyond the sameness and conformity I strived for in my own childhood. He has taught me to trust what feels right, to establish boundaries and hold others accountable to them, and to understand that expressing oneself authentically is the most powerful form of strength. Because of Sam, I have come to embrace a deeper, truer sense of self.

In the words of our participants

[My son] is the light of my life […]. We call him the sweetest giant because he's 6 foot 6[…]. He is just the sweetest, kindest soul, you know? He makes me so happy – Stacey Ann

He's the most fantastic child I've ever come across. Everybody that meets him is like 'he is honestly the kindest child I've ever met' – Brianna

She's brilliant. If you spoke with her, you'd probably be like, 'wow, I can't believe this girl is only seven!' – Sareeta

…[H]e's a very happy, affectionate, loving child – Linda

[I]t's so nice to just meet a group of ladies who are so excited and so proud of their children. Like, all of you have said how wonderful they are, how much joy they bring you […]. It's nice to meet likeminded mothers who are so passionate and who are so loving and caring about their children – Stacy-Ann (Focus Group 2)

We include these beautiful tributes to honour the fact that every single one of the mothers involved in this project came to us as their child's most passionate advocate and cheerleader. However, the key message that emerged from the experiences they shared with us is that this dedication sometimes came at immense personal cost.

As Imogen succinctly stated: *"Nobody sees how hard this is. No matter how much I love my children, it's still hard to work 24/7".*

The remainder of this chapter, and the entirety of the next, will analyse the various dimensions of the 'mother work' necessitated by the demands of supporting an autistic child and illustrate how existing at the intersection of marginalised identities of race, gender, and disability exacerbates that struggle. In encapsulating these challenges in the multiplicity of burdens framework, we seek to engender understanding, empathy, and a commitment to improved outcomes for Black mothers and their autistic children.

To that end, the following two chapters will summarise and synthesise the key findings that emerged from each of the research instruments. Where possible, interviews and focus groups will be quoted verbatim, in recognition of the importance that the co-researchers place on authenticity and of the belief, articulated so powerfully by one of our participants (Toni) that *"there's no one that understands our own experiences like ourselves".*

However, in the interests of brevity, where several participants have outlined the same, or closely comparable position, we will on occasion use a single quote to convey a collective experience. Alternatively, we may choose to summarise a perspective that recurred multiple times across most, or all, of the stories that were shared with us. Our thanks go to Sareeta, a participant in our research, who inspired this approach by expressly requesting that we create a *'tapestry'* of Black women's voices, of the type she lamented never having seen in existing autism research.

The survey

As was highlighted in the previous chapter, the relatively small number of viable responses to the survey precludes us from claiming that the resulting quantitative data are statistically significant in their own right. However, initial findings certainly provide grounds for further investigation.

- Of 26 respondents, 7 (27%) stated that they were autistic, with 5 (19%) identifying themselves as having ADHD, and 2 (8%) stating that they had PDA. This reinforces the sense that many of our participants are advocating for their children while contending with the impact that neurodivergence has on their own lives.

- 10 of 26 respondents (38%) shared that they suffered from anxiety and 9 (34%) stated that they lived with depression. These findings support our view that mothers with complex caring responsibilities often rely on emotional and psychological reserves which are already strained by mental health challenges.

- 35% of respondents strongly agreed and 12% agreed with the statement *"I feel that education services would have treated me differently if I were not Black"* – a total of 48%. 8% disagreed and 12% strongly disagreed – a total of 20%. 4% of respondents stated that they had not accessed education services in respect of their child's autism.

- 35% of respondents strongly agreed and 27% agreed with the statement *"I feel that healthcare services would have treated me differently if I were not Black"* – a total of 62%. 15% disagreed and 4% strongly disagreed – a total of 19%. 12% of respondents stated that they had not accessed healthcare services in respect of their child's autism.

- 27% of respondents strongly agreed and 27% agreed with the statement *"I feel social care services would have treated me differently if I were not Black"* – a total of 54%. 12% disagreed and 8% strongly disagreed – a total of 20%. 31% of respondents stated that they had not accessed social care services in respect of their child's autism.

These findings indicate that a large number of participants believed that their racial identity had impacted their advocacy journey, and that many had not engaged with social care services as part of that journey. This suggests that there is much that professionals might learn from a closer engagement with the lived experiences of Black mothers of autistic children.

Notwithstanding the caveat regarding sample size, the semi-structured and open questions which invited respondents to elaborate on the answers they had provided elsewhere produced results which accorded closely both with the collective autoethnographic vignettes and with the subsequent interviews and focus groups.

As such, direct, verbatim, quotations from these responses are embedded into the analysis of each of the five 'burdens'. They are included as a means to reinforce and contextualise the statements shared by the six participants who completed all three phases of the research and who are, therefore, cited more frequently and in greater detail than other respondents.

The three interviewees who, owing primarily to issues of availability, were unable to join the focus groups, also provided extremely useful insights that are quoted throughout our analysis.

In what follows, we are at pains to indicate where a given statement has been shared anonymously via the quantitative survey, where it is explicitly attributed to one of our six 'principal participants' (i.e. those who completed all elements of the participant research), or to one of our three additional interviewees. Of course, we recognise that the anonymous nature of the survey ensures that some of the responses to open-ended questions

will have been provided by those who went on to participate in subsequent phases of the research. However, we see intrinsic value in those participants having had the opportunity to express their views via a variety of different mechanisms, since this would have encouraged them to speak freely about their experiences.

Basic biographical information pertaining to all interviewees is listed below.

The participants

The co-researchers:

Claire
Age range: 40–44
Born: UK
Lives: South Wales, UK
Children: • Daughter (13), diagnosed with autism, ADHD, and learning disabilities   • Son (3), awaiting assessment
Relationship status: In a heterosexual marriage with the children's father
Employment status: Employed (part-time)
Health issues: Anxiety, insomnia

Mel
Age range: 40–44
Born: UK
Lives: London, UK

Children:
• Son (8), diagnosed with autism and SPD
• Son (5), awaiting assessment for autism and PDA
Relationship status: In a heterosexual marriage with the children's father
Employment status: Employed (full-time)
Health issues: Depression, anxiety, adenomyosis

The focus group participants

Sareeta
Age range: 30–34
Born: UK
Lives: London, UK
Children:
• Daughter (7), awaiting assessment for autism
• Son (6), diagnosed with autism
Relationship status: Living with and co-parenting with former partner (children's father)
Employment status: Employed (part-time)
Health issues: Hypertension, stomach ulcers, complex PTSD, dyslexia

Toni
Age range: 35–39
Born: Jamaica
Lives: London, UK
Children: • Son (11), diagnosed with autism and awaiting assessment for ADHD
Relationship status: Lone parent
Employment status: Full-time carer
Health issues: Diagnosed with autism; awaiting assessment for ADHD

Brianna
Age range: 35–39
Born: UK
Lives: Cheshire, UK
Children: • Son (10), diagnosed with autism • Son (3), undiagnosed (likely neurotypical)
Relationship status: Living with/engaged to children's father
Employment status: Employed (full-time), currently retraining
Health issues: Awaiting assessment for autism and ADHD

Imogen
Age range: 45–49
Born: UK
Lives: Greater Manchester, UK
Children: • Son (28), autism (undiagnosed) • Son (25), diagnosed with dyspraxia • Son (21), diagnosed with ADHD • Daughter (19), diagnosed with autism and PDA • Son (17), diagnosed with autism and depressive disorder
Relationship status: Lone parent
Employment status: Full-time carer
Health issues: Chronic fatigue, chronic pain, autism, ADHD

Linda
Age range: 35–39
Born: Angola
Lives: London, UK
Children: • Three children, including son (6), diagnosed with autism
Relationship status: In a heterosexual marriage with the children's father
Employment status: Full-time carer
Health issues: Ehlers-Danlos syndrome, Type 3

Stacy-Ann
Age range: 45–49
Born: USA
Lives: London, UK
Children: • Son (21), diagnosed with autism
Relationship status: Lone parent
Employment status: Employed (full-time)/Doctoral researcher
Health issues: Chronic fatigue, autoimmune issues

Additional interviewees

Matilda
Age range: 35–39
Born: UK
Lives: London, UK
Children: • Daughter (7), neurotypical   • Daughter (5), neurotypical   • Son (3), awaiting assessment for autism
Relationship status: In a heterosexual marriage with the children's father
Employment status: Full-time carer
Health issues: None disclosed

Laura
Age range: 55–59
Born: UK
Lives: London, UK
Children: • Daughter (27), undiagnosed autism   • Son (23), diagnosed with autism
Relationship status: Not disclosed
Employment status: Employed (full-time)
Health issues: None disclosed

Ayesha
Age range: 60–64
Born: UK
Lives: West Midlands, UK
Children: • Three children, including daughter (30s), undiagnosed autism and PDA
Relationship status: In a heterosexual marriage with the children's father
Employment status: Employed (full-time)
Health issues: Anxiety

As the above biographies indicate:

- Participants range in age from early 30s to mid-60s

- There is extensive variety in their geographical locations.

- The bulk of the participants were born in the UK but Toni, Linda and Stacy-Ann all shared that they moved to the UK as children (from Jamaica, Angola, and the USA respectively).

- The data includes perspectives from women who are married to the fathers of their children, and from women who are lone parents.

- Five of the eleven participants are employed on a full-time basis, two on a part-time basis, and four are currently full-time carers.

What this demonstrates is that, while all participants share a common identity, as Black mothers raising autistic children in the UK, there is also considerable demographic diversity among those who contributed to the research. This is significant because it means that the challenges identified by participants transcend considerations such as age, geography, and socio-economic status that might otherwise be considered to have been significant causal factors.

A further word on 'resilience'

It is important to note that in unpacking the individual components of the multiplicity of burdens, we also draw attention to some of the strategies that our participants have devised to navigate and withstand them. While this decision is partially borne of our determination to honour the diligence, dedication, and resourcefulness of the mothers who shared their journeys with us, we consciously do not valorise conceptions of 'resilience', viewing them instead as an extension of the 'Strong Black Woman' trope that our research revealed to be profoundly damaging to Black mothers of autistic children.

In further elucidating the multiplicity of burdens model, we expand upon an emerging literature which recognises the toxicity of resilience-based narratives, and the harms that they visit on Black women.

As Liggins-Chambers (2024) asserts:

> The expectation of resilience can lead to an excessive emotional and psychological burden. Black women are frequently expected to shoulder not only their own struggles but also those of their families and communities, often without adequate support. The pressure to be resilient can have detrimental effects on their physical and mental health. Chronic stress and the need to constantly appear strong can contribute to higher rates of mental health issues such as depression as well as health-related problems (e.g. hypertension), among Black women.

Similarly, Bentley-Edwards (in Banks, 2024) also makes the case for moving beyond a focus on resilience, affirming that:

> Nurturing resiliency among Black youth was intended to provide a stop-gap measure to deal with societal ills, but it should not be a substitute for addressing systemic problems [...]. [S]ociety relies on Black women to be resilient [...]. Often times, we focus on just changing people's behaviours and habits and not the systems that put these inequalities in place. We need to ease that burden. Otherwise, it's people always adjusting to chaos.

We wish to go further than this by expressly stating that, very often, labelling Black women as 'superhuman' provides a veil for continuing to treat us as if we are, in fact, *less than human* and, therefore not worthy of human kindness, compassion, and care. As such, we are unwilling to endorse 'resilience' as a so-called 'coping strategy' in the face of systemic neglect and institutionalised racism. Within dominant neoliberal frameworks, resilience is framed as an individualised capacity to endure hardship, often divorced from the structural conditions that produce that hardship. This framing places undue pressure on Black mothers to perform strength and perseverance, rather than interrogating or addressing the systems that perpetuate harm. In doing so, it shifts responsibility away from institutions and onto individuals, effectively privatising trauma. The emotional, physical, and psychological costs of navigating racism, ableism, and misogyny are thereby rendered personal burdens to be silently managed, rather than collective injustices to be redressed. It is from this perspective, that we will now further explore the multiplicity of burdens faced by Black mothers of autistic children.

Breaking down the multiplicity of burdens

Physical burden

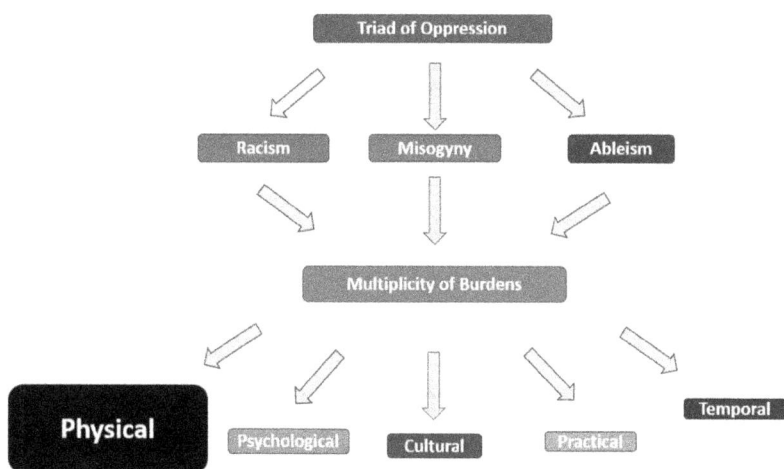

Figure 7: Focus on the physical burden within the multiplicity of burdens

Our findings in this study define the physical burden as the embodied effects of birthing, mothering, and advocating for our autistic children. We note that the effects of the racism experienced by racially minoritised individuals cannot and should not be perceived as being purely psychological. There is increasing evidence emerging that demonstrates how a social identity such as a racialised one, that is "stigmatised by the dominant culture as inferior, threatening, other, or in some way undesirable, shapes the lived reality and health of each person who is defined by it" (Geronimus, 2023, p. 134).

In the following sections, we illustrate how the mothers in our study have experienced this burden.

Mel's story

Becoming a mother changed me in physical ways that I hadn't ever expected.

My pregnancy with Sam was challenging. I didn't properly realise it at the time, as I hadn't got far with my previous pregnancy, losing that baby just before ten weeks. After the loss, I was told I had a large fibroid located at the rear of my uterus. Fibroids—non-cancerous growths in or around the womb—are more common and severe among Black women than other racial groups, with studies indicating that 80% of Black women develop fibroids by the age of 50. They are often accompanied by other gynaecological conditions, compounding the burden.

With Sam, I developed anaemia, carpal tunnel syndrome, De Quervain's tenosynovitis, recurrent thrush, and high blood pressure. Some of these terms were new to me; others, I'd never imagined would be part of my life. When people asked how I was, I often brushed it off, saying, "Oh, pregnancy is just hard on the body." But deep down, I was frightened, already aware of how my body felt strained by the weight of this journey.

The next year and a half after Sam was born brought a new wave of challenges. I experienced sharp abdominal pains after eating, which escalated to unbearable levels within 15 months. My doctor was convinced it was Irritable Bowel Syndrome (IBS), prescribing Buscopan™ and advising me to cut out dairy. In October 2018, my husband found me curled up on the bedroom floor, crippled by pain. A trip to A&E that day finally provided an answer: an ultrasound revealed my gallbladder was full of stones. The sonographer was surprised I had endured the pain as long as I had. My gallbladder was removed in November 2018.

Still, the diagnoses didn't stop. Four years later, three years after the birth of my second child, I was diagnosed with Non-Alcoholic Fatty Liver Disease (NAFLD) and adenomyosis. NAFLD, often unrecognised as a public health issue, is directly linked to metabolic syndrome—a cluster of conditions like abdominal obesity and hypertension (Riazi et al., 2022). Adenomyosis, on the other hand, occurs when cells from the uterine lining are found in the uterine muscle, leading to heavy, painful, and prolonged periods. Research suggests Black women face disproportionately higher rates of adenomyosis compared to White women (Onchee et al., 2020). These conditions were markers of the toll my body had endured over years of cumulative strain.

Making significant dietary changes like cutting out alcohol and dairy reversed my NAFLD diagnosis, but adenomyosis remains an ongoing battle. My periods are heavier and longer, the pain sometimes immobilising. Add to that the kidney stones I've endured, and I feel as though my body is shouting back at me, weary from carrying too much for too long.

I can't ignore the toll on my body, what scholars of racial inequities call weathering. The daily stress related to raising and advocating for an autistic child in an unwelcoming environment amplifies this toll. Every battle for access to therapies, every microaggression faced at school gates, and every insensitive comment about my child chips away at me and resides somewhere deep inside my body. I exist in a constant state of hypervigilance, navigating systems that were never designed for families like mine.

Reading about the role of chronic inflammation in many diseases that disproportionately affect Black women, how it triggers autoimmune diseases and facilitates cancer growth, makes me scared, not just for myself, but for the future of my children. What world will my autistic child inherit, and how will his experiences affect his body in ways he may not even realise?

Motherhood has deepened my understanding of my own fragility, not as a weakness, but as a reminder that this body, this Black body, is always at work, resisting and surviving. But I don't want survival to be the only legacy I pass down to my children. I want them to thrive in a world that does not see their identities as burdens but as parts of their whole, vibrant selves. Until then, I carry the weight of this fight, physically and emotionally, knowing the stakes have never been higher.

Claire's story

As discussed in our introductory chapter, Lennard Davis (1995) promotes an understanding of disability which foregrounds 'normalcy'. Davis states that, "the 'problem' is not the person with disabilities; the problem is the way that normalcy is constructed to create the 'problem' of the disabled person" (1995, p. 24). In our home, the counterweight to this problematic construction is to embrace Mae's needs and behaviours as an integral part of who she is, and to create space for them to play out in whatever way may be necessary for her to maintain a semblance of emotional regulation. The flipside to this, however, is that the consequences of those behaviours have been 'normalised' for the rest of the family, to the point where their damaging impacts are often vastly underestimated.

A case in point is that I have not had a full night's sleep in 13 years. This is partly due to the irregular hours that Mae herself keeps, but it is also the consequence of my own constant state of hypervigilance. The light sleep of the 'newborn phase' of parenting is one which I have not been able to safely leave behind because, if Mae wakes in the night – which she is frequently inclined to do – she immediately becomes a potential danger to herself and to her little brother. Even into her teens, she has no sense of danger, and an extremely limited capacity for self-care. She wanders, she climbs, she attempts to run herself a bath, she seeks out an iPad which, if she had her way, she would stare at for the remainder of the small hours. If she is awake, she needs me to be too.

So, my 'sleep routine' – such as it is – is as follows: once Mae goes to bed, a process which usually takes until at least 11pm, I am left with no opportunity to unwind from the stresses of the day. No downtime, no 'me' time, no time to spend with my husband, even when he's not working a 12-hour night shift. I take the day's anxieties, both personal and professional, and tuck them in next to me. I do my best to observe sleep hygiene… I never drink coffee, I block out the light with expensive blackout blinds, I ensure that my phone is not within reach to tempt me with a nighttime 'doom scroll'…

Despite these efforts, sometimes sleep evades me altogether. Sometimes I collapse immediately and go out like a light. Either way, I will be awake by 1am, and until 5am. I might be tending to one or both of my children, during this time, or on a 'good night', I may just be staring at the ceiling ruminating on an endless list of incomplete tasks that await me with the dawn. The hour between my body finally capitulating and my alarm sounding at 6am passes in what feels like a heartbeat, and then the day begins anew.

The physical toll of 13 years of this crushing insomnia is now inescapable. I appear to have little to no resistance to coughs, colds, and infections (many and varied), I am plagued by headaches, and sore and aching muscles, and I am devoid of the energy that I should be using for exercise, the almost chronic lack of which completes the vicious circle of sleep deprivation. I know that all of this puts me at increased risk of hypertension, heart disease, cancer, and any number of other life-limiting conditions, but this is my 'normal' and I have long since given up hope of finding ways to change it.

It is 'priced in' to my experience of raising an autistic child, just like the bruises and scratches that cover my arms and legs, from ill-fated attempts to ensure that my daughter's daily meltdowns result in injuries to me, not to her.

My body wears the scars, both literal and metaphorical, of meeting her needs at the expense of my own.

Physical weathering

Our stories, and the stories of our participants, exemplify the effects of 'weathering' (Geronimus, 2023), which is itself based on a compelling rallying cry to address extreme disparities in health outcomes for Black communities.

Geronimus (ibid., p. 1) posits that weathering "afflicts human bodies – all the way down to the cellular level – as they grow, develop, and age in a systematically and historically racist, classist society". Crucially, weathering is not the consequence of 'moral failings', or poor decision-making. Neither is it 'natural' or 'inevitable' that certain populations should have markedly worse health outcomes than others. Instead, Black bodies are impacted by historical legacies of racism, slavery, and colonialism, but also by contemporary inequalities and the many stressors to which White supremacy disproportionately exposes them.

Furthermore, access to the kind of support which might enable Black people to mitigate the effects of weathering is also stratified along racial lines. Per Geronimus (ibid.), "Racialisation is a powerful means by which the dominant culture sets groups apart as more or less deserving of, or entitled to, resources, esteem, or power; or instead as worthy of contempt, punishment, deprivation, stigma, oppression, and exploitation".

In the case of Black women, whose intersectional identities are linked with both race and gender, the consequences of these ingrained inequalities are borne out in countless examples that speak to the real-world manifestations of weathering.

In March 2023, the Faculty of Life Sciences and Medicine, at King's College, published the outcome of its four-year study of 'Multiple Morbidity' in South London communities. It revealed that, compared with White women, "Black women have twice and in some cases three times the rate of long-term conditions including chronic pain, anxiety, hypertension, osteoarthritis, diabetes, and morbid obesity" (Soley-Bori, 2023).

Similarly, "research by the Mothers and Babies: Reducing Risk through Audits and Confidential Enquiries across the UK (MBRRACE-UK) collaboration considered the data on women in the UK who had died during or up to one year after pregnancy in 2018–2020" (House of Commons Women and Equalities Committee, 2023). The study revealed that Black women were at the highest risk of any ethnic group and were "3.7 times more likely to die during or in the first year after pregnancy than White women" (ibid.), a statistic which remained stable in their subsequent 2020–2022 findings (Knight et al., 2022).

The prevalence of heart disease has been illustrated by the Centers for Disease Control and Prevention (CDC) in the US, which found that roughly 50% of Black women suffer from some form of this condition, a factor in the 3-year life expectancy disparity between this population and its White counterparts (Collier and Smith-Johnson, 2024).

These statistics paint a bleak picture of significantly reduced health outcomes for Black women, in both the UK and the US. However, we contend that Black mothers of autistic children are at even graver risk. In the first instance, this group is exposed to a disproportionate number of physiological stressors, by dint of their identities and their caregiving responsibilities. Secondly, they are 'marked' as unworthy of meaningful support because of their race, their gender, and their attachment to the 'unproductive labour' of raising children who are both racialised and potentially limited in their ability to mature into 'income generators' in a capitalist society.

The lack of targeted research obscures these disparities, forcing Black mothers of autistic children to internalise the stress and normalise the resulting physical health issues. Conditions such as fibromyalgia, chronic fatigue syndrome, obesity, and women's health issues such as adenomyosis, tend to be under-researched and misunderstood, and can therefore be erroneously linked with a sense of 'moral failure' and used to perpetuate stereotypes of Black mothers as lazy or irresponsible. This further diminishes the empathy that othered mothers receive from healthcare professionals and society. Several of our participants shared details of the tolls taken on their physical health:

> [E]verybody knows what their limits are and their capacity. And I would say, actually, I've far exceeded my capacity. It really did put me in a very dark space… genuinely, like I was losing sleep for a while. I couldn't eat. It really, really affected me[…]. It's really having an impact on my physical wellbeing. […] I have high blood pressure and I do think this… just ongoing fight. […] is extremely strenuous and stressful on both the mind and the body. And yeah, my blood pressure, unfortunately my dad passed away from hypertension as well, only at the age of 53. So, I know well

that this is something that is in my family and that we need to be careful of – Sareeta

It's taken its toll on my mental health, and on my physical health. […] hair falling out, or feeling weak, or tired, or all of those things… It really used to physically take its toll on me because you're, you know, you're breaking down – Stacy-Ann

I'm so tired […]. Obviously, anyone else in a sort of typical situation, if they weren't sleeping for years, you'd be like 'oh no, this is really not good for you'. But you have no choice – you just have to crack on – Linda

I've got two health conditions that feature chronic fatigue […]. Black women's physical pain is ignored to our significant detriment… to the point of harm and death. […] You're just supposed to carry it. You know, you're just supposed to deal with it […] No one gives a shit about your pain – Imogen

The vicarious physical burden

Several of our participants also spoke at length about the experience of enduring physical pain vicariously through their children. Accounts of restraint and injury, specifically in a school setting, recurred across multiple interviews, with two participants currently involved in legal proceedings against schools which they felt had failed to adequately protect their sons.

Three boys punched him, but he didn't tell us until ages after [because] he couldn't communicate it – Linda

[T]he very first time that my son had a major outburst at school […] and they're calling me and they're saying 'Ok, well, he got really upset at lunchtime […] and he was

throwing food and we had to use physical restraint'. And I'm saying 'why did you have to use physical restraint?' [...]This is a special school, so you are equipped and knowledgeable to work with children that have a variety of challenging behaviours'. Whatever behaviour he's demonstrating or exhibiting, it's because he's trying to communicate something, and I'm expecting them as the experts [to understand that] – Stacy-Ann

[A member of school staff] manhandles him and they try to restrain him[...] and there's two members of staff that were outside holding the door handle so he can't open it from the inside. [...The staff] didn't tell me nothing about the restraining – Laura

As detailed in accounts of the 'Cultural' and 'Temporal' burdens, participants identified this increased vulnerability to physical violence as being part of a wider culture of hostility and racialisation facing their children.

The accounts highlight the severe physical toll (vicarious or experienced) that mothering and advocacy place on Black mothers, exacerbated by systemic neglect and a lack of empathy from healthcare professionals and society. The chronic stress, exhaustion, and health conditions they describe illustrate how their struggles are dismissed, reinforcing the broader pattern of ignoring Black women's pain and well-being.

Analysis now turns to the 'Psychological burden', which illustrates how the anxieties that participants expressed about the impact of such profiling on them and their families greatly contribute to the poor mental and physical health outcomes that they report experiencing.

Psychological burden

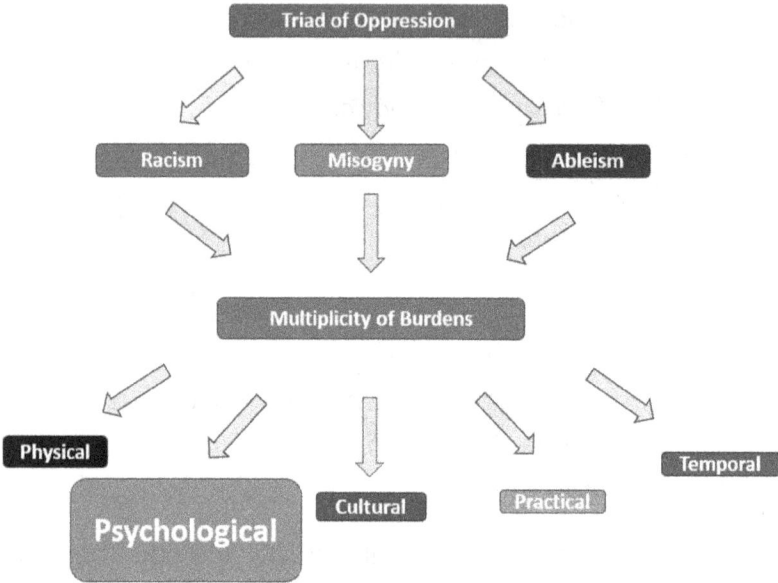

Figure 8: Focus on the psychological burden within the multiplicity of burdens

The psychological burden in this study refers to the ongoing emotional and mental strain that arises from mothering and advocating for autistic children. The following sections examine how this burden manifests in the experiences of the mothers in our study.

Claire's story

To delineate all the psychological impacts of my parenting journey would require a book of its own, but if I were to try to boil them down to one overarching theme, I'd say it's the feeling of inadequacy – of failing on multiple fronts, all at once.

In part, it's the 'Mum Guilt' that goes hand-in-hand with being the primary caregiver in a household with two children. In part, it's the

plate-spinning of trying to hold down a demanding job, one in which unpaid overtime and expectations of 'outperformance' come with the territory.

But it's more than that. It's also the way that I'm buffeted by the tropes of Black womanhood. I am expected to be strong, but not too strong. If I'm too strong, then I might seem angry. And no one likes an 'Angry Black Woman'. If I'm not strong enough, then I'm vulnerable. And if I'm vulnerable then so are my children.

The legacy of the messages conveyed to me by the 'assimilation generation' of which my Jamaican father is a part still rings in my ears. I know that it's not enough to be average, not enough to get by. I have to be the best because anything less provides a veil for racism and discrimination. "Never give them an excuse" is a mantra that 40 plus years of socialisation has embedded in my very core, and which has been consolidated by the range of ways in which services that purported to support my family, have routinely failed us.

Mae is a sensory seeker – most of the time – so I have to do everything I can to help her access spaces that will enable her to compensate for the dopamine deficit that is constantly taunting her brain. But, just as my identity as a Black woman necessitates a finely tuned balance, so does my daughter's nervous system. Inadvertently tipping into overstimulation is a recipe for immediate disaster, with Mae's gossamer thin 'window of tolerance' collapsing in the face of even the most low-level or arbitrary trigger.

In the absence of a capacity for emotional regulation, or delayed gratification, and labouring under the weight of her own complex sensory diet, she will drop to the floor, let out a blood-curdling scream, growl, scratch, kick, punch, and attempt to run away. This occurs on an almost daily basis, often for hours at a time, and only sustained deep pressure, well-rehearsed responses to her echolalic 'scripts', and a preternatural level of patience, will see her through such a meltdown.

This is hard enough in the safe space of our home but, in public, in a White-majority area where racist clichés about Black mothers are never far from certain people's minds, I can only brace for the judgemental side-eyes of strangers, and hope that no one reports us to the police. Again.

The emotional fallout from these incidents is difficult to articulate. It's a toxic soup of self-recrimination, resentment, and profound sadness, tinged with envy for my friends whose neurotypical teens are finding much more traditional ways to torture their parents.

I wish I could claim that the anger I feel in these moments dissipates immediately, but that's not entirely accurate. Because I'm conditioned to know that none of this is Mae's fault, and because my only priority is to help her recover from the exhausting effect that the meltdown has had on her, my anger is swallowed… shelved… suppressed in pursuit of well-rehearsed co-regulation strategies that enable me to give her the love and reassurance that she requires to find her way back to some kind of equilibrium. But I can't lie to my body which, despite my best efforts to remain calm, stores that anger away along with its favourite bedfellow: guilt.

Over the years, I have found a dizzying array of ways to hold myself responsible for Mae's autism and the ways in which it affects her. I won't dignify them by listing them here because I know, in my heart, that they're irrational. That doesn't stop them from troubling me, though, especially during those endless sleepless nights.

Family, friends, and even the professionals assigned to us will often offer empty platitudes along the lines of "I don't know how you do it". It's just another way to congratulate me on my 'resilience' because it's easier than acknowledging the depth of my trauma, and their own impotence in helping me to manage it.

I do it because I adore my child. And because I have no choice… since no one else can do it for me. But that's no protection against the harms that it visits upon my mental health. There's only so much one 'Strong Black Woman' can take.

Mel's story

Since Sam's diagnosis, I have begun to recognise that I very likely have undiagnosed neurodivergence myself. Yet, growing up in the 80s and early 90s with autism and ADHD not being as well-known resulted in 17-year-old-me being diagnosed with Generalised Anxiety Disorder (GAD) and 'mild' depression instead.

Reflecting on my own mental health, I see now that the challenges I've faced stretch back to infancy. My mother often recounts how I cried incessantly as a baby and toddler. For her and others in my family, it was easy to dismiss this as me being "too sensitive." By my teenage years, I had internalised that message, teaching myself to suppress my sensitivity so it would no longer be an inconvenience to others. But instead of disappearing, it re-emerged in other, more harmful ways: severe anxiety and depression, an eating disorder, and self-harm.

Years of therapy helped me gain insight into these struggles, equipping me with tools to better manage my mental health. By the time I had Sam in 2017, I felt more mentally stable and self-aware. But stability doesn't mean resolution. My need for control and structure, a common thread throughout my life, remained ever-present. It hid beneath the surface, manifesting in subtle but undeniable ways. For instance, when Sam was just a week old, I decided to prepare a fillet mignon for the first time in my life. I think I did this not because I was craving pastry-coated beef but to prove to myself that I could excel as a new mother and still be an exceptional wife. In hindsight, it was an early indication of how I channelled my anxiety into rigid standards and unattainable expectations.

Sam's autism diagnosis came during the Covid-19 lockdown: a time of unprecedented stress but also togetherness for our family. My anxiety skyrocketed. I became hypervigilant about hygiene and developed some obsessive routines. Every time my husband returned home from taking Sam out for two- or three-hour walks in the forest, I would essentially hose him down, scrubbing away the imaginary threats of contamination. For three months, I refused to leave the house. My world shrank to the four walls around me, and within that space, I threw myself into understanding my son's needs. I joined every autism parenting group I could find and compulsively consumed information. During late-night breastfeeds, I would scour articles, watch webinars, and devour research. I told myself that knowledge was power and that being the best possible mother for Sam meant becoming an expert on autism. But in reality, my fixations were less about empowerment and more about control; a desperate attempt to impose order on a situation that felt utterly overwhelming.

Sam's meltdowns, occurring four or five times daily, left me emotionally shattered. Witnessing your child harm themselves, *headbutting walls or clawing at their skin, creates a kind of pain that is hard to put into words. You feel powerless, heartbroken, and sometimes paralysed by guilt, wondering if you could be doing more or better. It consumes energy and leaves little room for anything else.*

The fight for Sam's diagnosis was just the beginning. It was followed by the battle to secure him a place in a specialist provision, and then the ongoing struggle to ensure that provision adhered to the requirements of his Education, Health, and Care Plan (EHCP). Each fight took a toll, damaging what was left of my mental reserves. By the time I began to see signs of neurodivergence in my second son, I was already burnt out—cognitively, emotionally, and mentally exhausted.

Psychological burnout has become a recurring state for me, an ever-present shadow that I struggle to shake. Maintaining the order and routine that my children and I both need feels like an insurmountable challenge some days. I know I need time to rebuild myself psychologically, but the demands of parenting—and especially of raising autistic children in a world that is often hostile to their needs—leave little space for recovery.

One of the phrases I absolutely detest is when 'well-meaning' people tell me that "I cannot pour from an empty cup". I hate the phrase because it is just not true. I pour from a near-empty cup every day. There is no time or space to fill my cup. Recognising my own likely neurodivergence is little comfort, though I am always grateful to my children for that revelation. It has given me greater insight into my own struggles and a deeper empathy for my children, but it has also illuminated just how much I have neglected and continue to neglect myself.

I will say though, there is something left in my cup, the love I have for my boys. It is the fuel that keeps me fighting with the same intensity and determination I have for the past eight years.

Psychological impact

In reviewing the ways in which participants addressed the psychological impact of supporting their autistic child, there emerged a series of stressors against which the majority of parenting experiences could be mapped. These included:

- dismissal of early concerns
- diagnostic delays
- impact of diagnosis
- lack of post-diagnostic support
- lack of opportunities for self-care
- the impact of the tropes of Black womanhood ('Angry Black Woman' and 'Strong Black Woman)
- (in some cases) managing a child's self-harm or suicidal ideation
- racial discrimination

Dismissal of early concerns

Our findings indicate that in every case in which a mother had been successful in securing an autism diagnosis for (at least) one of her children, the process had been extremely attenuated, with parental concerns significantly predating the diagnosis itself. All six of the principal participants described a pre-diagnostic period in which they felt that they had been dismissed by the professionals and service providers assigned to their family. This sentiment was also echoed in responses to the anonymised survey.

We'd seen a lot of professionals […] and they had all fobbed me off – Linda

I didn't feel heard… I didn't feel listened to – Toni

I felt very powerless, you know? They were the ones that had all this knowledge and this information. And I thought they were the experts. And here's me as the mum where I'm quickly getting shut down in appointments… You know, it's like in and out of the door and I'm like 'you're not even looking at him' – Stacy-Ann

I did start asking those questions at the age of 2 [when] I noticed that his language wasn't developing typically. I involved health visitors […] but it was just very much brushed off – Brianna

[E]very one of my concerns has been borne out. Like, everything I've been concerned about has been correct… and I've been dismissed."[.. I was] just made to look like I'm just pathologising my own children and all my concerns have, unfortunately, been validated in really painful, awful, ways. – Imogen

I was dismissed by several GPs, ENT specialists, health visitors, and initial speech and language therapist. – Survey respondent, anonymous.

These experiences illustrate a recurring pattern of parental concerns being overlooked, leading to delayed diagnoses and prolonged uncertainty. The consistent dismissal by professionals not only intensified the emotional and logistical burden on mothers but also reinforced systemic barriers to timely and appropriate support.

Diagnostic delays

While acknowledging that the nature of autism, as a developmental disorder (undetectable through, for example, blood tests or brain scans) can complicate the pursuit of a diagnosis in early years, the mothers in our study nonetheless reported extended periods during which no support was made available:

> *There was no support for months. It was a constant battle to get any kind of support or acknowledgement that my son needed the additional help. – Survey respondent, anonymous*

Furthermore, four of the participants stated (independently of one another) that they had had to re-refer their children into services that had 'lost' their notes.

> *But there was some mix up with that referral that I had to chase up. –* Matilda

> *They just couldn't find his [SALT] referral. –* Linda

> *They lost his notes several times. –* Imogen

> *I put his referral in. [SALT] took a year and then they said they never received it […] so we had to re-refer him and that took another year. […] I worked for the speech and language company and saw that they'd requested speech and language information, so they definitely received the [first] referral. –* Brianna

It is noteworthy that diagnostic delays were found to be even more lengthy for those mothers seeking recognition of autism symptomatology in their daughters. A pattern emerged of late, or misdiagnosis, continuing to be worryingly common among autistic girls. This reflected a trend identified by researchers at Swansea University who reported, in 2022, that girls wait an average of six years longer than boys to receive an autism diagnosis, with the average age of diagnosis standing at 10–12 for girls, and 4–6 for boys (Thomas, 2022).

Laura shared that:

> *My daughter is undiagnosed, but it's very clear*

Similarly, Imogen detailed the delays in receiving a diagnosis for her daughter, despite her having presented with what might be considered 'classic' autism symptomatology (speech delay, limited social communication, reduced capacity for emotional regulation, etc.) from a very young age. Although *"when she was in nursery, they highlighted suspicions of autism",* Imogen's daughter was not formally diagnosed until the age of 14.

> *… It just seems so obvious to me why children mask and why they don't mask… and also the complex intricacies of gender.*

These 'complex intricacies' have also resulted in a delayed diagnosis for Sareeta's daughter:

> *My 7-year-old [daughter who is undiagnosed] is… very sociable. She kind of, I would say, is almost like a bit of a chameleon. She really likes to… she's a real social pleaser. [Her brother who is diagnosed] is like 'This is what I like. If you don't like it, I'm not interested in you' where she's very much so accommodating to other people's needs. She has really high empathy. She really cares about how she's perceived in social groups.*

These diagnostic delays further contribute to the challenges faced by mothers whose daughters are not even entitled to the minimal support that might otherwise be made available to their family, on their behalf.

Irrespective of the gender of their children, however, mothers consistently reported that during what was often a years-long wait for a diagnosis, they experienced feelings of frustration, isolation, and self-recrimination. Far from being reassured by professionals (erroneously) claiming that there were no issues with their child's development, our participants recalled blaming themselves for 'failing' a child whom they were being falsely told was neurotypical.

> I felt like it was my inadequacies why my child was clearly suffering [...] and I was ridden with guilt because I felt like no matter how hard I'm trying; it just wasn't enough. [...] There's so much self-blame and I absorbed it. – Toni (Focus Group 1)

> Because there was such a lack of involvement from professionals in the beginning and because everything was brushed off, I genuinely believed that it was my fault and it was something that I had done and honestly, for the first seven years of his life [...] I tortured myself thinking it was me and that affected my mental health massively... massively and I genuinely believed that he would be better off with another mother, in somebody else's care and I wasn't enough. [...] When you've had that sort of mindset for such a long time, it's very hard to break that. – Brianna

Impact of diagnosis

Mothers in the study craved clarity and support for their children and fought extraordinarily hard to secure a diagnosis.

Nevertheless, the confirmation that their child was, in fact, autistic felt to many like something of a double-edged sword. On the one hand, there was a sense of relief, as expressed by Toni who explained that, at the point of her son's diagnosis (when he was 10 years old):

> I literally threw myself on the ground and bawled like a baby cause that's how much I was holding it in.

On the other hand, for many of our participants, feelings of guilt and self-blame were, in fact, amplified at the diagnostic stage:

> You're trying to manage this, but also managing it within the idea that somehow this is… this is something about you. You know, either you've genetically created this 'badly behaved child' or, […] it's your parenting. […] I think there's like a big impact around guilt and responsibility because… these are my genes that created these issues… or decisions that I've made. – Imogen

Mothers also reported that this sense of self-blame was immediately filtered through profound concerns about how living at the intersection of racialisation and disability would affect their child. This sentiment, which featured in several interviews, is summarised by Stacy-Ann who asserted:

> It took me a long, long time to really process that because as I said, he's my only child. And you know, I think as any mother does, when you're pregnant, you've got all these dreams and you kind of almost plan their life for them. And everything changed in that moment […] And for me it just… everything stopped. I just remember looking at my son thinking 'what is his life going to be like now?'… and

I think it was a combination of the fact that he is now going to be labelled as this young person that has this special, you know, special needs. But then he's also a Black person that has this special need.

Lack of post-diagnostic support

Crucially, the post-diagnostic support provided by professionals was reported as having been sparse and inconsistent, leaving mothers – who were still reeling from the diagnosis itself – little choice but to find ways to meet their children's complex needs alone:

[The Health Visitor] … didn't refer me on for any support, or information, any education, any anything. I had to look for everything [...so] I can't really say that I had support… because I had to seek that all on my own without anyone telling me [...] They didn't give me anywhere to turn to. They're like 'OK, wait a few months for an appointment… off you go.' – Matilda

I was literally told 'your child has autism' and then I was handed a book. There were courses to go on, but they were more about my parenting than my child. – Survey respondent, anonymous

I recognised that I needed to take matters into my own hands. If I was gonna get him the support that I could clearly see that he needed. – Toni

I have always felt left in the dark when it comes to available support for my sons. From the moment of diagnosis, rather than have anyone reach out to me, I've been handed a pile of leaflets and left to get on with it. No shoulder to cry on, no way of trying to make sense of things. – Survey respondent, anonymous

I think a lot of us, we end up doing so much reading or training… or just that learning… [so we can have it] with us in our toolbox at home. [...] I feel like a professor, compared to three years ago. – Linda, (Focus Group 2)

As well as the immense pressure to acquire a vast amount of knowledge and skills to enable them to meet their child's needs, participants also spoke to the isolating effect of realising that their child's developmental trajectory would be different from that of their neurotypical peers. The diagnosis brought with it a period of adjustment as mothers reflected on how much of this journey they would have to face alone.

The minute [my son] got that diagnosis, it was very different. You know, your phone doesn't ring as much. People don't come around as much as they used to, and it's always an excuse or it's always a reason, or whatever the case may be, and I think it opened my eyes to just really seeing how lonely it can be, how isolating it can be… – Stacy-Ann

It can be terribly isolating and lonely in the journey of advocacy. – Sareeta

Lack of opportunities for self-care

While all the participants in the study spoke candidly about the extreme toll that raising their autistic child without adequate support had taken on their mental health, few were able to point to examples of how they balanced meeting their child's needs, with prioritising self-care. Instead, they conceded that their own health, well-being, and identity were routinely compromised.

In order to give him that support and nurture him, I need that for myself because I'm lacking that. – Matilda

I think as a parent of someone that has autism [...] you can get lost in that, you know, that becomes another part of your identity. Yeah. And people don't see you. People don't see you anymore and people don't care to know what it's been like for you. – Stacy-Ann

A powerful example of this loss of individual agency emerged from a discussion during the second Focus Group, in which all three participants shared that they had suffered recent bereavements but had not been able to process their own grief, for fear of the potential impact on their children:

[M]y mum passed away [...] and, during this time of me grieving, I feel I can't drop the ball. – Stacy Ann, (Focus Group 2)

I lost my brother. [...] It was really sudden. [...] You have to give off that image that you're fine all of the time. I mean, [my son] is always so attuned to how I'm feeling. I can't... I can't show him any emotion. [...] That's been the hardest challenge of this year – trying to just be ok when dealing with my own grief. – Brianna (Focus Group 2)

I had to schedule in a bit of time to have a cry to myself each week because [...] my priority is my child. – Linda (Focus Group 2)

As well as being driven by the need to 'stay strong' to support their children's emotional regulation, mothers shared with us the reasons that they were reluctant to speak with professionals about the extent of their own mental health struggles, fearing that doing so would subject them to additional scrutiny from services which they felt they could not trust to have their best interests at heart:

[T]here's this fear where whenever it's anything to do with him and his needs… whether it's school, dealing with social workers, or dealing with anyone, anything to do with him and his autism… I feel like I have to be strong, right? I feel like I cannot afford to let my guard down. I cannot show any signs of weakness […] I cannot show that I'm struggling. […] because the minute that I do, I feel like they've then instantly put me into this bracket where 'yes, she can't cope… she can't handle it, you know? What are we going to do?' You know, it's this fear of 'will they take him away from me?' Just all these sorts of things that go on in my mind. So, I'm constantly masking that I may be struggling… that I may be finding it difficult to cope. – Stacy-Ann

Among mothers who did attempt to engage social care professionals, there were also negative or unsatisfactory outcomes:

I'm currently in a stage 2 complaint. The social workers breached my confidentiality – told my employers I have a disabled child and that I am seeking support. They then called my family 'complex' without a thorough assessment and then tried to initiate Child Protection proceedings. No support at all. Very Eurocentric and discriminatory in the approach and practice. I have two letters of apology from my local social services regarding the social worker's practice. – Survey respondent, anonymous

I've been trying for years to get a social worker and respite, and we're constantly turned down for it, even though my son's needs are extremely complex. None of them have been any help. When I tried to ask a social worker to investigate my son being manhandled by a teacher, they ended up investigating me instead. Of course,

I was completely vindicated but it was still an incredibly traumatic experience. I know of plenty of people whose kids' needs aren't as complex as my son's but they seem able to get help. I just get told that my older children should be able to help out with him. – Survey respondent, anonymous

Trauma, neglect, incompetence, poor practice… Considerably more harmful than even just ineffective. – Survey respondent, anonymous

The impact of the tropes of Black womanhood

All of this speaks to the 'weaponisation of resilience' and to the damaging impact of the 'Strong Black Woman' trope, which functions to isolate Black mothers of autistic children, trapping them in what one of our participants (Toni) termed *"[a] recurring cycle of distress".*

All of our principal participants discussed the expectation that they should 'suffer in silence', something which was summarised by Imogen who stated:

It's not just about them disbelieving me about what the kids' diagnoses were […]. It's also about how I am expected to manage extreme things. […] No one gives a fuck about my mental health and how I manage it all. I've just got to keep dealing with it.

In framing this experience in such raw and honest terms, Imogen was also conscious of embodying a second trope of Black womanhood – the Angry Black Woman.

Again, the impact of this trope is multi-faceted. Some participants shared that their concerns about being perceived as 'angry' or 'aggressive' caused them to modulate their tone and behaviour, even in the face of what they considered to be unreasonable provocation. Reflecting on her then 6-year-old son's teacher labelling him as a *'potential gangleader'*, Toni asserted:

> *Can't come across as that Angry Black Woman. But it's a very triggering situation… but at the same time you don't want to cause a scene or to make things worse, when essentially you want to make things better for your child. So that is my end goal. And so having to kind of massively manage this trigger that is happening within me.*

Similarly, Stacy-Ann stated:

> *I was always cautious because I think 'if I go in there all guns blazing, I'm the Angry Black Woman… and that was already going to shut the door.*

Indeed, there were examples where participants found that once the 'Angry Black Woman' label had been attached to them, it had negatively impacted their ability to advocate for their child.

For instance, Sareeta explained that, without explanation or justification, teaching staff at her children's school insisted that they would only meet with her on a 2:1 basis. Similarly, a survey respondent discussed being told by the teachers in her (non-speaking) son's Specialist Resource Base that she was only permitted to contact them via a generic whole-school email inbox and then await a reply at their convenience. This stipulation was not applied to any other parent, but she was nonetheless advised that violation of it would see her barred from school grounds.

In both cases, the mothers had initially contacted the school to express concerns that their child's needs were not being met and, in both cases, communication with the school immediately declined further, serving only to exacerbate such concerns.

It is also noteworthy that participants who identified themselves as being naturally 'passive' and 'non-confrontational' shared that their attempts to navigate systems which they had found to be ineffective and non-responsive had driven them to become 'angrier' in their interactions with professionals. Interestingly, Linda used the same expression as Stacy-Ann ('all guns blazing') to convey a different version of the 'Angry Black Woman' narrative:

> I'm quite a soft… probably more passive personality type – my natural disposition is always softly-softly… [but] now I have to just go all guns blazing and like 'OK formal letter, complaint letter, stage two'. In an ideal world if people do things properly you could be reasonable [but…] when they get pushed over the edge, that's when people go from 0 to 100. […] You know, you've had that really stressful week, and you've just looked at the email from the SENCO and just like 'Oh my gosh… I cannot reply because I'm going to cuss you out'. […] The rage, the rage that is drawn out of me. I mean, I don't know how someone can make me so angry […]. 'Are you just trying to be horrible? Do you hate my child? Do you hate me? It takes a lot of effort to not let the inside thoughts come out – Linda (Focus Group 2)

Toni expanded on Linda's observations to claim that, as pervasive as the trope may be, it does not reflect that, in situations of continually failing advocacy efforts, the 'Angry Black Woman' isn't born, she is made:

> So, the institutions come together against you. You're not meant to react. […] All of that is naturally gonna make

you angry. Your child is affected. Full stop. That's angering. You're screaming for help, and you're not [getting it] …. Your advocacy just ain't doing it. That is gonna make you angry. The pressure that they're applying doubling up on you… everything that's happening is supposed to make you angry, but you're made to feel like your anger is misplaced. And it's your fault because you're the angry person – Toni (Focus Group 1)

In all instances, our participants described experiencing, expressing, or repressing anger in a way which negatively impacted their mental health. This throws into sharp relief the suggestion that Black mothers of autistic children are at particularly acute risk of the physical and psychological impacts of 'weathering' (Geronimus, 2023) associated with internalising the physiological effects of anger and stress.

As Imogen asserted *"[t]here's a huge racialised component to increased anxiety"*, something which has been reflected in some of our participants' experience of mental health crisis:

I just fell into this deep depression – Stacy-Ann

And just… I stopped functioning. I couldn't… I couldn't do anything anymore – Ayesha

Managing a child's self-harm and suicidal ideation

Just as mothers reported being impacted by their children's experiences of physical pain, supporting a child through intense psychological trauma is also something which can be absolutely devastating for a caregiver. The close interconnection between neurodivergence and anxiety ensures that mental health conditions are common comorbidities for those with an autism presentation. In some cases, this can manifest in suicidal ideation, which can be expressed by autistic children from a very young age.

> *He had a lot of psychological problems when he was little. He was expressing suicidal ideation. [… Help was not made available] in circumstances where it's been clear that, you know, he could have… he could lose his life because the impact of all of that is so severe* – Imogen

> *He had said that he wanted to kill himself, which I found so upsetting* – Sareeta

> *She's been suicidal.* – Ayesha

> *He has just attempted suicide and CAMHS was basically saying 'yeah, it's not serious enough'. Like that literally was their report – their 'crisis report'. Like, how many times do we need to go through this for it to get to be serious enough?* – Toni

The prevalence of suicidal ideation among the children of our participants provides an alarming indication of just how high the stakes are for mothers seeking support for themselves and their families. In the absence of effective professional engagement, participants (and co-researchers) rely on their own hypervigilance to protect their children from the impact of mental health crisis, but the stress and exhaustion in which this results continually compromise their own health and limit their capacity for basic self-care.

Racial discrimination

Many dimensions of the 'psychological burden,' as outlined so far, are not necessarily unique to Black mothers. Extensive evidence demonstrates the physiological and psychological toll that complex caregiving responsibilities impose on all individuals who undertake them. As Clauser et al. (2021) note, the resulting stress is typically greatest for mothers, reflecting the unequal distribution of caregiving roles within families and the broader societal expectations placed on women.

However, our participants highlighted some of the ways in which their racialised, intersectional, identities as Black women with close proximity to disability, introduced additional variables into an already extremely emotionally fraught and psychologically challenging situation, thereby further undermining their well-being, even relative to other caregivers.

Importantly, in conveying these experiences, we have made a conscious choice not to dilute these accounts with the caveat that racial discrimination was 'perceived' or 'felt' by participants. We relate their stories, as they did, with the conviction that their race *was* a definitive factor in the treatment they received. While this may invite accusations of a lack of objectivity, we see no value in denying our participants an opportunity to speak their own truth, especially given that such experiences emerged as a consistent thread across the research sample.

As explored under 'Cultural Burden', colour evasiveness and the denial of racism often serve as tools to silence Black women who have experienced discrimination, and this is something which we are at pains not to endorse.

As Stacy-Ann stated:

> I think people are very – especially in this country – they're very careful [...] to make sure that their bias is not as overt. It's very... undercover but [...] I know when someone's

treating me differently because of my race. I know when someone's talking to me differently because of my gender… and I don't need them to spell it out

On this basis, one of the additional challenges facing Black mothers of autistic children relates to the effects of minoritisation, with several participants discussing how it felt to have so few opportunities to interact with professionals whose backgrounds were comparable to their own:

I feel like… it's hard when you're outnumbered – Brianna

It's really, really challenging, especially when you're trying to advocate for the best for your child and then it feels like you're… You're the Black person. This has been my experience in the room and everyone else is White and it's like, are you hearing me? Are you seeing me? Do I matter to you? If I don't, then how is my child gonna matter to you? – Toni

Others asserted that racist tropes concerning Black mothers' promiscuity or irresponsibility, as well as preconceived notions of Black children's behaviours and capabilities, contributed to biased treatment by professionals:

Being a Black lone parent [...] you get treated in a very specific way – Imogen

So, you'd get the comments when his dad couldn't make a meeting. Oh, you know, are you…? Is there anything changed at home? As in, you know… 'are you still together'? And I'm thinking 'what has that got to do with anything?' and I come to realise especially speaking to other Black parents especially mothers who were single… that that was the first thing. So, the minute that they knew that you were a single parent, things changed. And because of that, even when his dad and I split a few years ago, I was reluctant to tell them because I didn't want them to try and use that against us – Stacy-Ann

Almost all providers focused on the fact I was a single parent. There was constant prejudice throughout and that put a huge strain on my family. They broke a once happy home – Survey respondent, anonymous

And I just felt not supported or anything. So that made me feel really, really, crap […] So, I did kind of think 'oh, you know, these so-and-so people, they look at me, or they look at us, and they don't take it seriously.' And sometimes, I don't know if in the back of my mind I think, 'oh, it was another person who maybe looked like them, they might have done a bit more…' – Matilda

[…T]hey'll be like 'ok, Mum, well… you know, typically in Black communities…' […] and it would be the little backhanded comments and the little microaggressions… – Stacy-Ann

I have experienced really targeted and deliberate, institutional racism from the school. They have been awful and they have had seriously detrimental effects on my mental health […] I certainly think that I have been treated unfairly and it's because of my race – Sareeta

So far, research outcomes have demonstrated that the 'mother-work' attached to caring for an autistic child becomes even more demanding when professionals deploy racialised lenses in their engagement with Black families. The impact of this racialisation permeates all aspects of othered mothers' physical and psychological well-being and is, all too often, borne with extremely limited external support.

In the next chapter, we explore the ramifications of this inadequate support, in light of three further 'burdens': cultural, practical and temporal.

4
The multiplicity of burdens: Cultural, practical and temporal

This chapter explores the final three 'burdens' facing Black mothers of autistic children: cultural, practical, and temporal. It begins by challenging perceptions that there is a reluctance, among Black mothers to make themselves and their families known to service providers, and problematises the tendency to vilify 'Black culture' rather than explore the understandable reasons why this already marginalised group may feel disinclined to expose themselves to potential scrutiny and criticism.

It then constructs an account of what day-to-day life looks like for mothers who expressed that they were being constantly called upon to compensate for inadequacies and inconsistencies in the systems that ostensibly exist to support them and their families.

From the pressure to develop exhaustive knowledge of autism and the SEND system, to a lack of career progression and the associated financial hardship, to extreme time poverty, and concerns for the perils that may face their children as they enter adulthood, participants shared with us the strategies they have developed for managing their children's complex needs, and the ways in which their most egregious challenges are often exacerbated by systemic failures that are beyond their control.

Cultural burden

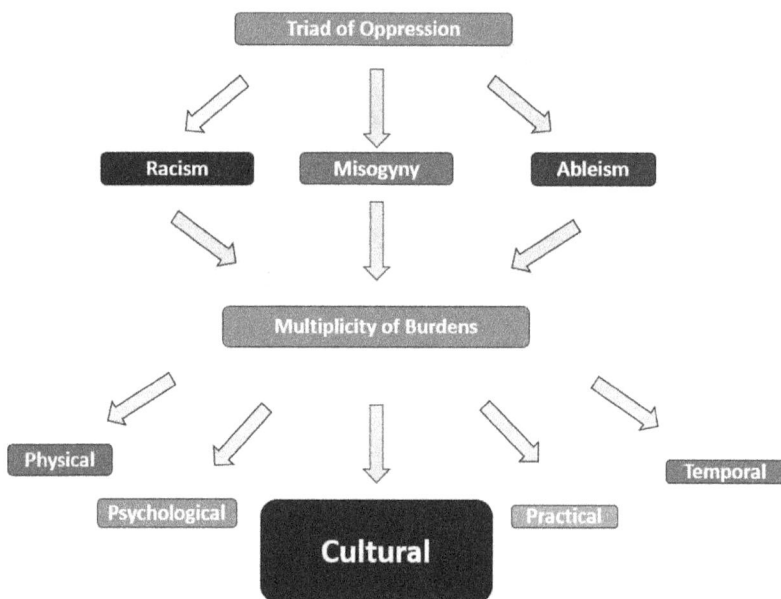

Figure 9: Focus on the cultural burden within the multiplicity of burdens

The cultural burden encompasses the additional pressures Black mothers face in navigating societal expectations, cultural stigmas, and community perceptions while advocating for their autistic children. The following sections explore how this burden shapes the experiences of the mothers in our study.

Mel's story

A trend amongst my Black millennial friends seems to involve them breaking "intergenerational curses" or reducing "intergenerational trauma." This idea resonates deeply with me, particularly as I navigate the complexities of raising two autistic children. For many of us, breaking these so-called curses means doing the emotional labour of self-awareness, reflection, and healing, often without a blueprint or wider community support. But raising an autistic child brings its own set of challenges that are layered with cultural expectations and systemic inequities.

I made two close mum friends during Sam's early years. One, a White woman in an interracial marriage raising mixed-race children like me – we met in our National Childhood Trust (NCT) group, an antenatal group many mothers attend primarily with the goal of making other mum friends. She and her family have been a part of our lives ever since, celebrating each of our children's birthdays together. Her three children are all neurotypical and she is wonderful at hearing me and trying to understand the differences in our lives despite never having had the experience of raising a child who needs to do laps of a building if it is unfamiliar to them. The other is a Black mum I met at a baby signing class. Her son has since also been diagnosed as autistic, and she remains one of the few people who truly "gets it". Having friends who can witness your struggles without judgement and walk alongside you in navigating this path is a lifeline, but these connections are rare.

I have rejected friends who've demonstrated an inability or unwillingness to understand autism. One such friend asked me for advice on teaching her son to "tolerate" a child like Sam. As I tried to explain Sam's needs, she interrupted, finishing my sentence with, "I bet you wish he wasn't born like that." It was like a punch to the gut. How do you maintain relationships when people fundamentally misunderstand your child's humanity?

Family, too, can be a source of friction. My husband and I have an interracial family (his side is White Irish-British, and mine is Black Jamaican). While both grandmothers are involved in my children's lives, understanding autism has been a different story. My husband's father passed away the year my youngest, Daniel, was born, and my own family dynamic has always been small as an only child raised by a single mother. My husband's brother lives in South-east Asia and has never had any children of his own. The absence of extended family support feels particularly stark when cultural expectations collide with my children's needs.

For instance, my Jamaican grandmother, who lives thousands of miles away, once asked why Sam didn't wave or look at her during a video call. I found myself justifying him, explaining his sensory sensitivities, even hoping against hope that he might behave differently that day, just to avoid her disappointment. But no explanation seemed to satisfy her. Her expectations, and the weight of cultural norms around respect and social engagement, made me feel as though I had to defend my son's very existence.

Even within my husband's family, challenges arise. Some relatives question whether Daniel needs a diagnosis because he is intelligent and highly verbal. There is little understanding that autism is a spectrum, and that his social and emotional needs are just as significant as Sam's. While trying to advocate for my children, I often feel as though I am also advocating for myself. I need to assert boundaries, defend my choices, and centre my sons' needs in a world that insists on minimising them.

One of the few spaces where I find solace is within SEND-specific communities. An online parents' forum conducted through Facebook and WhatsApp was the place I ran to when Sam started smearing. The local SEND community group 'The Together Space' has been the only place I have been able to take my children with the sole purpose of socialising with others. This space where other children have physical, neurological and learning differences has provided us a rare sense of comfort and understanding for the past three years. In these environments, autism isn't the headline, it is normalised. It is everyday. At one event, Sam became so excited about a water play area that he soaked himself through to his nappy. New nappy on and no trousers he ran from play station to play station, laughing on the bouncy castle, balancing expertly on the zip line. No one batted an eye at a six-year-old who was not yet toilet-trained. There were no disapproving stares or whispered judgements. It was a moment of pure joy for him and a reminder for me that there are places where my child doesn't have to apologise for being himself.

Yet these spaces are not the norm. Outside of them, I am constantly balancing cultural expectations with my children's reality. As a Black child, mixed-race or not, I am fully aware that the first thing people see in my child isn't autism; it is misbehaviour at best, deviance at worst. As a Black woman, I constantly feel the pressure to raise children who meet the standards of respectability; standards that my children, through no fault of their own, may never conform to.

Claire's story

As we have indicated throughout this book, one of the things that inspired us to undertake this study was the paucity of pre-existing literature in the field of SEND and race. What alarmed us even more than this dearth of research, however, was the tendency for those discussions that did foreground a racialised viewpoint on SEND children and parents, to fall back on racist dog whistles concerning ableism, ignorance, and a 'lack of engagement' among the Black community, in respect of autism diagnoses and symptomatology.

A particularly egregious example of this came to our attention when Marsha Martin, founder of the London-based community group 'Black SEN Mamas', an organisation which seeks to support 'othered mothers' such as ourselves, was flagrantly misrepresented in an article in The Guardian.

The article's headline "UK's black children 'face cultural barriers' in accessing help for autism and ADHD" (Ofori, 2024), along with its drop header which identified "stigma within [the] black community" (ibid.) as the principal reason that such matters were not discussed, took an all-too-familiar deficit-based approach to understanding the experience of Black autistic children and their families. The focus was agential, rather than systemic, with a tone of blame and condescension which painted the Black community with a broad brush and sustained problematic claims that we already knew were belied by our own lived experience and our ongoing research.

More pertinent and revealing statements were buried much later in the piece, so that the vital sentiment that "a lot of us in Black SEN Mamas have a very similar story. And it really has a lot to do with the lack of support from the local authorities, from the school and the education system…" (ibid.) read almost like an afterthought.

In response to the article's publication, Martin took to Instagram to explain that her views had been editorialised and that she "definitely did not want [her] contributions to the article to support a focus on the ignorance perpetuated within the Black community surrounding disability" which "greatly pales in significance, compared to the pervasive, systemic racism, interwoven into the fabric of the foundation and framework of our society" (Martin of Black SEN Mamas, 2024). As important as this clarification was, it is impossible to know how much harm the article's clickbait title had already done to perceptions of Black SEND parents, or how many people were reached by Martin's attempt to course correct it.

What is clear, however, is that it formed part of a broader tendency toward assigning 'blame' to the Black community for not sufficiently understanding or accepting autism. This narrative seems to us to be a convenient way in which to absolve professionals of their responsibility for effectively supporting Black mothers. For this reason, we were somewhat reluctant to explore, at length, the contention that 'Black culture' itself precludes such support.

That said, we would be remiss if we failed to acknowledge that not all the stigma, hostility, and exclusion that Black mothers of autistic children face is from beyond our community.

From a personal perspective, however, the greatest 'cultural burden' I have encountered has come from professionals and service providers lacking awareness of the ways in which their perception of me has been filtered through racist and misogynist lenses. While service providers have no choice but to ask certain questions about a family's circumstances, the range of racist (micro)aggressions to which I have been subjected has done nothing to increase my confidence in the 'support' they claim to provide.

Questions such as '…and… is Dad living in the family home?' (something which I have been asked by the same individual on no fewer than four occasions, despite me already having made clear that I am married to the father of my children), thinly-veiled jibes about how autism in children might be linked to the use of recreational drugs during pregnancy, and comments such as 'children whose parents don't read to them are more likely to experience speech delay', have proven much more offensive than any judgement that I have ever received at the hands of members of my own family or community.

A 'culture' of systemic racism

As intimated in our earlier review of extant literature, there have been a vanishingly small number of attempts to explore the experiences and perspectives of Black parents of autistic children. The most substantive account to date is a doctoral thesis submitted in 2022, which became publicly available in early 2024. In it, Eli Gemegah (2022, p. 4) describes the aims of her study in terms similar to our own. Specifically, "to demonstrate the gaps in support services in familial, contextual, and systemic contexts that if considered and implemented, would benefit parents' psychological well-being and aid in the child's holistic development".

However, the thesis goes on to posit that the principal hurdle preventing autistic children in the Black community from being availed of the support and resources that they require for survival and flourishing can be attributed to cultural barriers *within* the community itself. Gemegah recalls her own experiences as a "teacher with learning responsibilities for students with SEN (sic)" who witnessed "some Black Parents' refusal to acquire a diagnosis for their child, which led to experienced difficulties in navigating their child's challenging behaviours in schools, whilst others had received an autism diagnosis for their child but rejected the diagnosis, which created some tension between parents and professionals, and led to diminished communication and strategies on how to support children in school and home" (ibid., p. 11).

Gemegah speaks to what she sees as the "cultural dissonance" (ibid.) that impacts Black parents of autistic children and calls upon professionals and service providers to develop a richer understanding of Black culture which might enable them to transcend the resulting communication and behavioural barriers.

This narrative of parents within the Black community being reluctant to acknowledge, and therefore unable to meet, the complex needs of their autistic children, is one which has gained significant traction in the media and in policymaking. As well as the aforementioned Guardian article, a recent response to alarmingly high school suspension rates for Black pupils in the North London borough of Islington saw local councillor Ilkay Cinko-Oner affirm that: "We have to understand some parents from Black and ethnic minority [groups] do not recognise their children have anything wrong with them (sic) […]. We need to address this and explain that their children are not 'rowdy'. They may have ADHD or autism, for example" (Steen, 2024).

In addressing the fact that 37.9% of suspended pupils, in the borough, were Black Caribbean (compared to the national rate of 23.5%) with 37.2% of suspensions issued against children with SEND, Cinko-Oner appeared to add, only as an afterthought that "Parents are really afraid of diagnosing their children, and it's schools persistently, constantly calling them just 'badly behaved'. It doesn't work." (ibid.)

We acknowledge that there are sections of the Black community in which 'autism denial' remains a pressing issue. Neither do we contest the proposition that targeted support and intervention to help better develop understanding of neurodiversity, via community groups, or places of worship, would be a welcome and effective tool in helping to bridge some of these gaps in terms of knowledge and acceptance.

That having been said, our research indicates that this focus on 'cultural dissonance' as endemic and endogenous in Black parents is an oversimplification, which can itself facilitate racial profiling and provide a convenient rationale for professionals and service providers to dismiss Black mothers as being disengaged from their children's well-being and 'hard to reach'.

In contrast, the mothers in our study shared extensive evidence of their experience of struggling to overcome systemic barriers that often made it all but impossible to secure a diagnosis or associated resources for support. Our participants shared with us a reluctance, not on their part, but on the part of educators and service providers to see beyond racialised views of Black families and children.

For instance, Stacy-Ann stated that, in her capacity as a SEND teacher, she observes that:

> *[I]t's always the young Black children with autism that are in the hallways [having displayed] challenging behaviour, but yet there's another child from a different background that's in the classroom tearing up the whole classroom... but they won't be excluded. They won't be suspended. They won't be put outside. And when I go and challenge my Headteacher and [...] I'm like, 'OK, so why are we not looking at this through the lens of race, ethnicity, etc?', it's always 'Oh, we haven't considered that, really'. You haven't considered that all of your Black children are ones that you're calling the parents up every day, and there's always a 'problem' there...?*

The correlation between Black children and high rates of school exclusion manifested in Stacy-Ann's personal, as well as her professional life, when her own son began to display challenging behaviours in the specialist educational provision that he was attending. She cites:

> *[t]he shock that the first thing that they thought about was suspension. And then when I met with the Headteacher at the time [...] she was very quick to say, 'oh, well, you know, we expect this. I'm sure you know, about Black boys and underachieving, you know, that the research is there'. [...] It was the fact that she even mentioned that because I thought to myself again, 'you're correlating challenging behaviour with his race. Why? What has one got to do with the other?*

Several other participants recalled an unwillingness among staff at their children's schools to recognise the autism symptomatology that was leading to challenging behaviours, asserting that instead of support, their children were met with punitive measures:

> *Things escalated to where it was a daily thing where the school would be complaining to me about some behavioural issue that my child had, you know… he was hitting another child, or he wasn't following instructions, or… but these are all… when you look at them individually, you know, it may seem like this child is bad, you know? But when you look at them collectively, they all paint a picture of somebody that's got some additional needs that need to be looked at and instead of them doing that, they were starting to exclude him from activities* – Toni

> *I was told [by a teacher] when he was 4 years old, my son has 'an attitude of non-compliance'* – Laura

> *[My son's] mainstream school were clueless and applied punitive interventions* – Survey respondent, anonymous

> *My son's meltdowns would just be perceived as aggression… this aggressive little mixed-race boy', sort of thing* – Sareeta

> *[My son] left school with no GCSEs after being in and out of formal education, being mistreated and presumed badly behaved (not over stimulated) and was suspended 9 times* – Survey respondent, anonymous

Conscious of this hostile attitude toward Black children with SEND, Linda explained that she took a preventative step to control the kinds of language that professionals would use in reference to her son:

> *I incorporated that into the EHCP because I do not want my Black child just labelled as 'the naughty boy'. I was like 'I basically don't want any mention of 'naughty' because*

that's just always been the go-to. That's why so many Black children have been so let down for so long. Because rather than thinking,' oh, they might have extra support needs', they're just 'naughty'

Our participants also noted that the adultification underpinning these labels appears to vary along lines of gender, with Black boys presumed to be 'aggressive', and Black girls treated as if they are 'rude' or 'sassy'.

My daughter attends mainstream school. I've been made to feel that I should have the answers to my child's behaviour/ presentation from class teachers. There is also a perception that my child is deliberately defiant rather than considering her diagnosis… [She] has been labelled negatively by the class teacher – Survey respondent, anonymous

Despite the conviction among many respondents that their children's racialised identities had played a key role in shaping their schooling experience, mothers often found it difficult to seek recognition or redress. Brianna notes that, in a majority-White school, the response she received when she raised issues related to race and racism was one of denial and 'colour evasiveness':

[I]t was often just dismissed. So, if it was about race… just dismissed. I mean, we live in a predominantly White area and he's the only Black child in his school. I found that that was dismissed and maybe they didn't know how to deal with certain issues and had never had to deal with it. […] A child in [his] class had been saying things about [my son's] skin colour and I took that to school and it's like… there's just nothing done

An extension of the failure to recognise Black children's additional needs is a tendency to assume that challenging behaviours, or academic underperformance, can be attributed to parenting deficits. Again, Brianna provided an insight into some of the microaggressions with which she had been confronted when her son began to show signs of delayed speech:

> [H]e was sort of non-verbal and I've had comments like 'well did you not speak to him when he was little?' [...] It's all of those ignorant comments, you know? 'Why don't you get out and do more with him? That's the best way for them to learn language.' And I'm like, 'I do. I promise you, I do.'

Here, our participants, who were sharing experiences from a range of different geographical locations, across different forms of educational provision, and from a combination of personal and professional perspectives coalesced around an account of school environments in which their children's racialised identities were both minimised and weaponised, resulting in a seemingly contradictory experience of invisibility and hypervisibility for both mother and child. This account stands as a counterweight to the alternative narrative, seemingly more palatable to educators and policymakers, that Black parents are simply not willing to accept the possibility that their children may have additional needs.

Furthermore, the evidence that Black children with SEND are marginalised in schools has ramifications for Black mothers' engagement with other services. In discussions of the role that social care professionals played in her child's life, Linda explained why she had gone to great lengths to avoid their involvement:

> ...[t]here's some fantastic, amazing professionals [in the council where I worked]. But I also saw there are some

disgusting 'you shouldn't even have a job' professionals there. And for that reason, I've never wanted to get support in case I got rubbish ones. [...] I'm not saying that it's most people. I'm not saying it's even half, but I'm like, 'there's too many I've come across that I would not trust'... And very overworked and all the rest of it. And to cut corners, you know, you can get thrown under the bus as a parent. Your child can get thrown under the bus. So, I have never wanted to seek any [social care] support

Both Laura and Stacy-Ann echoed the sense of suspicion and trepidation that Black mothers can harbour towards professionals and support services:

We come to the table with the 'oh, you know, this is how Black people are treated' [...] whether by health, education... [...] we come with that energy and then we are met with it... we already know it's there – Laura

I come from a Caribbean background. So our family network is everything, you know. You definitely do everything within the family. So, we didn't have any social care or support [for my son] up until at the age of 18 and that was because I didn't really trust the system and I still don't to a degree. I'm very cautious about what I let them know and what they don't know because I need to be sure that they are genuinely allies... that they're in it for the right reasons – Stacy-Ann

A culture of parent blame

Hostility toward Black autistic children and their caregivers is reflected in the racially stratified experience of parent blame. The fear of being blamed for an autistic child's behaviour or symptomatology is a significant and persistent issue for all parents seeking support for their autistic children. A 2024 report, *'Blamed Instead of Helped'*, published by the Autism and Parent blame Project (Ferguson and Hollingsworth, 2024), found that 86% of parents of children with autism face blame when asking for support from healthcare, education, and social care services. The study, which was not disaggregated along lines of racial identity, included parents, carers, and guardians living in England who had sought assessment or support for their children, whether formally diagnosed with autism or not, and revealed that 78% of parents experienced judgemental or discriminatory statements about their parenting.

In our study, experiences of parent blame were echoed across multiple participants:

> *You ask for help and then if anything's to go wrong, then you're blamed. This is what I don't understand. So, if you go there, you say 'my son, you know he's experiencing this and I can't manage this by myself', there's no help. But if anything was to have gone wrong – if he was going to get caught in anything – then it's you know 'what were you doing as a mother?' – Abby*

> *The view or the perspective was shifting from looking at my son and why he might be feeling this to kind of like looking at me [...]. This parent blaming and parent shaming is so strong in education at the moment, and I mean you speak to so many parents and they're sort of echoing the same thing – Sareeta*

> *You're meant to collaborate with the teachers against your child. That's what I think they wanted from me. For me to stand firm, working with the school. It meant that I was*

supposed to be agreeing with the teachers against my son. But because I won't do that, they then clamp down on me because if it's not the child's fault, it's the mum – Toni (Focus Group 1)

All of this highlights the broader issue of how systemic neglect or ignorance is often framed as a personal failing of the parent, rather than a reflection of inadequate systems and services, or a lack of understanding from the institutions that are meant to help. It also places into context Ferguson and Hollingsworth's (2024) troubling finding that 72% of parents seeking support faced open criticism of their parenting abilities, an experience captured in the earlier quote from our participant, Linda, and her concerns about being "thrown under the bus" by the professionals assigned to her family.

Similarly, Sareeta described how schools often dismissed autism as a behavioural issue, stating:

The school will make out like it's not his autism, it's like… it's him, or it's your parenting, and they won't accept how autism presents in children of ethnic minorities, particularly Black children.

This dismissal of autism in racially minoritised children points to an underlying bias, whereby the intersection of race and disability amplifies parent blame, which is then experienced even more acutely by Black families than it is by White caregivers.

Furthermore, 81% of parents from the *Blamed Instead of Helped* study reported that they weren't believed about their child's autism presentation, figures which align with the experiences shared by participants in our study, where several mothers felt they were not taken seriously when describing their child's struggles. The belief that a parent is either too strict or too lenient creates an environment in which parents cannot win, leading to a constant state of self-doubt and frustration and fuelling parent blame.

For some of the parents in the *Blamed Instead of Helped* study, this blame took more drastic forms: one in four (27%) were subjected to safeguarding referrals. This harrowing experience is familiar to Claire, who, after months of petitioning her family's social worker for help to manage Mae's escalating acts of self-harm, found herself subjected to a MARF (Multi-Agency Referral Form), also known as a 'Harm Statement', generated by a member of the CALDS (Child and Adolescent Learning Disabilities Services) Team. During a home visit, which Claire herself had requested, she drew the team member's attention to Mae's swollen lip – a self-inflicted injury sustained during a meltdown. Claire was later horrified to discover that the form subsequently submitted in respect of her family began with the question: "What did the parent do, or not do, to cause harm?". After filing a complaint, Claire was offered only the initial 'assurance' (issued over the phone, rather than in writing), that a MARF is the only form of documentation available for professionals seeking to source additional support and resources for struggling families. In other words, irrespective of whether a parent has caused harm to their own child, the simple request for help is enough to trigger 'safeguarding concerns'. The social worker and CALDS team member (both White women) demonstrated no appreciation of the stigmatising impact of Claire, as a Black woman, being ostensibly labelled as a potential threat to her own children. The respite hours which were promised as a response to the form never materialised, and only a lengthy and involved complaints procedure eventually resulted in the referral being expunged from the family's record.

Blamed Instead of Helped also revealed that one in six parents in the study (16%) were accused of Fabricated and Induced Illness (FII). The experience of being accused of FII is a particularly distressing form of parent blame, as it involves the assumption that parents are causing or exaggerating their child's condition. This was a fear expressed by Linda, who reflected:

> *One of the lessons I'm learning now is when you get a medical report back and you're like, we didn't say that. Well, that's not quite accurate. But you're like, well, at least they've got this in it. At least it says the diagnosis, or at least it says this. So I didn't challenge it. I've never challenged a medical report or letter. And now I'm like, I really wish I did. Because now if I need to go to tribunal, I could have used that letter. I can't use it now because that says this.*

Linda's experience illustrates the compounding frustration of being dismissed by professionals, only to later realise the consequences of not challenging inaccurate portrayals of her child's needs.

For Black mothers, the experience of parent blame is often compounded by racial stereotypes. The intersection of Blackness and autism can create an even harsher judgement, where Black mothers are not only blamed for their children's behaviours but also face additional scrutiny due to prevailing racial biases. The cultural stigma surrounding Black parenting often intersects with misunderstandings about autism, amplifying the blame placed on mothers. This unique form of intersectional oppression makes it all the more difficult for Black mothers to be seen as credible and competent in advocating for their children's needs and high-lights how the structural racism embedded in healthcare, educa-tion, and social care services further marginalises them.

The dismissal of early concerns, the constant scrutiny of par-enting styles, and the racial biases that exacerbate these expe-riences feed into a culture of racial hostility which, in turn, creates an environment in which Black mothers are set up to fail. Not only are they blamed for their children's challenges, but they also face systemic barriers that prevent them from accessing the support they need. This is a vicious cycle of blame and dismissal that leaves Black mothers not only fight-ing for their children's well-being but also for their own dignity and credibility within a system that fails to recognise their lived experiences.

Again, the narrative that emerges here is not one of Black moth-ers denying or failing to meet their children's needs. Instead, there is a pattern of mothers (already managing the physiological and psychological challenges of raising an autistic child) feeling com-pelled not to access the limited services that might otherwise be available to them, for fear that racial profiling and damaging tropes regarding their parenting will place their children in harm's way. In other words, the prevailing toxic 'culture' at play is one of institutionalised racism, rather than 'non-engagement' on the part of the Black community, with the media-fuelled discourse which erroneously states that Black mothers are 'hard to reach' disguising and perpetuating this experience of oppression.

Why culture does matter

Crucially, however, it is vital not to underestimate the specificities of Black culture(s) and their importance for, and impact on, Black mothers of autistic children. The sense of having to balance different elements of their own cultural identity was something that mothers reported as an additional challenge they faced in their parenting journeys.

For instance, a recurring theme among participants was the sense of being 'caught' between conflicting parenting styles. Stacy-Ann spoke to the need for professionals not to rush to judgement but to be cognisant of the ways in which child-rearing may be perceived differently in different ethnic and racial communities:

> *I think they definitely would need to recognise our culture, our background, the way that we were raised, the way we do things […] Someone might speak to their child with a raised voice because that's how they were raised, or you know, just little nuances that I don't think people really get. Understand our culture, understand our heritage… understand why we do things in that way. You know, there's a lot of talk at the moment on the 'gentle parenting' and 'soft parenting', things like that. And I'm thinking 'yeah, that's great, but that's not how I was raised, so I might raise my child in a very different way*

In contrast, several other participants endorsed 'gentle' and 'conscious' parenting but added that their commitment to it can sometimes put them at odds with other family or community members:

> *We try to be conscious of that… and we, as a couple, we do try to pull each other up with 'Actually, do you think*

this would work better? [For example, with our son's] very restricted diet. We started off literally doing the 'oh, you're not hungry, right? You don't eat that, you get nothing'. [...] And also when our parents tried to tell us the same thing like well 'what happened to just eat what you're given?' and it's like, 'Yeah, that's not really gonna work'. [We decided] we're not gonna stay [at our parents' houses] because it gets me really mad – Linda

I've had somebody even say to me that I could beat him to stop him from tiptoeing. But [...] like, I'm coming from just a completely different school of thought – Sareeta

And then my family joined in as well and says, 'oh, it's because you're spoiling him' because they saw how much I was overcompensating, but they didn't see the real challenges behind... the real journey behind that. And so, they blame me for spoiling him. And they're like, yeah, you just need to beat the child. And of course, it got to the point where I did listen, and I did, you know, discipline my child in that way, and I felt even more guilt because I could see how scared he was. I could see... literally, the pain I felt doing what the family said was the right thing to do because all of my tools were just constantly failing – Toni

In this respect, the 'cultural' and 'psychological' burdens intersect as Black mothers of autistic children can find themselves torn between contradictory expectations and troubled by feelings of guilt and inadequacy when they feel that they have fallen short of the standards set for them by themselves and others.

[M]y guilt is probably when you reach that capacity and then you're like – you know... you're not as gentle with your

parenting. And I feel like, 'oh no, that's the African Mum coming out.' And [then] I feel so guilty. And he's gone to bed and it's, you know, it's like, 'oh, I didn't have a very good mum day today' – Linda

If your mother was Black and you see, you know like in your aunts and your grandmother and you see people doing that stuff that's, you know, 'you can't possibly let your kid go out with a hole in their tights…' – Imogen

The effects of this dual burden are worsened when the services that mothers have to engage then fail to demonstrate a level of cultural competency commensurate with the challenges faced by those who are balancing the demands of intersecting identities. In other words, managing this 'clash of cultures' becomes yet another task that Black mothers of autistic children have to face with little to no support.

Raising children with an awareness of their own culture

A further dimension of the 'cultural burden' was expressed by participants who were concerned about how they could foster a sense of Black identity in, and for, their children:

My parents are part of the Windrush generation. My dad came from Barbados. My mum came from Saint Vincent. They said everything for us was about our culture. You couldn't get them to tell us otherwise. Our race, ethnicity and culture […] How do I get to support my son in the same ways? How do I get him to understand the value and you know, these things that I grew up with culturally in the way that's most accessible for him? – Stacy-Ann

Here, Stacy-Ann highlighted the difficulties that othered mothers may encounter in their attempts to acquaint their children with their own Blackness. This focus on positive racial identity development is a much-needed counterweight to the ways in which the insidious discourse of 'colour evasiveness' encourages denial and obfuscation of racial difference and racial discrimination. The expression 'I don't see colour' is an intrinsically problematic contention, often uttered as a way for those who are not impacted by racism to abdicate responsibility for its existence, or understate its consequences for those who are racially minoritised. However, in the case of Black autistic children (particularly those with a high support presentation), processing the layers of abstraction and meaning attached to racial identity, in other words truly 'seeing colour', can be enormously challenging.

As we have acknowledged throughout this book, institutional racism permeates the systems that Black mothers are attempting to access for their children. This racism shapes policies that, despite their intended purpose, disproportionately disadvantage racially minoritised children and systematically deny social and economic support to their caregivers (Hill, 2004). This suggests autistic children should be provided with opportunities to learn about systemic racism, how it affects them and their families, and how to challenge it in their daily lives.

Challenges in raising culturally and racially aware autistic children can result from the ways in which autism may give rise to an atypical version of 'Theory of Mind'. Theory of Mind is defined as the ability to attribute mental states to oneself and others and to understand that others may have different beliefs, desires, intentions, and perspectives (Berenguer et al., 2018). Yet, since Theory of Mind research has primarily focused on White children, its manifestation across different ethnicities remains largely unknown (Modirrousta and Harris, 2024), making it important to acknowledge that not all autistic children experience these challenges in the same way. While some may genuinely struggle to perceive or interpret the social significance of racial identity, others may develop a deep awareness of racial dynamics through alternative cognitive and communicative pathways. This variability highlights the need for nuanced approaches to discussing race and identity with autistic children that are adapted to their individual ways of understanding the world.

It is crucial that such work be undertaken since an appreciation of the nature and implications of racial identity is a key element of the well-being of Black autistic children. Firstly, this is a safeguarding issue because Black children need to be aware of the ways in which their identity may be weaponised against them. Secondly, they deserve the opportunity to celebrate their community and themselves, and to take pride in their Blackness. This latter consideration is particularly vital given the established link between positive racial identity development and self-esteem in Black children. Hughes et al. (2006) highlight the critical need for guidance on how to support Black autistic children in cultivating a strong sense of racial identity. This is a particularly urgent issue for those Black mothers who find it challenging to know where to start when it comes to exploring abstract concepts related to race and racialisation with their autistic children.

However, support and guidance in this area are often over-looked by professionals who fail to account for the significance of Blackness and Black cultural perspectives in their work with autistic children. Without access to culturally competent support and resources that consider both autism and racial identity, Black autistic children risk being excluded from opportunities to develop a secure and affirming sense of self.

Religion

Fostering this appreciation of Black culture also links with the relative prevalence of religious belief within Black communities. Four of our principal participants explicitly referenced their faith and it was clear that it was a significant component in helping them to navigate the challenges they face.

> *You know, I keep thinking 'maybe God wants me to learn something through my son'* – Stacy-Ann

> *One of the main things that comes to mind [as a coping strategy] is faith. I think this has been, for me, just a stronghold […]. Sometimes I think of it this way… that maybe God has given me this specific set of circumstances and this scenario, so I can use my voice to help other people* – Sareeta

However, Linda illustrated that perceptions of her religious belief can sometimes contribute to the poor treatment she receives when advocating for her child.

> *I think with me being Muslim, visibly Muslim, I think there's people acting based on stereotypes* – Linda

An additional challenge which can face Black mothers of autistic children concerns how best to reconcile membership of religious groups and organisations, which can sometimes adopt a somewhat regressive attitude toward disability (disability as 'test', disability as 'punishment', etc.) (Jegatheesan et al., 2010, p. 98) with the comfort that can be derived from spiritual belief.

Gemegah (2022, p. 44) states:

> *Despite the strong reliance on positive religious beliefs and spirituality to understand and accept autism, parents complain that religious organisations perceive disability, particularly autism, negatively and display insensitive attitudes towards the challenges of raising a[n autistic] child.*

This lack of understanding and acceptance may explain studies which indicate that "Religious activities were associated with more negative and less positive outcomes: mothers who reported a greater frequency of involvement in religious activities reported higher levels of parenting stress and lower self-esteem, [and reduced] psychological well-being, positive affect, and control of internal states" (Ekas et al., 2009, p. 713).

The possibility that Black mothers of autistic children may seek solace in religious belief, only to experience rejection or misunderstanding from within their religious community, represents a further dimension of the cultural burden that can face some othered mothers.

Practical burden

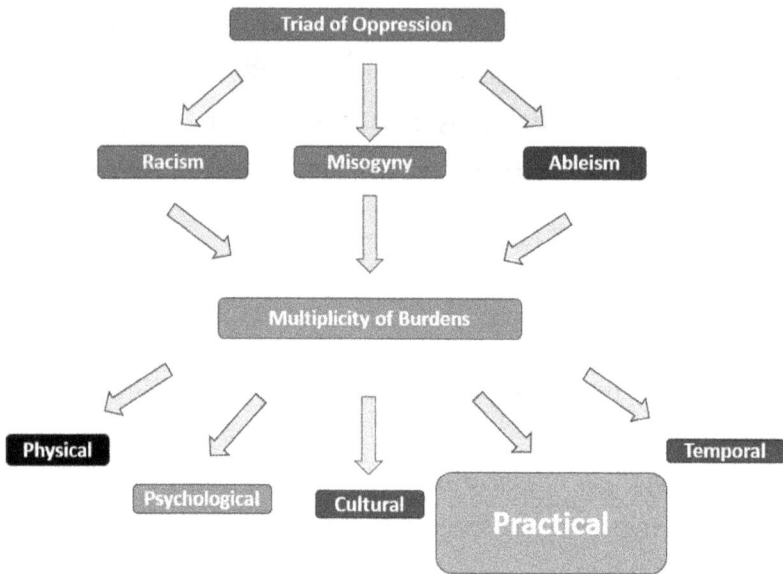

Figure 10: Focus on the practical burden within the multiplicity of burdens

The practical burden refers to the relentless demands of managing daily responsibilities, coordinating care, and securing resources while advocating for autistic children. The following sections detail how this burden impacts the mothers in our study.

Claire's story

The 'life admin' associated with raising a teenager and a 'threenager' is the stuff of nightmares. For instance, I have a working theory that 'World Book Day' was invented by someone conducting an experiment to find the exact breaking point of mothers everywhere.

Doctors, dentists, parents' evenings, poorly timed growth spurts that necessitate the replacement of a full wardrobe roughly every 17

seconds, non-uniform days, school trips, empty cupboards ravaged by inconceivably large appetites, at-home training camps for a toddler who seemingly has ambitions to compete in the UFC… it never ends.

But this is what I signed up for. I always wanted kids and the thought of being their full-time PA, cleaner, court jester, therapist, and punch bag was a privilege I looked forward to for years. It bears repeating that I still love (almost) every moment of it.

As in all things, though, I have my limits, and factoring in a wealth of additional appointments: Paediatrician, Speech Therapist, Occupational Health, Educational Psychologist, Child Psychiatrist, Social Worker, Physiotherapist, Podiatrist… ensures that they are permanently strained. This struggle is particularly acute when so many of the appointments result in little, to no, progress or support.

Relatively simple matters, such as grocery shopping, are complicated by the fact that Mae has a restricted diet. We are extremely lucky in that she is willing to eat a reasonable range of fruits and vegetables, but all hell breaks loose in the event that the only brand of mozzarella stick that she's willing to eat doesn't find its way onto her dinner plate every single night, along with the obligatory chicken nuggets and chips.

Travelling any distance is some fresh hell, since we must find space for a veritable entourage of toys, blankets, and wildly inappropriate outfits, as well as listen to a 'playlist' of the same half a dozen songs we've been looping for the last six years. Meltdowns in the car place us all in imminent danger and often force us to pull over into every service station known to man where we can do nothing but batten down the hatches and hope that the worst of it blows over relatively quickly. Often, it does not.

In such instances, it is arguably Joshua who suffers the most, both from exposure to the meltdown itself and from its consequences in terms of derailed plans. He has begun to express the frustration that this causes him ('why is Mae's screaming?', 'it's too loud') and has even taken to admonishing his much older sister ('No, Mae. No shouting', 'Mama said wait, Mae'). It's heartbreakingly difficult to find ways to acknowledge and validate his feelings, while also making clear to him that it is not his responsibility to draw boundaries around his sister's behaviour. Equally, the caring way in which he tries to comfort her when she is distraught is a credit to him, but it is also an indication that he has seen far too much for a child of his age. I worry about his tendency toward 'peacekeeping' and 'people pleasing' and whether, in and of itself, it speaks to a degree of trauma from witnessing such turmoil while he is still so impressionable.

This is why I pour so much energy into 'prevention'. The extent of pre-planning and logistical forethought that all this necessitates has, once again, been 'normalised' for us, but this does nothing to detract from how exacting it is, and, even with all this preparation in place, it is impossible to control for every contingency, with family trips frequently abandoned due to some unanticipated exogenous factor that we could not have been aware of in advance.

Of course, the 'we' in this account is doing a lot of heavy lifting and my husband would be the first to acknowledge that the lion's share of these tasks falls to me. Even with a partner as supportive and dedicated to his children as he is, the default of 'Mum as primary caregiver' has still managed to take hold, and it is a huge contributory factor in the physical and mental health challenges that feature elsewhere in the multiplicity of burdens.

Mel's story

At the beginning of the summer holidays in 2024, Sam climbed out of a ground-floor living room window while I was sitting in the same room. Within minutes, he had scaled a wall and ended up in a neighbour's garden five doors down. He was missing for 15 to 20 minutes— minutes during which I truly felt as though I was losing my mind. His abscondment led to a series of urgent changes in our home: installing a camera on the front of the house to complement our existing video doorbell and fitting internal locks on all downstairs windows that require a key to open fully, a precaution we had already taken upstairs.

When the police arrived, they directed all questions to me, ignoring my husband almost entirely despite my visible distress: sobbing, wailing, barely coherent. The implicit assumption that I was solely responsible added another layer to the guilt I already felt. I was in the room with Sam when it happened. I was the one distracted, laptop open, working on my EdD thesis. Even though the missing window locks were an oversight on both our parts, it felt like my failure alone. While he was missing, I kept repeating the same thing over and over, "he's just in his nappy!". The guilt was compounded by the other milestones Sam has yet to reach, like being fully toilet trained. I carry it daily.

By November 2024, I had reached a breaking point. Managing Sam's after-school meltdowns or needing to provide his sensory diet to assist him with regulating after a full day of socialising became overwhelming. On top of that, there was the endless paperwork involved in the process of removing him from his current specialist provision, and the emotional labour of navigating this system left me exhausted. I reduced my working hours to five hours a day, aligning with the time my children are at school. A temporary reduction in working hours obviously meant a reduction in salary and while it was a decision borne out of necessity, it meant having to scale back even more during a cost-of-living crisis. I made peace with that reality.

Everyday tasks for our family require levels of planning that others might find unimaginable. A simple trip to the supermarket or the dentist necessitates social stories, countdowns of sleeps, and detailed conversations with my husband about who will look after which child and when. Our home, meanwhile, has been transformed into what feels like a fortress. Locks are installed on every door and cupboard, and cameras monitor all rooms except the living room, though we're now planning to add one there too. These measures may seem like a luxury but are essentially a lifeline that ensures Sam's safety in a world that often feels perilous.

Then there is Daniel, my five-year-old, who I know to be neurodivergent but who has very different needs to his brother. Daniel doesn't yet fully understand Sam's needs or the permanence of his differences. He frequently says things like, "When Sam gets older and starts talking…" and each time, I explain this may never happen. Slowly, Daniel is beginning to recognise that his interactions with Sam cannot mirror those he has with his peers at school. Yet watching his attempts to engage, when his hopeful gestures are sometimes met with no response, and witnessing his disappointment is painful.

In many ways, Daniel has taken on the role of an older brother, even though he is almost three years younger. He tries to help, to care, to take responsibility for Sam in ways that are far beyond his years. While I am proud of his compassion, it also worries me. Childhood is not meant to carry this weight, and I struggle with the knowledge that the dynamics of their relationship may never align with what society views as "typical." Daniel's disappointment, his caretaking instincts, and his occasional frustrations all remind me that autism shapes not only Sam's life but all of ours. Yet it also means I feel immense joy in the mundane, like when Sam laughs at Daniel's antics or when they hold hands while jumping on the trampoline. A different hypervigilance is required here: the constant looking for the different ways they show each other love.

Practicalities for Black mothers

Across the nine participant interviews and two focus groups conducted for this research, the word 'fight' (or a derivative thereof, such as 'fighting' or 'fought') was mentioned 54 times. The sense of constantly battling to advocate for their child was something that emerged from virtually every participant account, despite the co-researchers electing not to include such language in the initial interview questions.

The physiological and psychological impacts of a life beset by battle were detailed at length throughout the previous chapter, but there is an additional dimension at play: the sheer weight of the practical demands of advocacy.

The gendered division of labour

In all cases, mothers – as the primary caregivers in their respective households – expressed that it was they who shouldered the bulk of responsibility for those demands. This held even for those in two-parent households, with Sareeta neatly summarising the theme of a gendered division of labour and the ways in which it consolidates the already overwhelming task of meeting the complex needs of an autistic child:

I'm lucky that their dad is present, and he is around. But yeah, ultimately the lion's share does fall on my shoulders and much of the advocacy is very taxing.

Participants also shared the additional frustration that when their children's fathers did participate in meetings and appointments, it often resulted in noticeably different outcomes to those they had been able to solicit alone, something which accords with earlier observations regarding the treatment afforded to those perceived as Black lone mothers:

One thing I do is to make sure that my husband comes with me where possible. So that's… maybe that's… I don't know if that's just because as a woman…, but he doesn't even have to open his mouth. Him… just a man being there, I get treated better. I get a better outcome. Just him being sat there – Linda

[I]t was always interesting to me when I went with his Dad, they'd have a little bit more time to sit and listen to what I had to say than whenever I was going on my own… – Stacy-Ann

Sareeta highlighted the effect of her children's father's race on such interactions, explaining that (much as the co-researchers had identified through their own collective autoethnographic research) he was positioned to secure support for their children in a way that she could not:

[I told their Father] 'you need to use your White privilege. Now use your voice to support your Black children, because this is how they're treating your Black children in these environments, and you need to speak up more'.

Creating a safe environment

Rendering the environment as safe as possible is not simply a task for outside the family home. One of the most common forms of autism symptomatology is inflexibility, which is itself often both the cause and the consequence of the comorbidity between autism and anxiety. The need for predictability, routine, and control over the environment and over the (otherwise potentially mystifying) behaviours of others can make it extremely difficult for an autistic person to respond to unexpected changes or demands. Thus, while anticipation and pre-planning are crucial elements of any parenting experience, for those raising autistic children the 'margin of error' is substantially smaller.

As Brianna asserted, in explaining the lengths to which she has to go to legislate for her son's need for consistency:

> [N]obody really understands that. They don't have to make sure everything's in place every single day and everything's perfect.

Participants shared that creating and sustaining an environment which could be responsive to their child's needs numbered among their most important considerations, and that they were continually under pressure to develop strategies in support of this priority.

As Toni stated:

> I'm constantly second-guessing myself. I'm constantly having to expand the toolbox trying to find new resources.

As difficult as this task may be, it is not something that participants felt able to avoid, since the only alternative would be to cut their children off from the world, denying them opportunities for socialisation and the development of life skills.

Stacy-Ann summarised this by stating:

> [W]e're not doing that. We're not going to stay at home and not experience real life. No… you're going to go to the supermarket. You're going to learn how to shop. You're going to do all the things that you enjoy. We're not going to lock you away. You're not some animal that can't be let out of a cage…

Going it alone

In discussing the possibility of deferring to healthcare, education, and social care professionals for help with and resources for managing the practical burden, a consensus emerged that support was largely unavailable or unfit for purpose.

Per Brianna:

> [T]here is no support around I don't access anything. There's nothing. I wouldn't even know where to go for support. Everything that he needs, I sort of cater to myself from what I've learned.

In fact, Linda affirmed that compensating for the limitations of professionals was a practical demand in its own right, one which she highlighted as the most difficult of all the tasks she faces:

> I think it's definitely the fighting with professionals… trying to advocate for your child. Get your child what they need. Constantly checking people are still doing what they're supposed to be doing […] It's a lot mentally. It's a lot. It's a lot of admin.

'Life admin'

Participants shared that much of this 'admin' involved form-filling, a process which was often extremely time-consuming and dis-heartening. Toni and Imogen both explained why this specific task is particularly challenging, given the statistical likelihood that mothers of autistic children are already faced with their own experience of neurodiversity:

> I really advocated for [the school] to complete a referral form. And they gave me the form to complete. For me, I'm neurodiverse (sic). I struggle with forms.... why are you giving me the form to complete? – Toni

> A large amount of mothers of neurodivergent children are neurodivergent themselves, and you've got to do really difficult things – Imogen

Much of this form-filling has to be undertaken in order for moth-ers to access the minimal resources to which they and their families are entitled. However, another theme that emerged in discussions of these processes, concerned the deficit-based viewpoint into which these mothers are then forced, through the design of such forms and associated appointments:

> Even just sitting down doing the [Disability Living Allowance] form is just so draining and upsetting because you're only focusing on all the negatives. You're only focusing on all the things that they have challenges with or struggles with. So, it's not even a balanced reflection of your child – Linda (Focus Group 2)

> I have regular med reviews with my 16-year-old with his Consultant Psychiatrist. And it's always, you know, it's

always the chat list of negative stuff, you know, not the positive stuff, you know… just risk stuff and it's like… 'this is depressing' […] everything is a negative interaction – Imogen (Focus Group 1)

Here, once again, the psychological and the practical burdens intersect as mothers find that the only means by which they can advocate for their children, is to continually elucidate the ways in which they are 'deficient' by neurotypical metrics. This speaks to the damaging persistence of the 'medical model' as the principal framework through which autistic children and their caregivers are recognised.

Appeals and tribunals

While participants identified referrals and form-filling as significant triggers, what was even more demanding for a great many mothers in the study was the regularity with which such referrals were denied. A theme emerged of re-referrals, appeals, and complaints as a regular feature in their everyday lives and as a time-consuming and expensive undertaking.

Both co-researchers have experience of having to engage with SEND Tribunals in order to guarantee an appropriate educational provision for their children, so it came as little surprise to learn that this had also been an issue for several participants.

I found the school chose to parent blame and gaslight me about [my son's] needs when in fact they're not trained in autism and were not in the position to identify his needs […] In the end, I had to raise a discrimination complaint including adultification for them to be seen to take his needs a little more seriously – Survey respondent, anonymous

[I]t culminated with my deciding to go to tribunal to get him into a special school – Laura

I had to fight to get his EHCP and in the end I took it all the way to appeal and won. The school refused to recognise him as a child with neurodiversity. It has been exhausting – Survey respondent, anonymous

The EHCP itself is not fit for purpose and now I'm having to go through the tribunal process – Toni

Teachers and teaching assistants have been very supportive. However, senior school leadership and all SENCOs have failed to follow the law and I have had to fight to get some of what he needs. The Local Authority have been the same, making mistakes and delivering a poor standard of work forcing me to go to tribunal. – Survey respondent, anonymous

However, it was somewhat alarming to note that 6 of the 8 interviewees whose children were old enough to have attended school (8 of the 10, if co-researchers are included), had had to withdraw them from one, or more, educational placements, with a further participant planning to do so in the near future.

We are seriously planning to home school once it is feasible for our household to do that – Linda

[I realised that] he needs to be in a school that understands him better and can provide and cater for his needs – Brianna

I took him out [of school] before he got excluded – Imogen

He's in his last year of primary school now, but he's been through three primary schools – Toni

This is their third school. And just to give you some context, my children are six and seven years old – Sareeta

Withdrawing a child from school, either with a view to home educating, or with the intention of switching their provision to an alternative placement, can be a difficult and protracted process even when all parties are in agreement about why it is necessary. Limited specialist provision and cuts to education budgets undermine the efficacy of the SEND system, to the detriment of children, parents, and educators alike.

For Toni and Sareeta, however, this process has been further complicated by a breakdown in relations between the school and parents, which has led to legal action.

Toni describes an incident in which her son was struck in the face by a teacher, during a martial arts lesson. Despite her son requiring treatment following this incident, the teacher faced no disciplinary action with the school initially denying (even in the face of medical evidence) that any injury had been sustained and then concurring with the teacher's assessment that the incident had been caused by the child's 'hyperactivity'. The practicalities of the ensuing legal dispute, in which Toni has taken umbrage with what she sees as the weaponisation of her son's autism and ADHD symptomatology as a means to avoid accountability for his having been injured, have proven to be enormously exacting and have been ongoing through resulting periods of home-education, and even now that her son is attending an alternative provision.

Sareeta points to what she characterises as a sustained campaign of harassment, which began when she raised pedagogic concerns with her son's school. As a teacher herself, she found the school's response to be defensive and unhelpful and was taken aback when relations deteriorated to the point where staff would only agree to speak with her on a 2:1 basis. Among the issues for which she is now seeking legal redress, Sareeta cites an incident where she pointed out to staff that a hole that had been ripped in the seat of her son's school trousers had gone unnoticed and unresolved by them, despite spare clothes being available. Thereafter, Sareeta states that staff began a daily routine which they described as 'checking [him] for holes', something which she deemed to be degrading, invasive, and a disproportionate response to the concern she had flagged.

> I said 'you're dehumanising him, you're humiliating him' and that's what made me realise that by using my voice – which is why I stopped using it – I'm basically putting my son in harm's way.

Therefore, in addition to the multitude of tasks and responsibilities already facing them as mothers of autistic children, Toni and Sareeta describe the additional burden (practical and psychological) of supporting their children in settling into new educational settings, while still managing the *"expensive"* and *"exhausting"* legal ramifications of a dispute with their previous school.

Both spoke to the sense that the legal proceedings have generated a legacy that continues to impact them and their children:

> But you know what's really difficult is legacy, that kind of stays with you. Even if you move school […] and how individuals who are also maybe of that school of thought, or leaning, can utilise the way you have been classified or vilified – to ultimately silence you – Sareeta

> When the next school then used the data that the previous school put on… I've actually got it in writing that the

next school is telling me when I start to raise objections and challenges and complaints against them… I've got it in writing where they are now telling me that they have reports from the previous school about my behaviours and my attitudes – Toni

Home-educating

One means by which mothers have sought to navigate the practicalities of their children's education has been to add this to the list of tasks undertaken in the family home. Six of the eight interviewees with children old enough to have attended school (eight of the ten, if the co-researchers are included) reported that they spent a period of time home-educating their children. This is in addition to the period during the COVID-19 pandemic when they were mandated to do so, due to school closures.

For most, this was a mixed experience with some relief from the usual anxieties that their children might experience distress or harm in the school environment, but alternative concerns were also generated, regarding how to support their children in effectively accessing the curriculum.

Another key disadvantage to home-educating was that mothers found that it was even more difficult to access other forms of support, without school staff being in a position to co-sign the need for it:

[My son needed…] occupational therapy, speech and language, bearing in mind that he was at home. I had to fight to get [it] – Laura

In contrast, Linda, who asserted that she plans to home-educate her son in the near future, expressed that she feels well-placed to do so, since she is already having to maintain such an active role in his education by undertaking research on behalf of his teachers:

> …*seeing that I'm researching strategies and then essentially sharing that learning with staff, I think that's a bit wild.*

The expectation that mothers should effectively design their own curriculum, even when their child is attending school, was also expressed by a survey respondent:

> *I struggle with constantly having to create ideas for them to use in class with my child rather than the support coming from themselves; calls home are frequent for nonsensical reasons – Survey respondent, anonymous*

A related observation from Sareeta was that the resort to home-educating was often symptomatic of broken systems:

> *… [T]his is not sustainable and this is why so many of us are homeschooling […]. Also [in homeschooling] we are then creating solutions to [the schools' problems]. They don't want us and we're kind of… tidying it up for them […] and that's not fair. The strain that places on families and those wonderful mothers […] that are doing that. It isn't fair. We should have systems that work, but they're not working. And even educators are saying that themselves.*

It bears repeating that while many of the challenges of navigating such systems are faced by all parents of children with additional needs, the experience of being racialised by professionals and service providers renders them even more difficult to manage for Black mothers of autistic children. The 'Strong Black Woman' trope is particularly insidious in this context because it fuels an expectation that 'resilience' will equip these women with the means to weather the storm.

It is for this reason that the extraordinary lengths to which some participants have gone to support their children represent a double-edged sword: an endorsement of their commitment to their families, and an indictment of the limited service provision that compelled them to meet their children's complex needs without meaningful assistance.

The impact on career

Examples of this commitment include Stacy-Ann who trained as an SEND teacher so that she could equip herself to support her son in accessing the curriculum. She states that her initial interest in doing so was borne out of the need to be able to monitor his well-being at school as closely as possible:

> [B]efore I even went into working in a special school [...] I only wanted to be a parent spy. Like I went to work in his school once because I wanted to see what you were going to do. [...] I wanted to go in.

Similarly, Brianna elected to retrain in order to be able to personally bridge the gap in the service provision that was available to her son:

> Speech and language was horrendous. Absolutely horrendous. Still is [...].He's never accessed any form of help really, apart from getting, you know, sort of assessments for the EHCP and for his diagnosis. Apart from that, it's hit and miss. There's just... there's nothing that's been sort of continual or continuous. So that's been absolutely awful, dreadful. And to be honest, that is... I was a teacher beforehand and I've swapped and I'm now in my final

year, I've been becoming a speech and language therapist because I just couldn't access the help … And I thought, 'well, OK, I'm going to have to do this myself'.

An anonymous survey respondent also recounted changing career, in order to provide her son with the care that she could not secure for him elsewhere:

…Non-existent support for Black carers. I took it on myself to educate myself and other professionals and trained as a social worker for information.

Even more common among participants, however, was an account of how the intensity of caring responsibilities had left them with no choice but to reduce their working hours, or even to leave their jobs entirely and become full-time carers.

Sareeta is a primary school teacher but the practical demands of supporting her autistic children are such that, at this stage in her career, she can only commit to supply teaching:

My career… I feel like it's definitely not where it could be, where I would ideally like it to be. But ultimately, I feel like I've had to kind of decide. 'All right, well, what do you want? What is the priority?'. There's so many things that I still need to get in order… and I've kind of put my career on hold

Toni and Linda have both left their jobs in order to enable them to focus entirely on their families' needs:

My career has been affected […] I came out of full-time employment, so I can more manage a work life with a family life, in terms of my son's needs. […] So, I'm a full-time carer at the moment – Toni

I've always... I've never not worked. So essentially, quitting work because it's just too stressful. It's like a full-time job even just doing the admin. Fighting, fighting for your child... Fighting professionals to do their job... 'Just please, just do your job'. [...]. So, my husband, he works full time. I don't work. So even things like you know you can't help but think about – as a woman – your financial security for the future. But the priority is, you know, our household unit, how we can... how we can best manage all elements of that – Linda

Imogen summarised the quandary facing many of the mothers in the study:

I'm currently not wage working because the care needs of my younger two children prohibit that. For a number of years actually. [...] You can't wage work because it's a full-time job just to administrate your child's life.

The financial implications of caring

Perhaps unsurprisingly, the theme of struggling financially was one which was broached by several participants. This was not only due to reduced earning capacity but also to the additional expense associated with raising a child with complex needs. Between the specialist provision that participants had to access to meet those needs, the expensive private healthcare that they had to seek out when free-to-access services had proven inadequate, and the additional expense of buying and replacing items, or accessing spaces, that their children rely upon for emotional regulation, mothers shared that their ability to manage their finances was continually undermined by what might usefully be thought of as an 'Autism Tax' paid on family life.

Participants shared the following indicative examples of the financial burden generated by their caring needs.

> I've had to sign him up for private physio because the NHS won't do physio with him [for his idiopathic tiptoeing]. That's so expensive, it's like £165 per session, which is ridiculous [...] I'm paying £165 and I'm basically co-facilitating this session with her in order for him to get the most out of it. – Sareeta

> He's discovered that he likes to rip his clothes into the smallest amount of pieces and it just gives him a certain peace, you know? – Stacy-Ann

> I knew that secondary school was right around the corner and I couldn't sit back and wait any longer. I definitely wasn't prepared to wait on CAMHS waiting lists, so I don't know where I got the money from [to pursue a private autism diagnosis]. Rob Peter to pay Paul. Whatever bills didn't get paid, whatever food we had to cut back on. I found that money – Toni

The financial dimension of the practical burden is, of course, exacerbated for those who have more than one child. However, this is only one component of the challenges associated with managing sibling relationships in a neurodivergent household.

Managing sibling relationships

It goes without saying that raising multiple neurodivergent children is liable to consolidate the effects of the multiplicity of burdens. However, participants shared that raising children in a home where one child is diagnosed, and the other is either neurotypical or undiagnosed, can also render it enormously difficult to manage sibling relationships.

Ayesha recalls this challenge from when her (now adult) children were younger:

> I was always trying to placate… I was always trying to distract. And, of course, that also has an impact on the other children. So, they kind of just grow up by osmosis, taking all of this in

Sareeta, reflecting on her current experience, shared that:

> [H]is sister does antagonise him and I say to her that you know her words really impact him, and his response is like… it's like a switch has been flipped [….]. But it's really difficult actually trying to explain to her because he has the diagnosis. You know, if you say, 'it's your brother', it's gonna be a trigger in her response because she [says she] hates her brother and she hates autism.

Thus, relationships between siblings, and indeed between their parents, can be a common casualty of complex caring responsibilities and are yet another practical consideration facing Black mothers of autistic children, one which can be further exacerbated by financial hardship and a lack of access to meaningful support.

While the pressures to meet the conflicting needs of more than one child are common to many parents, most can expect this challenge to ease as their children age. This is not the case for caregivers of children with additional needs, for whom increasing independence in later years is by no means guaranteed. It is this which informs our conception of the 'temporal burden'.

Temporal burden

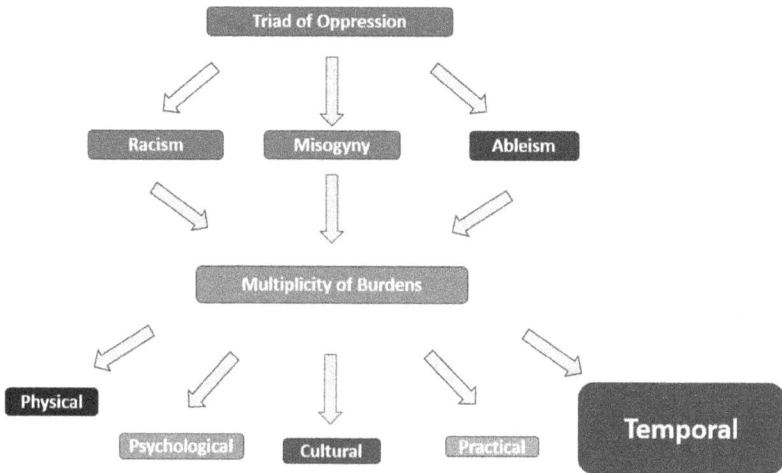

Figure 11: Focus on the temporal burden within the multiplicity of burdens

The temporal burden reflects the ongoing demands on Black mothers' time as they raise and advocate for their autistic children. Their parental responsibilities endure far beyond typical timelines, as care and advocacy often extend into adulthood. Additionally, their children's delayed or non-linear milestones create further strain, as rigid institutional frameworks fail to accommodate their needs. The following sections explore how these challenges shape the experiences of the mothers in our study.

Claire's story

The first time I met Mel in person, which doubled as only the third time I had ever spoken to her, we wandered back through the corridors of

the hotel where we had just attended a conference dinner. We spoke nineteen to the dozen, desperate to wring every last second from our discussion, before retiring for a sensible early night so that we would feel human for the next day's agenda. We had run the conversational gamut, over dinner, showing off pictures of our children, comparing notes on their diagnosis and presentation, gossiping about our workplace, lamenting certain 'testing' relationships with various family members, and I think it's fair to say that both of us had long since decided that the other was a 'keeper' in friendship terms.

As we arrived at Mel's hotel door, she made no attempt to open it and I made no attempt to leave, easily adding another 20 minutes to our enthusiastic exchange, before we realised that we should probably let our temporary neighbours get some sleep.

Our conversation came to an end on a note that would have sounded shocking to anyone who might have overheard it but which, to us, made perfect sense. Mel knew that my husband and children were waiting in my room, because there was no practical way in which I could have travelled without them. She explained that because she lived much closer to the venue than I did, her husband had been able to bring her children along to say goodnight to her, since she knew that they would be unable to settle into bed without first doing so. I can't remember which one of us jokingly pointed out that our children's dependency on us was such that we 'weren't allowed to die', but what I do know is that this led to a very matter-of-fact statement, endorsed by both of us, that we had no contingencies in place for long-term care for our autistic children.

With no one in our lives, besides our husbands, who understands our children's needs in the way that we do, no one who would be capable *of meeting them, and no means to save the vast sums of money that it takes to fund high quality adult social care, we each conceded that the closest we had to a planned future was… immortality.*

It was at this point that we first identified the 'temporal burden' facing us as othered mothers.

This burden takes two forms, both of which are connected with a lack of time. In the first instance, we are 'time poor' in our everyday lives. The practical demands of raising an autistic child suck up all the oxygen in the room and militate against long-term planning, as does the uncertainty of Mae's developmental trajectory.

There are simply not enough hours in the day to do anything but ensure that she is as happy and safe as possible, and everything else is sacrificed in this pursuit. My husband and I recently calculated that we have not been on a 'date' in over two years, and we often joke that much of our life is spent 'high-fiving in the doorway' as one of us heads to work, leaving the other with a 'to-do list' of logistics to ensure that our children make it through the day unscathed.

While this might be suboptimal, it is, once again, a great privilege in that we have each other with whom to arrive at this division of labour. What neither of us wants to consider is the second dimension of the temporal burden, which relates to the lack of alternative caregivers in Mae's life.

There are times when fears for the future are simply too overwhelming to countenance but ignoring them will not make them go away. Mae only has six more years in full-time education and I have no idea what the implications of this will be for my career, and for my husband's. What I do know is that neither of us can live forever, and that this reality cannot easily be reconciled with the fact that Mae will almost certainly not have the capacity to live independently, in our absence. I don't know what this will mean for Joshua.

Even if his needs prove to be low support, it is unfair to assume that there could or should be caring responsibilities in his future. All I am able to do for now is to save what little money I can and try to take the best possible care of myself, in a bid to delay the inevitable.

But, with all the other 'burdens' facing me in my role as a Black mother of an autistic child, finding the means to do this feels like one among many impossible tasks.

Mel's story

Writing a will is not something anyone wants to sit down and do. It feels unnatural to make plans for a future where you may no longer be present. Yet, for parents raising autistic children, particularly those with high support needs, I think it becomes a necessity far earlier than most. For me, it was not just about ensuring financial stability for Sam but also securing his care and protection in a world that has shown time and time again that it will fail him if he doesn't have an advocate.

The reality of writing a will caused fractures in our family. My mother and I fell out when I chose not to name her as Sam's guardian in the event of mine and my husband's passing. My acknowledgment that she did not understand enough about autism, and, by extension, Sam, to be his carer, despite the love she clearly felt for him, caused significant tension in our relationship. Despite the tension, our actual choice—Pete's younger brother—is far from ideal due to him currently living thousands of miles away. While my brother-in-law has assured us that he would return to England, if necessary, this is a promise made easily in his current circumstances as a single man without children. His future priorities, however, could shift. We know it and he knows it.

The more likely scenario, unspoken but deeply felt, is that Sam's care will ultimately fall to Daniel, his younger brother. This thought weighs heavily on me. It would be unfair to place such a burden on Daniel, who is already navigating his own neurodivergence. Yet it is likely that Daniel may grow to be more "productive" in neoliberal terms i.e. he is able to engage in education, employment, and other societal contributions in ways that Sam might not. But to frame it in these terms feels dehumanising, as though I'm comparing the worth of my children through society's narrow metrics of value. Still, I cannot escape the knowledge that Daniel's role will likely extend far beyond that of a sibling. He may become Sam's carer, his advocate, and his protector in place of his parents.

When my husband and I discussed another reality with my mother-in-law, she described us as morbid for suggesting that Sam would likely live with us for the entirety of our lives. Her comment stung but was unsurprising. Intergenerational living, while common in many cultures, is often viewed negatively in a society shaped by neoliberal ideals of independence and self-reliance. Yet the likelihood of Sam living independently feels inaccessible. The more probable scenario is that our home will remain his home, even as he grows into adulthood. This is something I am already at peace with and looking forward to.

Sam is only eight, but I am already preoccupied with what the world will look like when he is older. By the time he turns 19 and is no longer seen as requiring educational support, I hope to be working part-time or semi-retired, and able to dedicate more time to his care. But the truth is, I don't get to fully enjoy his childhood. I am acutely aware that Sam's childhood will be extended.

I feel like I am always living with one foot in the present and one in an uncertain future and this shapes every decision I make. It affects how I parent, how I plan, and how I interact with the world. It feels like our time is not our own; it is borrowed from the future. It is because I love Sam deeply and unconditionally that the weight of responsibility to make sure his life is comfortable when I am no longer here is inescapable. It is a constant reminder that my role as mother does not have an endpoint even when I die.

Time poverty

As above, the 'temporal burden' as expressed by our participants takes two forms. The first is 'time poverty', which is inextricably linked with the physiological, psychological, and practical burdens outlined elsewhere. Perhaps unsurprisingly, given all that the research findings have already revealed about the unsustainable load linked with the motherwork undertaken by Black mothers of autistic children, participants consistently reported a lack of time in which to prioritise self-care, career, or in which to socialise with their friends or partner. The overwhelming responsibilities of the 'life admin' undertaken to protect and support their children ensured that they were constantly at, or over, capacity and the physical and emotional consequences of this were palpable in the accounts they provided.

Sareeta shared an instructive example of the ways in which the interventions she pursues to support her son, result in additional work – and reduced time – for her. In so doing, she reflected a concern echoed among several of our participants about how unsustainable it feels for them to have to act not just as a parent, but also as an 'expert' in every arena of their children's lives and development, when the expectation is that the home is the best, or only, place in which such support can be provided:

> [Y]ou get to these clinics [...] and it's just like [...] 'here's some exercises', and 'this is what you do at home' and, like, 'see you in a year' sort of thing [...]. But when they're saying to me, 'go and do these exercises', just... how feasible is that every day? Because especially on the days I've been at work, so I get them from after school club at 6pm and I've still got to bring them back. They're starving. They're really grumpy. They need to have food. We need to do their homework because, you know, God forbid you forget that. So, we've got to get their homework done and then they've got to get in the bath and then they need a little bit of wind down time [...] got to read the story... and then it's bed. And like before, you know, it's like it, [the evening] is done... and then he's so resistant to doing the exercises.

Toni spoke to an issue highlighted by several participants when she described how much of her time is absorbed through the (often fruitless) appointments she has to attend on behalf of her son:

> I end up in so many meetings on top of everything else I'm going through, which... you shouldn't have to be in so many meetings. And... basically, the meetings oftentimes become ineffective. The right people aren't there, or they weren't aware of that information, so now they need to go away and investigate it more...

Brianna pointed to the difficulties of balancing the demands on her time, in a way which enables her to cater to the needs of both of her children:

> *It's hard trying to get everything correct the way he wants it, and sometimes I'm just not on my day. I've got a little 3-year-old that takes up a lot of time as well (Focus Group 2)*

The impact of caring on time management was also cited by participants as a reason that they had had to reduce their working hours, or even reluctantly walk away from their pre-motherhood careers. As Toni explained, a key factor in her decision to become a full-time carer was the regularity with which her son was being sent home from school. Reflecting on her last few months in paid employment, she stated:

> *I remember not wanting to take a day off work, you know? Like, you get the call from the school and you're… you're scared. And I'm thinking, 'OK, well, which one of us is going to be able to go to the school this time and how will that look? You know, if I take another day off…?' (Focus Group 2).*

Enduring parental responsibility

The effects of time poverty, like so many of the challenges facing othered mothers, are liable to persist far beyond the point at which those raising neurotypical children might expect the weight of their day-to-day parental responsibilities to steadily ease. It is this which throws into sharp relief the second component of the temporal burden; specifically, the fact that for many participants, the impact of the multiplicity of burdens will continue to shape their lives, even as their children reach adulthood. Given the lifelong impact of autism symptomatology (in both high and low support presentations), it is little wonder that participants coalesced over the fear they felt in respect of an inherently uncertain future:

> *You really think about everything for the future in a lot of detail – maybe a bit excessively so. You know, will they get married? What, you know, what their education could be like. How's their day to day at work going to be? Will they speak? How will the world treat them? What will I do when someone's bullying?… You know, all those things…* – Linda

> *I do still then think, 'OK, well, what happens after I go, you know? Who's going to then be there for him? Who's going to support him? Who's going to make sure that he is well looked after, that he is loved, and all of those things?'* – Stacy-Ann

These fears are exacerbated by an ongoing crisis in adult social care, which drastically limits the provision which is available for autistic adults:

> *You have to remember that once you become an adult with special needs, the services and provisions… stop* – Stacy-Ann

Three of the mothers in our study were able to discuss these concerns through the lens of current experiences, since they each had adult children. The theme of 'enduring parental responsibility' was one which united all three of these accounts.

Ayesha's daughter has what might be described as a relatively low support presentation and yet the effect that it can have on her ability to manage the demands of adult life is profound, and is experienced vicariously by Ayesha herself:

> *[S]he can't advocate for herself… for what her strengths are, for what she needs, y'know? […] And it's draining for*

me in particular cause I've shouldered most of that. Even things like… this is a smart person with a really good job, and yet she's phoning me while I'm at work about how to… what to say in an e-mail which is maybe a couple of things. And it's about how to communicate – the etiquette of communicating that she doesn't have. And yet she's asked me so many times and she's done it so many times. […] The thought of me not being there when she's going through all the things she's going through and not picking up the phone. You think… 'I don't know what she's going to do'? […] You have to navigate the world carefully. She finds it very difficult to navigate the world as a Black woman.

Similarly, Imogen indicated the ways in which the practical and temporal burdens intersect in her experience of supporting her adult daughter:

I have to help her manage it because sometimes she can't speak in front of other people. So, for medical appointments and stuff, sometimes I have to attend with her.

In both cases, the ostensibly 'low support' needs of the vulnerable adult are such that their mothers can only support them with their explicit consent. Given that both Ayesha and Imogen have adult daughters who display the symptomatology of PDA, such consent can often be withdrawn by their children at exactly the time when advocacy is most needed. This is a further source of anxiety for mothers who are forced to 'battle' not just the systems that are failing to meet their children's needs, but also with their daughters' own conceptions that they do not require support.

[A]nd of course, because she's an adult, I can't advocate […] I don't have the oversight to. […]She has to drive it – Ayesha

Stacy-Ann's fears for her adult child manifest differently. They relate to the culture of hostility that participants with younger children identified as currently impacting their Black sons at school and provide an insight into what the future might hold for those young boys and their mothers.

> *[When he was younger] I'd spend all my time worrying about the future, missing out on the present [...].Now that he's 21, I have that real fear – and I think many of us do, especially when you're raising young Black boys and young Black men – because we know what it's like out there. [...] You know, he's a 6 foot 6 Black man, walking the street. If I'm not with him, I'm petrified because I'm thinking 'whoever's with him needs to be clued up, know what they're doing [if...] heaven forbid, he has an outburst, he gets upset. [...] I don't want to have that fear for the rest of my life because it robs me of the joy that he has.*

Stacy-Ann's description of contending with anxieties that cause her to struggle to stay 'in the moment', and connected to the joy that her son brings her, closely correspond with Toni's concerns for her 11-year-old:

> *The hopes and dreams that I have for this child is that he makes it past each day alive. That he's not groomed by some gang. Or, you know, he never has to get stopped by the police because – yeah – like, I could never imagine how he would cope with the sensory overload and not being able to manage conflict and problem solve, and how he may come across to the police as a threat or intimidating. And who are they seeing when they see him? Are they seeing a 'big man' that they're threatened by, or are they seeing a young vulnerable child? Like, my heart wrenches for if that experience should happen...*

Imogen's experience of the school-to-prison pipeline illustrates the basis of concerns such as those expressed by Toni. In the case of one of her sons, Imogen asserts that the failure among key service providers to recognise and meet his needs at an early age played a key role in his eventual incarceration:

> [M]y [20-year-old] son has gone through the system exactly the way that it's supposed to be. He's in prison now, so…
> […] Teachers that thought he was involved in selling drugs didn't tell me, didn't report it to anyone who could have supported him, and he was just – you know – selling drugs at 14. [… I was] pleading with CAMHS even when he was like 6, 7, 8, saying he needs proper support [but…] he just never got any of the support to deal with his low self-esteem. Our children are vulnerable but they're not going to get protected from that vulnerability because [criminality] is the future that these institutions see for your child. You know, so you're out there trying to get the maximum options and outcomes that are positive but, if you're fighting on your own, it's almost impossible.

While Imogen may have detailed a particularly harrowing example of the future that can face a child whose identity sits at the intersection of race and disability, the statistical data outlined in Chapter 5, indicate that the trajectory she describes is by no means exceptional. Furthermore, even for those mothers whose children secure relatively positive outcomes through the school system, the level of focus and hypervigilance required to support them in effectively navigating their adult lives ensures that the multiplicity of burdens in one which many Black mothers of autistic children must continue to contend with for life.

This enduring burden is further compounded by the pressures of living in a neoliberal society that emphasises individual responsibility over collective care. Within this context, the challenges faced by Black mothers of autistic children often remain invisible, as they are pressured to manage their struggles privately, rather than receiving the communal support such circumstances demand. This phenomenon, which we term the privatisation of trauma, reflects how neoliberal ideologies shift the weight of systemic failings onto individuals, particularly marginalised groups, compelling them to internalise and suppress their pain. The next section critiques this dynamic, exploring how societal indifference and the dismantling of welfare structures have created an environment in which mothers are left to navigate their trauma in isolation, often at great personal cost.

The privatisation of trauma

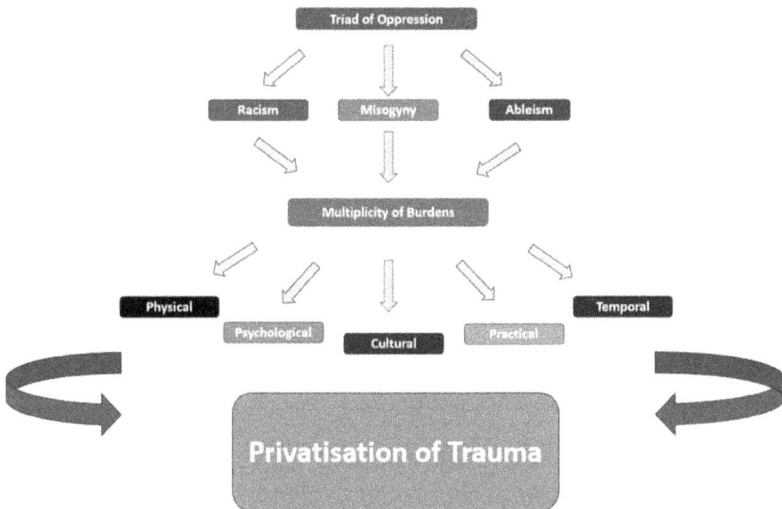

Figure 12: Focus on the privatisation of trauma which results from the multiplicity of burdens

The privatisation of trauma refers to the ways in which the pain, distress, and struggle of othered mothers are contained within the personal and domestic sphere, rendering them invisible to wider society. For Black mothers of autistic children, this manifests in the expectation that they must endure their hardships in silence, without adequate support from healthcare, education, and social care professionals, or from their own communities. The structural inequities they face, such as medical neglect, institutional racism, and the devaluation of their expertise as parents, are reframed as personal challenges rather than systemic failures. This enforced invisibility not only isolates mothers but also reinforces cycles of exhaustion, self-sacrifice, and emotional suppression. In the following examination, we reveal the privatisation of trauma through an overview of the othered mothers' experiences and how they are expected to absorb and manage the consequences of structural oppression alone, with little to no recognition or intervention from the very systems that purportedly exist to support them.

Claire's story

A little over two years ago, the delights of puberty hit us like a ton of bricks. All the strategies we'd been relying on for a decade, to support Mae with her communication and behavioural challenges were rendered completely unfit for purpose, almost overnight.

Any parent with a child of Mae's age will be familiar with the feeling that their little angel has suddenly been replaced by an untidy squatter with a short fuse and questionable personal hygiene, but this was more than your standard adolescent chaos.

Mae began to experience meltdowns on a hitherto unprecedented scale, with terrifying acts of self-harm – banging her head repeatedly against the walls and floors, balling her hands into fists and punching herself in the legs until welts began to appear, and kicking out at any and all objects in her vicinity. This is also when she began to lash out at me, a tendency that peaked at certain times of her newly arrived menstrual cycle. The sustained incidences of guttural screaming that accompanied these meltdowns were, and still are, an almost intolerable sensory assault that it's very difficult to describe to anyone who hasn't witnessed them.

Where Mae's window of tolerance had been expanding in tiny increments in the preceding years, she now had the emotional equivalent of a 'hair trigger' and it became almost impossible to predict when and how that might manifest. Her sleep was even more disrupted than usual, she lost interest in the physical activities that had always proven to be such a welcome distraction, and she would become consumed with anxiety any time that she was not in my company.

All this culminated in a meltdown so severe that witnesses driving past our family car during a panicked journey home from an abortive attempt at a day out, contacted the police, who turned up on our doorstep 20 minutes later to perform a welfare check on the child they assumed we must be abusing. Fortunately, Mae was in an accommodating mood, giving the officers a taste of the behaviour in question, and so they agreed that they had seen enough and took no further action. Nonetheless, after a lifetime spent studiously avoiding any interaction with law enforcement, even when I had been the victim of criminal activity, the sense of being 'on their radar' was deeply unsettling.

Put simply, I was desperate. Desperate enough to consider options that I had formerly dismissed. I contacted the Disability Team

Around the Family to request that they assign us a social worker. For years, I had feared the stigma of being a Black mother whose family required this sort of 'support' (for which read scrutiny), but it was the only way to be considered for respite care, something which all of us desperately needed.

I spoke with the Paediatrician about ADHD medication, but Mae's adverse reaction to stimulants was immediate and harrowing. Alternative forms of medication had little effect or resulted in increased blood pressure or a quickened pulse and so were withdrawn in short order. In extensive research, which I had to undertake with no advice or support from healthcare services, I discovered that Mae appeared to be exhibiting signs of PMDD (Premenstrual Dysphoric Disorder). For the uninitiated, think PMS on steroids. The recommended treatment for this disorder is an SSRI (Selective Serotonin Reuptake Inhibitor) administered as a low daily dose, or intermittently for two of every four weeks. Pursuing this on her behalf, however, placed me firmly at the unenviable intersection of racism, misogyny, and ableism: a Black woman pursuing a pharmacological intervention for a gendered condition that many doctors dismiss out of hand, that was affecting a child already rendered invisible by her disability.

The drug could only be prescribed following a referral to CAMHS (Child and Adolescent Mental Health Services), a service so overburdened that years-long waiting lists are the norm. In fact, I was told, in no uncertain terms, that Mae would not be considered for such a referral since she was "cognitively incapable of suicidal ideation", a statement as inaccurate as it was alarming.

This collapse of options forced us to seek out expensive private healthcare from a Child Psychiatrist who strongly agreed that the medicinal intervention was needed as a matter of urgency but, owing to Mae's young age, he cautioned that he could not sign off on it without approval from CAMHS. Once again, waiting lists loomed large and we were back at square one.

When the possibility of a referral was finally mooted, it was – much to my chagrin – issued for me… to attend a parenting course. When I pointed out that I had already completed no fewer than five such courses, withdrawing from a sixth only when the pregnant facilitator asked me, without a hint of irony, whether I might be interested in taking over her role when she went on maternity leave, this suggestion was thankfully rescinded.

Eventually, through a level of persistence that bordered on stalking, I was able to persuade CALDS (the Learning Disability wing of CAMHS) to add Mae to their caseload and provide us with the prescription we had, by then, been petitioning for, for almost a year.

Blessedly, the medication proved to be (relatively) effective but the time, energy, and psychological fallout linked with obtaining it left me battle-scarred beyond recognition. In order to advocate for my child, I had had to allow myself to become known to social services, who now engage in regular, fruitless and intrusive visits to my family home. I had suffered the indignity of having my parenting called into question by a clinician who accused me of seeking out "chemical restraints" for my autistic daughter, dismissing my efforts to support her as nothing more than drug-seeking behaviour. In pushing back against this characterisation, I had been labelled as "angry" and "aggressive", further consolidating the racial microaggressions that I had already endured. I was forced into debt by my attempts to circumnavigate a system which was keeping my child from the only medication that could meet her complex and increasingly dangerous needs. As a consequence of all of these stressors, my own physical and mental health declined sharply, resulting in me having to be signed off work for several months.

More than anything, my ingrained suspicion that opening up about the extent of my family's struggles would only increase our vulnerability, was borne out entirely. I now feel even less inclined to engage such services in times of crisis, choosing instead to internalise my trauma since – in the absence of culturally competent provision – this genuinely feels like the lesser of two evils.

Mel's story

When Sam first started smearing, my husband was horrified. It happened while both our mothers were visiting, during a period when Sam was struggling significantly at school. His room is his safe space, and with a camera installed, we allow him to spend time there unsupervised. We hadn't expected coming upstairs to ask Sam to say goodbye to his Nanas and find faeces smeared on his walls, windowsills, and wardrobes.

I say my husband was horrified, not because I wasn't, but because I was numb to it. Having previously taught in specialist provisions, I had seen this before. Smearing is one of those behaviours that many autistic children engage in during periods of dysregulation, and by the time it started happening, I had already internalised so much of the distress and chaos of our daily lives that it barely registered as something extraordinary. This is what happens when trauma becomes routine; you normalise it, suppress it, and keep going.

We normalised Sam's Pica to the same degree. Pica is the consumption of objects not typically intended to be eaten. Sam loves leaves, soil, and grass. We've looked up the toxicity levels of every plant, bush, and flower in our garden to ensure they are non-fatal to humans, just in case. While we've had some success distracting him with alternatives (crispy seaweed or wafers instead of leaves), it's that constant vigilance. Once, a neighbour reprimanded Sam for picking and eating an ivy leaf as we walked past their garden. I hadn't seen him do it, and while I was able to quickly grab it out of his mouth, I was embarrassed. I made a joke about it, ran indoors to Google it, and sat watching him for hours after finding that ivy is mildly poisonous.

In September 2024, just as Daniel began primary school, I would say our family descended into crisis. We had completely focused our attention on Daniel and celebrating his milestone so much that we hadn't expected Sam's escalating struggles at school. We had had a summer holiday that had been relatively peaceful, even joyful. But within two weeks of returning to school, Sam's behaviour suddenly shifted. He became violent; something we had never experienced before. My husband bore the brunt of it: black eyes, bruises covering his body, scratches across his face.

We turned to the school's family support services, desperate for help, but none came. Two messages were left, but no phone call was returned. We confided in our parents, only to be met with platitudes. "Poor Sam," they said. "Well, we hope things get better soon." Their responses, though well-meaning, were infuriatingly detached. They didn't grasp the depth of what we were going through—the sleepless nights, the constant hypervigilance, the emotional and physical toll. It was as though they expected us to simply endure, as though this level of strain was somehow normal, but I guess we were the ones who had normalised it.

We didn't want pity or for it to seem as if we couldn't cope with our children, so we endured. We isolated ourselves. We kept things private, kept calm and carried on. The trauma becomes something you carry alone, behind closed doors, because sharing it often leads to minimisation, judgement, or misunderstanding. There is an unspoken pressure to protect others from the rawness of your reality. We learn to frame things in ways that make others comfortable: "We're managing," "He's just going through a tough time," "It's hard, but we're coping." The truth, however, is often far messier.

Navigating public services privately

As diverse as the backgrounds and family lives of our participants may be, the consistencies among their experiences of advocating for their children are striking. All the mothers who shared their journeys spoke of their exhaustion and frustration and of the physical and mental toll taken on them by a system which had continually proven to be unfit for purpose:

[Y]ou're fighting in a broken system and for what you can get within that broken system… That's what it feels like. You're fighting for scraps – Linda

Everything takes so long. Everything's – you know – it's just so hard to obtain – Brianna

It just compounds and validates your own significant trauma – Imogen

[T]he system isn't designed to support us. […] It's constantly harming us. It's… it's a fucking maze. But

even when you understand it, and understand the right person to challenge, to then feel like you have the ability and capacity to make that challenge is a whole other level [...] You're trying to navigate a system that's essentially designed for your child to end up in prison, or six feet under... – Toni

Participants spoke of 'gatekeepers' that consistently blocked access to much needed services, and to a culture of parent blame and hostility that confronted them when they attempted to air concerns, or to seek out solutions.

Educational and social care services flout legislation and force many of us to spend energy and time pursuing formal processes to enforce this. Medically, given that autism is highly represented in Black communities, parents shouldn't be so frequently dismissed. I have also found that services have tried to make me feel guilty for taking up their time when they are so busy, and many other children are waiting to be diagnosed/supported. Additionally, I am made aware of the funding challenges of schools and the difficulty in obtaining speech and language professionals, so medical professionals are reluctant to report the full extent of needs because it will be rejected. This is bizarre to me – Survey respondent, anonymous

The Education sector and Local Authority seem to want to parent blame, rather than look at the fact they are unable to meet need and do not have the sufficient provisions for children in my local area – Survey respondent, anonymous

Untrained poorly equipped professionals who act as gatekeepers for assessment and support across education, social, and health care create barriers to appropriate assessment and support, and preferred to view my children's needs as behavioural and related to my parenting – Survey respondent, anonymous

In some cases, mothers had been explicitly told not to expect help in managing their own well-being and mental health challenges:

Still trying to get him the support he needs. Still trying to get me some support. You know, even speaking to his social worker and for her to look at me and say 'so you're gonna have to find your own support because resources are lacking at the moment' – Toni

In others, the most significant hurdle mothers faced was generated, not by their child's developmental needs, but by the additional practical and emotional labour of seeking action and accountability from the many health care, education, and social care professionals involved in their lives:

The biggest challenge for my mental health has actually not been really to do with how I support my child. It's been more all the professionals who aren't really doing their job and it just seems like such an unnecessary additional stress and strain […] trying to hold people to account [..] just for them to do the bare minimum for your child – Linda

Rapid staff turnover within the SEND system adds a further dimension to this struggle, with respondents reporting the adverse impact of 'losing' support systems that had previously proven to be effective:

I've had inconsistent experiences with SENCOs due to staffing concerns. Many people have left or have little

knowledge of my child. I keep having to repeat myself and start again. There is a lack of knowledge about autism from each teacher despite me trying to support them and educate them in understanding my daughter and the traits that she presents with – Survey respondent, anonymous

My son has only been known to social services for a short while, as a result of a self-referral. However, since that time, there has been a significant turnover of staff and so we have had to keep returning to the drawing board for help and support – Survey respondent, anonymous

Lack of staff and resources are impacting on their ability to support SEND children and meet their individual needs therefore, a lot of pressure is put on the parent – Survey respondent, anonymous

These institutional failings resulted in participants expressing a desire to withdraw from the very systems that are ostensibly designed to support them:

Our children are, unfortunately, in the hands of institutions which we know well to deeply distrust – Sareeta

[T]he system doesn't work together well with the different parts of the system […] It becomes really frustrating and overwhelming to keep on top of it and to keep being that open, hopeful mother who wants to keep working with everyone to make sure my son's got the right support and, you know, I kind of get sometimes in the mindset to be like, fuck everyone -I'm just gonna find my own way… – Toni

Thus the 'hard to reach' narrative appears to emerge only when Black mothers become so disaffected with the systems they are forced to navigate, that they elect to meet their children's needs alone, thereby consolidating the many burdens they already face. The tropes of Black motherhood turn Black women's 'resilience' into a license for professionals not to support them and to dismiss the righteous anger they feel when their children are failed, as baseless and irrational aggression.

Almost all of the research participants in this study had a relatively large amount of 'navigational capital' (Morgan and Stahmer, 2020, p. 25) given that among their number were qualified teachers, teaching assistants, speech therapists, and council workers. Almost all expressed concern about how mothers with fewer resources to call on could possibly be expected to manage the intricacies and foibles of the SEND system.

As Linda summarised:

> I'm educated to degree level. I've worked in a council. So, I understand some of the bureaucracy and, you know, the processes. I've done a little bit of advocacy work before. So, I feel like I'm actually in an ideal position to take on these challenges and [...] I'm finding this, you know... pretty solid. It actually fills me with such horror for other parents who are not in the position that I'm in.

The fact that women whose own lives are so relentlessly demanding retain a focus on others whose experiences may be even more challenging, speaks to the final trope of Black motherhood. The 'Community mother' bleeds not only for herself but for what her story illustrates about the pain of others.

> The tolls on physical and mental health and how that affects, I think, not just myself, but seeing how it

affects the community… seeing how it impacts the community impacts me because I feel like we're all in this together – Sareeta

We contend that it is partly through this focus on community that significant improvements can be made to a system which is currently exacerbating the struggles facing Black mothers of autistic children.

In the next chapter, we explore the recommendations for improved practice which we have derived both from our participant research and in discussions with community groups and organisations that are already working to support Black women's health and well-being.

5
Recommendations for improved practice

When we made the decision to write this book, we both agreed that we did not want the accounts we shared – our own and those of our research participants – to emerge as pitiable tales of 'Black suffering', to be consumed and discarded by those with little to no commitment to effecting change.

Coincidentally, during one of the first participant interviews conducted for the project, Sareeta echoed this conviction:

> I know that wherever this is going to go is probably on a lot of white seats and tables and laps. And how is that going to be received? Part of me wants it to be received with genuine empathy, with care, but also with a desire to want to do something about it rather than just sort of, 'oh, look at these 'poor black folk' and their tragic stories and lives'. I'm really just holding that thought in my mind when we are all kind of sharing our traumas, because that's exactly what this has been actually… So yeah, I want this to be about raising the voice of the women who haven't been able to come to this table.

In our discussion with practitioners who are already working to support women in the Black community, this sense of urgency around translating observation into direct action was a consistent rallying cry. Our heartfelt thanks go to two organisations in particular: 'Global Child and Maternal Health' and 'Black Mothers Matter'.

GCMH is based in London and was founded in 2021 by Agnes Agyepong. It defines its purpose as "*creating a Black led global body whose key focus is to research, inform, amplify and create solidarity with Black maternal health movements around the world*" (Global Child and Maternal Health, 2024). To date, GCMH has launched multiple initiatives and research projects that are concerned with disparities in health outcomes for Black women. Specifically, GCMH representatives Michelle Peter and Reyss Wheeler have co-authored two key reports: *The Black Maternity Experiences Survey: A Nationwide Study of Black Women's Experiences of Maternity Services in the United Kingdom* (2022) which examined Black maternal mortality (Peter and Wheeler, 2022) and the *Black Child SEND* report (Wheeler et al., 2024). The latter is of particular relevance to our own work regarding the experiences of Black mothers of autistic children and complements many of the recommendations we propose in this chapter.

'Black Mothers Matter' was founded in 2020 by Sonah Paton, Aisha Davies, and Yomi Oluwatudimu. The organisation is based in Bristol but defines itself as being "committed to supporting and celebrating Black pregnancies across the UK" (Black Mothers Matter, 2024). It shares with GCMH a focus on racial disparities in pregnancy and works directly with NHS staff to ensure that they are "more knowledgeable and better equipped to support all types of Black people giving birth" (ibid.). This perspective on engaging and training healthcare professionals in anti-racist practice is relevant to our recommendations for improving outcomes for Black mothers of autistic children.

A key point of commonality between GCMH, Black Mothers Matter, and the co-researchers is a determination to, in the words of Michelle Peter *"use our research by using evidence… but also by actually doing something about it".*

Her colleague, Reyss Wheeler concurred when she stated:

> We originally started from this kind of research perspective [but…] I personally reached the point where I was tired of watching the community that I belong to be researched and it not having the follow-on support, or the same sort of money go into implementation and actual change-making.

Sonah Paton took a very similar position when she asserted:

> I think there's a lot of people that work in research and are responsible for producing this kind of data that are [...] a couple of years behind, so maybe they've acknowledged the kind of headline data, [but] the headline statistics are not the full story, and they need to get a wider picture. And then they're like, 'OK, let's go find some Black women to talk to, to share all those traumatic things.' But actually [the key is] how that data is used.

With this in mind, what follows is a series of specific recommendations for policymaking and professional practice in the support of Black mothers of autistic children. These guidelines have been derived directly from the words of our participants whom we asked to convey to us how healthcare, education, and social care professionals could more effectively meet their needs, and from the experiences of community groups that are striving to actively advocate for Black women.

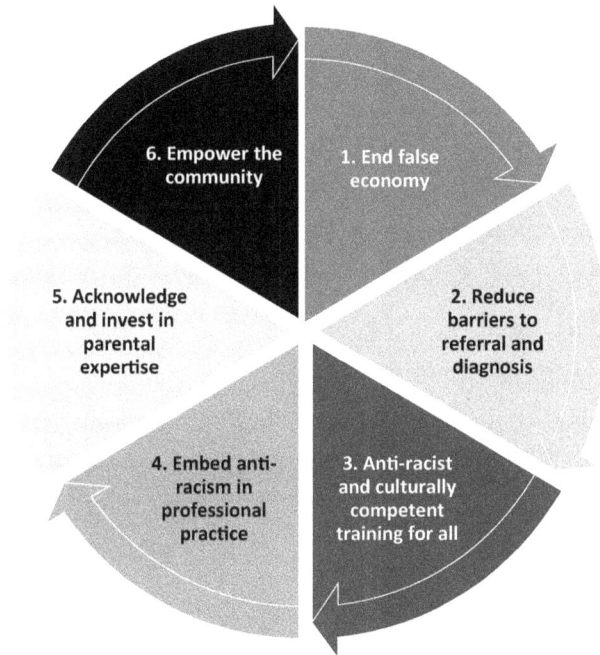

Figure 13: Mothering at the Margins research study recommendations

1. End false economy

Perhaps unsurprisingly, the most consistent response to questions concerning how to improve service provision was a call for increased investment and resource. Reyss Wheeler pointed to a "deficit mindset" in which professionals are social-ised into the assumption that *"we don't have resource. […]. You're just another number. I can't get emotionally attached to any of these families".*

This focus on the 'bottom line' undermines empathy and contributes to the dehumanisation of struggling families. Moreover, it results in a focus on 'false economy', in which opportunities for early intervention which could be crucial in the prevention of loss of income, family breakdown, school exclusion, removal of children from the family home, and even incarceration, are missed in a bid to reduce short-term costs.

An anti-welfare rhetoric, as Thomas (2021) observes, has intensified in austerity Britain, where individuals claiming support are often framed as apathetic, shameful, or irresponsible. These pejorative configurations seep into the experiences of families navigating support systems, where parents of disabled children find themselves resisting deficit-based narratives that diminish their children's worth and humanity. Yet, such resistance occurs in the context of a neoliberal society that fosters enmity and indifference towards disabled people and their families (Thomas, 2021). The premise of scarcity, a feature created and perpetuated by neoliberal policies, exacerbates these challenges, creating an environment where access to essential resources and support is perpetually constrained. Parents lament that this scarcity forces them into cycles of advocacy and self-reliance, where their efforts to secure what should be basic entitlements are met with institutional suspicion and societal judgement. In this climate, the structural barriers faced by families are compounded by the ideological devaluation of their struggles, leaving many to confront not only the practical difficulties of care but also the stigma attached to seeking help.

In this context, the difference between value and cost is aptly illustrated by the following statistics from across England and Wales:

- As of August 2022, there were 1.4 million claimants in the UK in receipt of Carer's Allowance (a 4.2% rise on the previous year) (GOV.UK, 2023). This is a benefit which can be accessed by those who provide a minimum of 35 hours of care a week to a disabled child or adult, and who earn below the designated threshold of £151 per week. Although the weekly payment of £81.90 is a relatively paltry sum, it may well be that more effective support for families of autistic children would prevent the need for mothers (in particular) to work as full-time carers, thereby enabling them to maintain wage-work outside the family home, and to remain net contributors to public finances.

- A 2023 report commissioned by the Disabled Children's Partnership and published by Pro Bono Economics (Jemal & Kenley, 2023) found that in the previous year, councils had lost 96% of the SEND Tribunal cases brought by parents, at a cost of £60 million. This figure represents almost 10 000 SEND unit placements that might otherwise have been made available to children who needed them (Henshaw, 2023), a disjuncture which illustrates just how much resource could be preserved if professionals were to work more cooperatively with SEND parents, rather than actively working against them.

- Suspensions and exclusions increased by 20% in 2023/24, with the cost to the state over a lifetime for a single cohort of permanently excluded children being estimated at £1.6 billion (IPPR, 2024). Children with SEND were overrepresented in these findings, with those in receipt of EHCP/IDP being excluded at a rate of 0.7, relative to a rate of 0.2 for the non-SEND cohort (Pepper, 2024).

- A 2024 joint research study from the Institute for Public Policy Research, and education charity 'The Difference', found that

Black Caribbean children and children of dual heritage (Black Caribbean and White) were twice as likely, relative to their White counterparts, to be excluded from mainstream school in favour of Pupil Referral Units (PRUs) (White, 2024). This is significant because the cost of PRU places is considerably higher than those in mainstream settings. In 2019, it was reported that the average cost of providing a place at a PRU was £21,051. This was more than three times the average cost of a secondary school place (£5,771) and over four times the cost of a primary school place (£4,864) (GOV.UK, 2019).

- Furthermore, those attending PRUs have been found to be at increased risk of contact with the criminal justice system, at an early age, and are thereby more likely to become "entrenched in the system", a risk further exacerbated by the symptomatology of neurodisability (Kent et al., 2023).

- For those for whom contact with the criminal justice system does result in imprisonment, the average cost accrued to UK taxpayers was estimated, in 2022/23 to stand at £51,724 per prison place in England and Wales (Clark, 2024).

- Social care placements outside the family home are also associated with astronomical costs. A 2023 survey of councils by the Local Government Association quantified the number of individual placements costing in excess of £10 000 per week and found that this figure stood at 1,510 (rising from only 120 five years previously). The proportion of councils with at least one such placement was found to have increased from 23 per cent to 91 per cent over the same period. This increase has been attributed to price gouging by private providers who are positioned to exploit the shortage in available spaces (LGA, 2023).

These statistics demonstrate that, even from the perspective of the 'business case' used as a justification for gatekeeping resources, the current model of relying on mothers to internalise their trauma and to manage the many burdens they face with vanishingly little support is one which cannot be defended. As well as the strong moral argument for improving access to services for struggling families, there is also a simple financial argument for a 'stitch in time' approach which directs relatively minimal intervention to families in need *before* their challenges escalate to the point of the spiralling costs that we have outlined.

In short, while mental health provision, respite services, and financial support for community groups may not come cheap, all are entirely more efficient uses of resource than the reactive strategies currently relied upon by policymakers.

Short-term cost-cutting measures in support services lead to long-term financial and social crises. Investing in early intervention, through adequate SEND provision, mental health support, and family services, not only upholds dignity and prevents harm but also saves public funds by reducing exclusion, imprisonment, and emergency social care placements.

2. Reduce the number of barriers to referral and diagnosis

There is a clear consensus that early intervention is key to enabling autistic children to fulfil their potential, and yet the majority of our participants reported that their families had spent years on

NHS waiting lists for referrals and diagnoses. Commonly, this had resulted in their seeking out private healthcare, at great expense, further exacerbating the financial challenges associated with raising a child with additional needs.

In December 2023, the average wait for an autism diagnosis via the NHS was found to have hit 300 days "up 53% from 12 months prior" (Fagg and Woodhead, 2023) and significantly in excess of the NICE (National Institute for Health and Care Excellence) target of 91 days. Even this damning figure is liable to be an underestimate, since it does not necessarily take account of the time it takes to secure an initial referral onto the assessment pathway. Such delays also continue to be stratified along racial and gender lines, with girls receiving a diagnosis an average of six years later than boys (Thomas, 2022).

While it has proven difficult to find robust data detailing the exact disparity in diagnosis rates between Black and White children in the UK, the lack of clarity around this issue is telling in its own right. Furthermore, datasets from the USA provide a useful indication of the scale of the problem. Mandell et al. (2007) found that "*African-American children with autism were diagnosed an average of 1.4 years later than White children and spent eight more months in mental health treatment before being diagnosed*" with Black children being 2.6 times less likely to receive an autism diagnosis than White children (Mandell et al., 2007).

Unnecessary diagnostic delays generate further waste within the SEND system. As Brianna observed:

> *Just everything starting earlier you know. So [...] referrals made earlier... We're not waiting for Reception age to start referring because it takes years and then they can't access*

SEND schools or Resource Bases or any sort of additional help in Key Stage One. [In my local area in the Northwest of England] there's just been a massive influx of Resource Bases opening and they're saying, 'well, nobody's in Key Stage One because the referrals are not done on time'

Despite the insurmountable evidence that there is a genetic component to autism diagnoses, there are no mechanisms in place to fast-track assessments for children who have a sibling who has already been diagnosed. There is also little to no appetite to provide short-term specialist placements to children who may, ultimately, be able to return to a mainstream setting. Access to meaningful support and resources continues to be contingent on a diagnostic process which is attenuated and inefficient.

It's always gatekeepers, when really [...] it should be more accessible – Imogen

The nature of autism is such that diagnosis can only be arrived at via consensus among several different professionals. As detailed elsewhere, depending upon the age of the child, parents may have to work alongside a GP, Health Visitor, Teacher, SENCO/ALNCO, Paediatrician, Occupational Therapist, Speech Therapist, Child Psychologist, and Educational Psychologist, before a formal diagnosis can be issued. Many of these professionals will remain in the child's life thereafter, with a roster of appointments contributing to the 'practical burden' explored in Chapter 4.

…They need to engage with each other, so you don't have to keep repeating yourself in every single appointment. It would be helpful to see the same person more than once, [...] people you can contact easily in-between

appointments. They need to prioritise appointments for kids with complex needs.

We contend that a more efficient and humane use of resources would be to ensure effective collaboration between all the agencies involved in the child's life by providing parents with access to 'Multidisciplinary Team Meetings' prior to diagnosis, something which our respondents and participants consistently cited as a small change that would make an enormous difference to their quality of life.

The sense of helplessness, and the immense psychological burden facing caregivers whose children are stuck in this diagnostic limbo needs to be prioritised among professionals, with a focus on interim resources and support, and an earlier acknowledgement of parental concerns. Redirecting investment away from wasteful initiatives which demonise and even criminalise autistic children – particularly those within the Black community – toward support groups for parents and multidisciplinary assessments involving teams of healthcare, education, and social care professionals is a vitally important step toward dismantling barriers to referral and diagnosis.

Delay is costly. Autism diagnosis delays place undue strain on families and create inefficiencies within the SEND system. A more effective approach to reducing long-term costs and ensuring timely access to education and care would prioritise early referral, fast-track assessments for vulnerable children, and integrate multidisciplinary teams to support families *before* diagnosis.

3. Improve training and professional competency across the SEND system

Redirecting resources and prioritising early intervention would also facilitate more effective and comprehensive training at all levels of the SEND system. As autism diagnoses steadily increase, existing models of healthcare, education, and social care systems are being exposed as unfit for purpose, and this necessitates a root-and-branch re-evaluation of their functions and limitations. Key to this is more extensive mandatory training in the field of autism.

As Michelle Peter observed, with reference to the interviews she conducted for Global Child and Maternal Health's Black Child SEND (Wheeler et al., 2024) report:

> [What is needed is] an injection of funding into the services that are required. I think it would also be a big push for education of professionals because one thing that came up in our interviews was that there are a lot of teachers who are going through their PGCE who don't have any training in SEND. That to me is mind blowing. I don't understand how you can only be taught about how to educate children who are developing neurotypically.

Our participants reported being alarmed by the lack of specific expertise among teaching staff and SENCOs/ALNCOs supporting their autistic children:

> The guy had no education training… so he's not a teacher. Not even at all. And he was saying 'I don't think he is [autistic]'. What do you know…? Also, SENCOs are often not

people with specific qualifications. They're just somebody who put their hand up in the staff room to say they'll be the SENCO, and that's part of the issue. They're not equipped and they don't feel supported – Imogen

This lack of specialised training is also an issue among health and social care professionals, and our research has indicated that it can lead to very difficult and traumatic encounters for Black mothers of autistic children:

I just found it hard because the speech therapist at the sessions, she would say, 'Oh yeah, you know, you've got to focus and get down to your child and speak with them, connect with them.' And I will try and explain to her, you know, in a corner 'I think he's on the autistic spectrum. I can't get him to focus on something. I'll get down on my knees. And he'll wander off to the next thing.' I felt that they didn't understand what I'm saying. 'I think he's on the spectrum… I can't engage with him that way […] That made me feel just not understood and not listened to… […] it was just feeling like I wasn't heard… which made me feel like a bad parent – Matilda

We assert that all professionals who are liable to encounter autistic children as part of their practice must, as standard, be extensively trained in, and assessed on their knowledge of, all facets of neurodiversity. This must include instruction in the common comorbidities associated with an autism diagnosis, the complexities of the sensory diet, and the manifestations of both 'low' and 'high support' presentations. Police officers, paramedics, dentists, ophthalmologists, and anyone employed in the fields of healthcare, education, or social care should be mandated to attend training sessions which are designed and delivered by those with direct knowledge of living with, or raising a child, on the spectrum. Crucially, to be effective, this training must take, as its foundational assumption, an understanding of the enormous diversity in the lived experiences of autistic children and their advocates, and of the impact of intersectional identities linked with gender and race.

Train to include, not exclude. A lack of autism-specific training across healthcare, education, and social care leaves autistic children, and their mothers, unsupported and misunderstood. Comprehensive, mandatory training designed by those with lived experience is essential to creating a neuro-affirming and culturally competent, effective, and equitable SEND system.

4. Embed anti-racism in professional practice

As Pellerone and Bellomo (2015, p. 63) state "racial identity and disability are separate issues, but both contribute to the multiple social identities that influence the outcomes of life". As such, when viewed through an intersectional lens, the failures of the current system are experienced even more acutely by those who are already contending with the impact of being racially minoritised. Targeting such communities with additional investment, at key stages of child development, would likely lead to improved outcomes not just for these groups but also for society as a whole.

As our participants stated:

> [W]]hen you come at it from a wider angle, it's already painting the picture of the limited resources available for children with additional needs. It's appalling to see the national budget that [the government] sets for these things. It's appalling to see their own understanding of children with additional needs. [...] So, you know raising that general awareness in the first place, but really kind of landing on those additional barriers that are there with Black mothers, how those further impact on them… being at the bottom of every measurable scale – Toni

> I mean, we know that there's a massive problem with all autistic children and access and support, but just that additional layer of how race does affect a lot of us and how dismissive teachers and healthcare professionals can be… It's just raising that awareness, so people understand where they're going wrong – Brianna

> We know that race and ethnicity matter. We know that race factors into all of these different areas, but they'll try and downplay it. They'll try and sugarcoat it, and I think that's something that we really need to push for more … [a]nd I guess one of the things that I dislike the most about the structures in society is that they don't consider our culture. They don't consider our race. They don't consider our ethnicity when they're thinking about things – Stacy-Ann

Acknowledging both the breadth and the specificity of Black women's experiences is key to ensuring that their needs and the needs of their families can be understood and met. As such, an approach to offering support which is rooted in 'colour evasiveness' and which, therefore, denies and obfuscates difference, is doomed to fail. In the simplest of terms, if professionals claim not to 'see race' then they will also fail to see 'racialisation' and 'racism' and the effects that these phenomena have on Black families.

Improving the SEND system is then, in part, a story of improved recruitment, retention, and representation from racially minoritised communities. Certainly, several of our research participants shared with us how much they had appreciated interacting with professionals who shared key elements of their identity.

> *We finally got a Black social worker and for me that changed the game because she was on it. She was listening. She understood. She was taking notes. She was making sure that anything that I asked of her was being done and she was feeding back to me. She was very, very efficient and doing her job. And I worry that, heaven forbid, if she leaves then we're back to square one again* – Stacy-Ann

> *Private paediatrician was brilliant and she was a Black woman with a specialist interest and expertise in autism. Dealing with her has been well worth it* – Survey respondent, anonymous.

> *I spoke to a clearly African sister, going by the name, and she was very, very, concerned about my son, so she was writing letters left, right, and centre. […] It was [a much higher] level of compassion and concern… and understanding. And following up promptly. She played her part […] but the next bit wasn't down to her* – Toni

> *My most recent (paediatrician) has been a godsend. I believe this is because she is Black, was non-judgemental, and tried*

to understand us as Black people – Survey respondent, anonymous.

However, these insights were shared advisedly, often with the cautionary note that 'skinfolk are not always kinfolk' and that, for as long as the 'deficit mindset' holds sway, racially minoritised professionals are socialised into a system which can see them internalise White supremacy to the detriment of the Black families they are employed to support.

Per Sareeta:

> *What we're talking about is White supremacy – an ideology, rather than an individual [and] the way in which it operates is just so insidious. [...My son] got a new teacher, the first Black teacher in the entire school [...] but she was an agent of institutional racism. She was awful [...] because all of her peers are White, and so she would perpetuate that racial oppression constantly.*

Reyss Wheeler shared her experience of undertaking advocacy work with Black women who felt similarly to Sareeta:

> *And so a woman who is at her wit's end, who is literally begging this institution for support via somebody that looks like her, who she, in her mind, might subconsciously feel safe with, then learns that she's not safe.*

Thus, as important as inclusive hiring practices may be, they are only one element of a holistic commitment to cultural competence. Another entails embedding anti-racism into professional practice through an explicit engagement with the harmful stereotypes, and structural barriers, that impact the treatment received by Black mothers attempting to advocate for their autistic children.

In the words of our participants:

> *First of all, they should have attended to and checked their unconscious bias before engaging with me and my family. These workers need to be multicultural and experienced […]. Assessments should look at how we experience the world being Black and disabled and/or caring for a disabled child. The support for Black disabled children is poor –* Survey respondent, anonymous

> *Actually engage with the tenets of anti-discriminatory practice. Genuinely care about combatting discrimination. Entirely change the structure and culture of their whole departments and systems. Have embedded service user participation panels. Employ a diverse (including neurodiverse) workforce. […] Gain an in depth understanding of what it's like to be a Black mother in the UK. Consider the soul-destroying pain and trauma that inadequate care causes –* Survey respondent, anonymous

> *That's the wonderful thing about British racism, right? Is that it's so invisible but felt ever so presently by people who experience it –* Reyss Wheeler

> *It's really important to recognize the different structures at play that perpetuate some of the challenges you have when you have a child that has special needs or when you think about our race, or you think about our gender –* Stacy-Ann

The thread that unites these observations is the call for systemic change, including culturally competent leadership at the very highest levels of practice and policymaking. As much as our research has indicated that motivated and empathic individuals, who demonstrate a commitment to the well-being of the families they support, can make a huge difference to the lives of struggling mothers, ultimately a reliance on individual 'out-performance' in an otherwise fractured system leads to inconsistencies in service provision and increased vulnerability for families who lose their advocates to the vagaries of staff turnover.

> It's a lottery of who you deal with. It is an absolute lottery. You get someone who doesn't care about their job and has no integrity, and then you get that person who absolutely just goes above and beyond and doesn't even get paid enough for all the hard work that they do. – Linda

As Reyss Wheeler observes, there is a lack of accountability built into the SEND system in which professionals are, by design, held at arm's length from their own local communities.

> The kind of the work that I do is all about being inside the very community that can hold me to account. And so, because practitioners usually don't, they don't even work in their areas [...] if you do something wrong, nobody can find you, right? So they have such a barrier, such a sterilisation between them and the people that they work with. And I would say remove that. I would say employ people that live and work in [the locality].

Building on this suggestion, we argue that those in leadership roles must render themselves accessible and answerable to their local community, with regular 'open surgeries', consultations, and 'you asked… we did' sessions, both in-person and virtual, in which SEND parents are provided with a forum to express their views and to ensure that they are being taken into consideration. Disaggregating such services and opportunities so that they can be tailored for specific communities should be welcomed as a means to ensure their efficacy, and assumptions of homogeneity among SEND parents should be interrogated for racial bias or colour evasiveness. In other words, there should be an explicit acknowledgement that racial minoritisation impacts the experiences of those working to advocate for their children and that this needs to be reflected in the provision available for those with intersectional identities. Recruitment to leadership roles should be predicated on an appreciation of this lived experience and the value that it can add in crafting and executing policy, and sustainable change should be targeted at the highest levels of decision-making.

Racial identity and disability, while distinct, intersect to shape the multiple social identities that profoundly influence life outcomes (Pellerone and Bellomo, 2015). These intersections demonstrate the importance of embedding anti-racism into leadership practices, enabling professionals to move beyond reductive labels like 'hard to reach'. Such labels often obscure systemic failings and the resulting trauma experienced by Black families.

In the words of Reyss Wheeler, who is a freelance social worker and advocate, as well as a representative of Global Child and Maternal Health:

> I've never found a Black family hard to reach. Same way I've never found a White one hard to reach. I've worked with mothers who were drug addicted, mothers who are working, mothers who have 100% of their time available for their children […] and I've never found any family hard to reach. There's always a way to connect with people. […] I will make sure I'm culturally competent for whatever family I'm dealing with. If that means I need to understand certain things about how they practise, I will know all of that so

I can reference that in conversation and allow that to kind of let the barriers break down [...]. That's the power and the point of social work. The most powerful thing about social work is the self. How do you use yourself in spaces? How do you use your ability to connect? [...] People who are struggling to find ways to reach Black families are not trying hard enough.

Michelle Peter, in outlining the findings of a series of practitioner interviews conducted for 'Black Child SEND' (Wheeler et al., 2024) reinforced this need for professionals working with Black families to contextualise their own perception of what it might mean to be 'hard to reach':

There will be a lot of families who will have disengaged from services based on their previous or prior experience with maybe that system, or other professional systems and areas where they have been just trampled over effectively. And so this is another person coming in into their space and treating them in a certain way and they have low expectations of those people. But rather than meet those families there and try to understand them and try to understand how to overcome those 'barriers' [...] I think a lot of professionals see them as 'You're just difficult. This is a difficult family and we don't have the time to engage with you'. And that I think is predominantly what the interviews told us. [...] It just really highlighted that actually if you don't understand the families that you're speaking to, you can never support them in a way that is going to benefit them.

We contend that labelling Black families as being 'hard to reach' is an extension of a tendency toward what 'Black Mothers Matter' founder, Sonah Paton, referred to as *"pathologising race"*. In other words, assigning blame to the Black community for its own over-representation in experiences of marginalisation, rather than identifying and addressing systemic racism and its consequences.

This speaks to a broader culture of parent blaming and shaming that perpetuates the oppression of SEND parents in general, and Black mothers of autistic children in particular. Dismantling this culture necessitates respecting and prioritising parental insight and expertise.

Intersectionality matters. Systemic racism and inadequate SEND provision compound the struggles of Black mothers advocating for their autistic children. Representation through inclusive hiring is not enough; professionals must be trained in anti-racism and cultural competence. Services must be responsive to the lived experiences of racially minoritised families. The narrative of 'hard-to-reach' families must be rejected in favour of addressing the systemic failures that exclude them.

5. Acknowledge and invest in parental expertise

Almost without exception, the mothers who participated in this project shared with us that they had recognised their children's challenges long before professionals had formally acknowledged them. Despite perceptions that Black families are intrinsically reluctant to seek out a diagnosis, our research indicates that attempts by Black mothers to articulate very real concerns regarding their child's development are often met with dismissal, or (implied) accusations of parental deficit. Sonah Paton summarised the experiences that Black mothers had shared with her regarding their attempts to secure an autism diagnosis for their children:

They feel like their concerns are being dismissed. The feeling for these women is that [they're being told] 'maybe they're a bit naughty' and you know, 'maybe it's home life. Is it a bit chaotic? What's home life like, you know?

This observation was consistent with the views expressed by our research participants, who stated that this dismissive attitude remained pervasive among the professionals they encountered, even after the diagnostic process:

'We are the educators and you are the parents'… and this is creating, like, this real… separation. Let's make this a collaboration. [I just want someone to say] 'This is your child – you know your child. You know what their needs are….' I think ultimately that in order for a lot of this to work, parents whose children have special education needs, are going to be the experts and are going to be the people that should be paid to put this idea and vision together because it's not going to happen with people who are sitting on the periphery. […] We are best placed to understand what our children need – Sareeta

I didn't feel like I was able to have that communication […] where they're actually listening and taking it seriously. I felt like I was being looked at in a patronising way. 'Oh, it's your first child'… Basically parent blaming like I'm the problem – Toni

Believe that the parent usually knows their child a lot more than you do. Understand that if they are asking for support [...] it is to benefit everyone, not just the parent. Prioritise children's mental health [issues] caused by not having their needs met – Survey respondent, anonymous

I feel like parental instinct should very much be taken into consideration when going through the pre diagnosis and assessment process. Instead of being generalised, I feel every case should be treated on an individual basis and parents should be empowered at such a vulnerable time. Professionals across the board should access autism training as diagnoses are increasing rapidly year by year – Survey respondent, anonymous

They will have to change their entire culture. They'd have to genuinely have regard for the intuition that Black mothers have about their own children. [...] It's got to be structured where they hear what you're saying because they don't... and they just want to be the expert. Parents are dismissed as having no expertise – Imogen

For a great many autistic children, the most effective advocate of all is the mother who is raising them. The necessity to gather information across every facet of a child's development, combined with an encyclopaedic knowledge of that child's individual needs and an unswerving devotion to ensuring that those needs are met, cannot be matched by even the best informed or most experienced practitioner. In failing to adequately foreground parental perspectives in all aspects of the SEND system, professionals risk generating a waste of resources even more egregious than the vast sums of money lost to bureaucracy and profiteering, namely the squandered opportunity simply to leverage the expertise of parents.

Our participants (including the co-researchers), shared experiences of being referred to 'parenting courses' following their child's diagnosis. Generally, post-diagnostic workshops relating to issues such as sensory processing, speech and language delay, or social communication challenges were initially found to be a useful means by which to demystify what autism might mean both for a newly diagnosed child and for their caregivers. However, once it became apparent that these relatively rudimentary workshops constituted the only support that would be made available to their families, participants grew increasingly frustrated at the sense that these referrals were being deployed as a means to gatekeep access to more specialised or individuated appointments, or that they were underpinned by assumptions of parental deficit.

For instance, Imogen shared that she had contacted CAMHS in response to her son expressing suicidal ideation:

> *And then I was sent on, like two or three fucking parenting courses by whatever it was before CAMHS – you know, the Primary Child Mental Health Team* – Imogen

At the time of writing, Claire has spent almost three years trying to secure Sensory Integration Therapy (via Occupational Health) to investigate Mae's daily self-injurious meltdowns, as well as specialist Speech and Language Therapy to unpack her Gestalt Language Processing. No such support has been forthcoming, with a recent invitation to attend 'Regulate to Participate' (a workshop that would have been the sixth such course that Claire has completed since Mae's diagnosis) being indicative of just how little regard there is within the SEND system, for the expertise that many parents have already accrued.

Our participants had all gone to extraordinary lengths to educate themselves about their child's needs and to develop strategies to meet them, with social media offering them access to a wealth of information more detailed and specific than that which had been available to them via the generic parenting courses to which they had previously been referred. For many, sifting through this information and working tirelessly to apply it to their own families is one of the most time-consuming aspects of the 'practical burden' detailed in Chapter 4.

As has been illustrated throughout this book, the trade-off for the intense commitment that SEND parents must demonstrate in advocating for their children is an increased risk of isolation, burnout, and physical and mental health problems on the part of these caregivers. Again, as our research has demonstrated, Black mothers of autistic children experience a multidimensional version of this assault on well-being. As such, parental support groups are a vital resource.

The data we gathered strongly indicated that engaging with organisations run for, and by, parents, had been an overwhelmingly more positive experience for our participants than had interacting with professionals.

> *Parenting groups both in person and online have been the best thing for me – I have learnt most of what I know on how to best support my son, how to manage school and the Local Authority, how to go through the mounds of*

paperwork without crumbling, how to juggle working and appointments – Survey respondent, anonymous.

Parenting Groups have mainly been my only support. They have provided me with training and meeting other parents – Survey respondent, anonymous.

Autism Family support groups were great! I was no longer alone, receiving tips, advice & support from others living in a similar situation – Survey respondent, anonymous.

The parenting groups have been extremely helpful in providing space to freely speak with people who understand the daily struggles & my child's behaviour – Survey respondent, anonymous.

What I found extremely helpful was a parenting group from the community that empowered and supported me to apply for the EHCP assessment as well as DLA [...]. Being able to meet other parents at their coffee mornings going through similar challenges made me feel like I'm not alone, and it's not my fault – Survey respondent, anonymous

Mel also views her local parenting forum, which she accesses through a WhatsApp and Facebook group, as a lifeline. She has accessed the group to better understand how to contact members of the local authority's SEND team, stay informed about SEND-friendly events, and share or receive legal tips related to SEND support.

With this in mind, as soon as our research was complete, we created a WhatsApp group that our participants have since used to keep in touch with one another. Within this group, these othered mothers share a 'shorthand' of intersectional identity and experience, and they have used it to offer one another the kind of support that professionals have so often failed to give them. They have proofread one another's appeal letters and complaints, shared links to helpful articles and resources, offered a sounding board at times of peak anxiety and distress, buoyed one another with their 'wins', and held space for themselves and each other in a way which has been unique and powerful. In this context, these women – so accustomed to their often thankless role of 'Community Mother' – have built a community of their own, one in which understanding and empathy abound, occasional displays of 'anger' are treated as defensible and righteous, and 'strength' and 'resilience' are acknowledged but never valorised at the expense of vulnerability.

We deliberately have not gathered feedback from our participants regarding the impact that this WhatsApp group has had on their lives, albeit – anecdotally – it has certainly been a boon to our own well-being. We reasoned that since our participants have already given us so much, it was vitally important to offer something to them that was a true gesture of reciprocity, quite apart from the initial research project. What we can share, however, is the joy that comes from being able to celebrate our children, in all their wonder and complexity, alongside others whose experience of parenting closely matches our own. This has proven to be a much-needed counterweight to the psychological burden of constantly being called upon by professionals to 'describe your child on their worst day' in order to secure even the most basic resource on their behalf.

However, significant caveats apply when praising the work of parenting groups. Firstly, a great many are run as charities, once again depending on the exceptional contributions of time and effort made by a relatively small number of individuals. Moreover, these groups are often providing an ad hoc solution to a challenge which ought to be the responsibility of policymakers and professionals. For instance, the Chief Executive of 'AP Cymru', a South Wales-based charity which Claire accesses for 'Autism Friendly' events, frequently shares an anecdote about contacting CAMHS to report that her family was in crisis and being reassured to hear that a local charity would be well-placed to help her. Unfortunately for her, the contact details with which she was then provided were for... 'AP Cymru', the organisation she herself had founded.

Similarly, in Mel's local North London borough, the webpage for the government-funded SENDIASS (Special Educational Needs and Disability Information, Advice, and Support Service) has been 'under construction' since 2020, with its 'Where to go for support' link leading only to the local Parent Forum.

Parenting groups are also often relatively free of moderation or are overseen by parents themselves rather than by trained practitioners and, as much as we have emphasised the importance of respecting parental intuition and agency, this lack of regulation is potentially problematic. It can expose such spaces to the threat of misinformation with, for example, long-debunked 'anti-vax' conspiracies, fad diets, or ableist ABA (Applied Behaviour Analysis) 'strategies' finding purchase among parents who are understandably desperate for answers to improve their lives, and the lives of their children.

In acknowledging the vital role these spaces can play in the lives of mothers raising autistic children, we argue that sustained government investment into groups run by and for parents should include training that community leaders can undertake, as well as training that they themselves can help to design and deliver. This would offer a means to combine the passion and lived experience of SEND parents, with the forms of expertise and access that only professionals can realistically provide.

Parents are experts, not problems. Black mothers of autistic children are too often dismissed by professionals who undervalue their expertise and intuition. True systemic change requires professionals collaborating with parents as part of the same team by embedding their knowledge into policy and practice rather than positioning them as passive recipients of care.

6. Empower the community to create genuine transformation

The recommendations we have outlined are envisaged as mechanisms for ensuring that consistent, practical, and easily accessible support can be made available to all SEND parents, and specifically to Black mothers raising autistic children. We contend that the imperative to reduce waste, redirect resources, minimise delays for referrals and diagnoses, and harness parental expertise can all be combined into one truly transformational initiative designed to effect change from within the community.

In truth, we cannot take credit for the suggestion itself because it has emerged directly from our research participants, who in response to the interview question *"If you could wave a magic wand to create the perfect service provision in your area (healthcare, education, and social care) for Black mothers raising autistic children, what would it look like?"* proposed variations on the same theme: a 'One-Stop Shop' of culturally competent resources, designed with and for Black families and made available via a locally-based Wellbeing and Advocacy Hub.

During her interview, Linda outlined the need for a space in which services and appointments would be both specialised and easily accessible:

> *So, if I think of all the types of professionals that you want involved with your child: Educational Psychologists, Nutritionist, Occupational Therapist with sensory processing as a specialty, Speech and Language, of course, various play therapies, Mental health support for child and for parent…. and I think having something specific because […] even me as a layperson I know that the proportion of autistic or neurodivergent children coming from Black and minority families [is high]. So, you need to make something specific because we're being let down as a massive group. So, I think that having something where there is a dedicated space […] would be so amazing*

Toni's proposal took the form of a Community and Information Hub that would combine peer and professional support:

> *[H]ave different community groups coming to speak as well as statutory services coming to share with parents what their rights are… And through that, parents can feel a sense of peer support. It provides a place to share their concerns but also a place to tap into whatever services they can access.*

She added that this would represent *"a safer space for Black mothers"* where issues pertaining to race and its impact on the parenting journey could be freely discussed:

When I'm in, you know 'Everyone Space', I feel like there are a number of elephants in the room… like 'let's not talk about that here' kind of thing. When we're talking about the challenges our children go through, it's no secret that there is a school to prison pipeline when it comes to Black children, and particularly Black boys, so I'm sorry but my concerns as a mother of a Black son are going to be different, from a different angle, with different lens, and different viewpoint. And, of course, race then becomes an issue and not everyone is comfortable to, allow, facilitate, enable, contribute to, support that kind of conversation. So let's just have these spaces where we can more comfortably have these conversations.

Similarly, Imogen highlighted the intrinsic importance of providing Black women with the space to support and elevate one another:

We need to be around people who can empathise and see how painful and difficult and hard and constant [it is], and what the impact of that is […]. There's just an innate value in being seen and heard and held up by other Black women

Sareeta also emphasised the need for communities to be empowered to create their own support systems, in ways that reflect their values and experiences:

Making spaces in which we feel valued and welcomed and also supported. Making spaces which are holistic, which are nurturing, which are supportive, which are embedded and rooted in community values, and which seek to uplift rather than this constantly criticising [us] and picking [us] apart. [… Spaces where we can] work cohesively as a community

*in order to achieve these aims and objectives and also keep
each other accountable*

In proposing the creation of such a Hub, our participants have
effectively posited a solution to the multiplicity of burdens elu-
cidated throughout this book, one which would foster the conditions for increased 'social', 'navigational' and 'resistant' capital
(Morgan and Stahmer, 2020, p. 25) for othered mothers.

While many of the challenges facing Black mothers of autistic
children are intractable, the impact that these issues have on the
health and well-being of caregivers can be significantly minimised if the correct interventions are put in place.

Black mothers raising autistic children have
identified the need for a locally-based Wellbeing
and Advocacy Hub, a One-Stop Shop, for
culturally competent support, professional
services, and peer-led guidance. Initiatives such as community
expertise and holistic, empowering spaces can alleviate
systemic burdens, reduce isolation, and create meaningful,
lasting change.

Physical burden

Since it has been established that certain health conditions are
particularly prevalent among Black women, especially those with
complex caring responsibilities, the Wellbeing and Advocacy
Hub would include a clinic offering check-ups and drop-in information sessions pertaining to health challenges such as autoimmune disorders, hypertension, and heart disease. Here the advice

and support would be tailored to take meaningful account of physiological and cultural markers that are too often overlooked, or pathologised, by healthcare professionals.

Sonah Paton, in referring to her organisation's work in the field of Black maternal mortality, offers a working example of why this more nuanced understanding of physical health is so desperately needed:

> [Take] gestational diabetes. You know how many Black women are, at an early stage, supported to manage that through diet? Not as many as White women, because all of the diet, and nutritional information, is based on a very Eurocentric way of eating [and] if that just doesn't fit, there's no other option for you. Then you're straight to […] a drug intervention.

There is a clear parallel here with the generic advice issued to SEND parents whose children have ARFID (Avoidant/Restrictive Food Intake Disorder), a common comorbidity with autism.

A greater focus on cultural competency and anti-racism in these areas would enable professionals themselves to unearth and overcome their own biases concerning why Black women and their families are overrepresented in (yet often underdiagnosed with) certain illnesses and would open up the possibility of ethical and effective research, conducted in partnership with the community. Crucially, we argue that professionals need to commit to learning *with* and *from* Black families, and that the only way that this can be achieved is to move beyond colour evasiveness into the co-creation of specialised services and provision.

Psychological burden

The weight of the psychological burden faced by Black mothers of autistic children is vast and complex, and we do not propose that this is a matter that can be resolved using a simple 'one size fits all' approach. However, as discussed at length in Chapter 3, there is a pressing need to explore the relationship between the psychological demands of caregiving and the physiological effects in which they manifest. With so much of the physical 'weathering' (Geronimus, 2023) that othered mothers face being linked with an outsized experience of stress and anxiety, any service designed to support Black women and their families must treat mental health as a key priority.

We propose that the Hub would offer free access to individual, group, and family therapies conducted by Black practitioners. This recommendation is based on the experiences of both co-researchers, who have benefitted enormously from seeking out psychological support from Black female therapists, and from our participants, including Sareeta who summarised the value of such an experience in her own life:

> [My Counsellor and I] sort of brainstormed together and she was also a Black woman, so she really got the institutional racism and what I was experiencing and how it was deeply affecting me. So, I would say that support and therapy from somebody you can relate to and who can also understand you is really important.

Again, we do not wish to suggest that Black women can only be 'reached' by Black professionals, nor do we believe that being racially minoritised affords practitioners an automatic defence against the conditioning impacts of White supremacy. However, our research has spoken to the damage inflicted by the tropes of Black womanhood, as well as the value in being able to air and dismantle them in safe spaces where their effects can be understood. This capacity for resistance is likely to be most effectively honed in collaboration among women with comparable lived experiences.

As Matilda stated:

> *[It would be] amazing to have something like that for Black mothers of autistic children, and maybe with the holistic approach as well. Talk, talk, talk, talk. For your child and yourself, that would be amazing.*

Cultural burden

We have been at pains to problematise the assertion that 'ignorance' and ableism in the Black community are the principal barriers to diagnosis and support for autistic children and their families. However, we do concede that the "cultural dissonance" to which Gemegah (2022, p. 11) refers remains a significant issue, particularly where there is a clash between parenting styles, spiritual beliefs, and cultural expectations concerning 'respect' and 'compliance'.

Although we maintain that it is racism – institutional and internalised – that fuels a culture of hostility toward Black families, both within and beyond the SEND system, we see intrinsic value in a Hub which brings together different members of the community to provide information about autism and its symptomatology and to help build and consolidate awareness and acceptance.

Such a space would be open to parents, extended family, as well as community and spiritual leaders and the focus would be on well-being and celebration. As Stacy-Ann stated:

> I'd love there to be, you know, more courses… more events and things that kind of bring families together. I don't know if there's enough of that in my community.

This would also help to address the desire, expressed by many of our participants and by the co-researchers, to find ways to proudly immerse our children in their Black identity, even when their comprehension of some of the abstract ideas associated with race and racialisation is potentially limited. Countering the negative messages awaiting them in the classroom, and in the wider community, with celebrations of themselves, their families, and their place in the world, would help to equip Black autistic children with the pride and self-belief denied to them by existing systemic frameworks in health, education, and social care.

Furthermore, just as in the case of the healthcare practitioners participating in the Hub, these cultural celebrations would also function as centres for research design and practice, informing improved training and increased competency among professionals working with Black families.

Practical burden

In outlining her vision for a Wellbeing and Advocacy Hub, Linda spoke directly to the ways in which its existence would alleviate the immense practical burden she faces in managing the needs of her autistic child:

[Y]ou could go to this Hub, or this Centre, and know 'ok, well actually… there's going to be a SLT drop-in, there's going to be an OT specialist, there's an Educational Psychologist, financial advisor, someone just to help out with admin… that can just do the DLA form [with you]. That's a weight off your shoulders and you can dedicate that time and have that capacity. […] Like a One-Stop-Shop… that would be a dream service.

We propose combining these drop-in services with access to affordable specialised childcare, giving mothers the opportunity to take real advantage of the services on offer. In addition, there would be support in writing complaints, appeals, and Tribunal cases, a 'lending library' of books and sensory equipment, areas where children and parents could take part in physical activities to promote fitness, and events designed for (neurotypical) siblings of autistic children to build friendships and enjoy respite. Extended opening hours, interpreter/translation services, and online access to information repositories and appointments would render the facilities as accessible as possible and ensure that they could meet the needs of a large number of families.

It would also offer the ideal location for affiliated Parent Groups to meet and for caregivers to advise and support one another, albeit with engagement from professionals across the various dimensions of the SEND system.

Temporal burden

The practical and emotional support on offer through a Wellbeing and Advocacy Hub of this kind would go some considerable way to relieving othered mothers of the burden of time poverty, which all our participants pointed to as being a source of considerable anxiety.

As Linda intimated, this would enable an increased focus on self-care, emotional well-being, and physical fitness, all of which are currently compromised for mothers whose energies are dedicated overwhelmingly to the practical tasks of meeting their children's needs.

Moreover, the fear of how our autistic children will fare without us is one of which we cannot be divested, but being given the means to prepare as effectively as possible for that inevitability is vital. For this reason, the Hub would offer advice services in respect of will-writing, trust funds, and adult social care.

More broadly, the change that these Hubs would effect within the community, and within the training and practice of professionals in healthcare, education, and social care would foster a cultural shift in understandings of autism which would reduce hostility, and increase awareness and empathy. In so doing, these services would facilitate not just improved outcomes for individual families, but also the systemic transformation needed to make society safer and more equitable for autistic children and adults.

In our concluding chapter, we revisit our initial research questions and explore how the findings and recommendations that they have informed can provide the basis for further research and reinforce the case for the establishment of a network of Wellbeing and Advocacy Hubs for Black autistic children and their families.

6
Conclusions

In many respects, we envisaged this project as an exercise in *resistance through vulnerability*. Faced as we are with the constant pressure to 'perform resilience' in all aspects of our lives, we challenged ourselves to be transparent about the limitations in our capacity and to provide our fellow othered mothers with an opportunity to do the same. In so doing, we have laid ourselves bare as women, as parents, and as academics, even as we remain conscious that to do so is to invite criticism and scrutiny on all three counts.

In drawing our work to a conclusion, we seek to anticipate some of these critiques and to create a blueprint for extending the scope and scale of our research. Although we believe that our work so far represents the beginning of an important and long overdue conversation, we also acknowledge its limitations. Given the opportunity to undertake the research again, we would hope for a larger sample size for the quantitative survey, one which would help us to source perspectives and experiences from the whole of the UK, rather than just England and Wales. We are also conscious that, in general, respondents are more likely to provide feedback on their experience of engaging a given service if their opinions are either very favourable, or very negative, with those who are reasonably satisfied being understandably less motivated to respond to a survey or to participate in an interview. This is an issue which has the potential to impact any form of self-selection among research participants and is part of the reason that qualitative data cannot be straightforwardly generalised.

We welcome those who have engaged with this research to replicate, or adapt, our approach to take account of alternative perspectives on parenting and autism, and would hope that such projects might include:

- Studies which foreground the experiences of Black mothers in the LGBTQIA+ community
- Longitudinal studies which unpack the 'temporal burden' in more depth by exploring how autistic children's support needs evolve over time and the impact that this has on their caregivers
- Research which explores fatherhood roles in the context of raising autistic children in the Black community
- Cross-cultural research which explores how Black mothers raising autistic children in, for example, the USA encounter and navigate the multiplicity of burdens outlined throughout our research
- Explicitly policy-oriented research, which focuses on streamlining autism assessments for racially minoritised children
- Research which expands upon the objectives of this book to develop culturally tailored autism interventions for racially minoritised children and their families

What we do maintain, however, is that the decision to design our project around the specific experiences of Black mothers raising autistic children, rather than to introduce a comparative element with, for example, the experiences of White women, has been vindicated by the research findings. The multiplicity of burdens framework has enabled us to demonstrate that Black women face a unique confluence of challenges, in advocating for their autistic children, and that this merits extensive reflection in its own right.

In light of this conviction, the concluding chapter revisits the research questions that underpinned the study, providing a summary of the data we have gathered and of the recommendations we have outlined.

What are the common experiences of Black mothers in the UK raising autistic children?

The initial phase of our collective autoethnography surfaced extensive commonalities in our own experiences. Even as accomplished women, with successful careers, reasonable economic means, supportive husbands, and any number of other forms of social advantage and cultural capital, we found that professionals' responses to our intersectional identities, linked with race, gender, and proximity to disability, were fundamentally undermining our ability to advocate for our children and to tend to our own basic well-being.

Motivated to explore the extent to which other Black mothers of autistic children had endured experiences that resonated with our own, we expanded the project to incorporate participant research. Our 26 survey responses, 9 semi-structured interviews, and 2 focus groups (featuring 3 participants each) revealed a clear pattern of common experiences, with gaslighting, racial profiling and gatekeeping cited by participants as key factors in their reduced physical and psychological health outcomes. Participants also revealed common experiences of time poverty, and difficulties in securing support for their children. We systematised these concerns into the multiplicity of burdens framework and explored the damaging and unsustainable 'privatisation of trauma' in which it resulted.

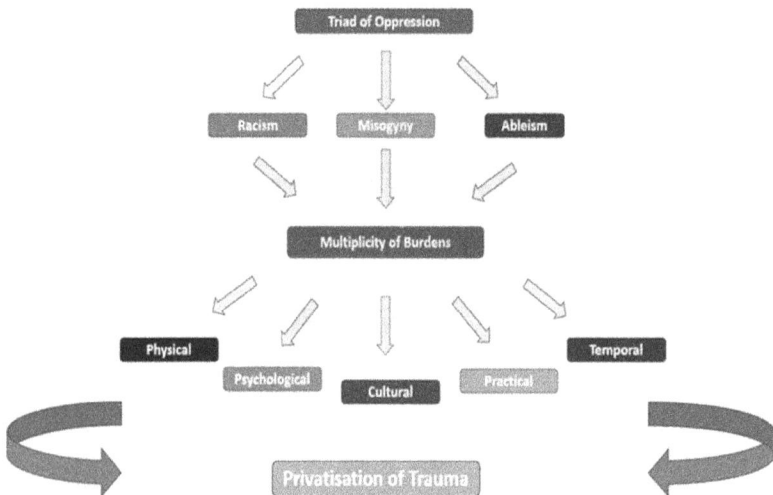

Figure 14: Multiplicity of burdens leading to privatisation of trauma

How do Black mothers perceive and navigate the UK healthcare, education and social care services for their autistic children?

Participants characterised their engagement with the professionals involved in their children's care as a 'constant fight' in a 'broken system'. They highlighted lengthy delays, 'lost' or rejected referrals, redundant appointments, rapid staff turnover, generic/inappropriate advice, defensive responses from professionals, and a culture of 'parent blame' as some of the barriers they faced in attempting to meet the needs of their families.

Both the parents and the practitioners whom we interviewed asserted that the structural flaws in this underfunded and over-stretched system perpetuated a 'deficit mindset' in which even the most desperate pleas for help fail to pass muster, and in which resource is a lottery, and accountability a fallacy.

These are failings not just of practice, but of policy, with successive damning reports into the SEND system and its many flaws yet to advance discussion beyond the governmental fixation with 'value for money', even as politicians of all stripes continue to shamelessly fuel narratives of opportunistic parents seeking to 'game the system' so that their children can secure additional time in exams, or free taxi rides to school. The notion that, in the words of the current Conservative Party leader Kemi Badenoch, an autism diagnosis "offers economic advantages and protections" which, by implication, are being erroneously sought (Courea, 2024) and secured on behalf of undeserving children, is insidious and divisive, and arguably intended to undermine empathy and understanding for disabled children and their families.

Equally, the Labour Party's insistence on cleaving to the uncritical assertion that the best way to reset the "broken relationship between schools and families" (Adams and Stacey, 2024) is by tackling pupil absences continues to vilify, and potentially criminalise, parents whose children's needs are simply not being met in the school environment, resulting in valid grounds for school refusal. Treating the adage that 'school is the best place for children' as aspirational, rather than factual, would inform policies that pursued mainstream 'inclusion' only where this is a viable option for a child, not where it is (often incorrectly) assumed to be the cheaper alternative. It would also necessitate an acknowledgement of the extent to which schools can be extremely hostile environments for autistic children, particularly those with racially minoritised identities. However, Labour's proposed roster of radical cuts to disability support (Watson, 2025) speaks to a profoundly flawed understanding of the failings of the current SEND system. It also appears to offer confirmation that an ill-advised obsession with austerity for its own sake continues to predominate on both sides of the political aisle. These policy directions are deeply rooted in a neoliberal ideology that individualises responsibility and frames systemic failures as personal shortcomings. Within this framework, trauma, particularly that experienced by racially minoritised and disabled families, is privatised, stripped of context, and rendered invisible in public discourse. Rather than addressing the structural conditions that produce school refusal, poor mental health, and educational disengagement, parents are left to absorb the blame, often without support, resources, or recognition.

Our participants drew attention to the impact of this hostility on their attempts to advocate for their children, and they also detailed equivalent experiences in the arenas of health and social care. Their perception was that these systems functioned, not in service of disabled children and their families, but in service of a cost-cutting agenda in which a proliferation in autism diagnoses is treated as a threat to the bottom line, rather than an opportunity to reconfigure provision in a transformative and sustainable manner.

How do Black mothers perceive the role of racial and/or gender identity in their experiences?

It is clear that all SEND parents are contending with the ramifications of this failed policy agenda, and its impact on practice among healthcare, education, and social care professionals. However, our participants drew attention to the ways in which their intersectional identity as Black women compounded these struggles.

Overwhelmingly, there was a sense that institutionalised racism was informing:

- professionals' assumptions of parental deficit ('Lazy/Irresponsible Black Woman'),
- defensive responses on the part of professionals to reasonable requests from parents ('Angry Black Woman), or
- professionals' failure to recognise the extent and urgency of a family's needs ('Strong Black Woman').

These racist tropes were also weaponised against Black children, who were characterised as 'aggressive', in the case of boys, or 'sassy' and 'disrespectful', in the case of girls. Adultification attributed intent and malice to behaviours which might otherwise have been correctly perceived as being consistent with autism symptomatology.

The internalisation of these tropes, as well as cultural pressures to overachieve, to keep one's own counsel, or to emulate parenting styles that emphasise compliance and respect, was found to further exacerbate the burdens facing Black mothers of autistic children.

Moreover, the lack of provision and support which could take account of the specific challenges of othered mothering contributed to feelings of failure, isolation, and anxiety, undermined "community cultural wealth" (Yosso, 2005), and exacerbated the racialised effects of physical and emotional weathering.

What specific recommendations do Black mothers have for improving healthcare, education, and social services for their autistic children?

As detailed in Chapter 5, the key recommendation that emerged from our participant and practitioner interviews was increased investment in the SEND system in general, and in culturally competent and anti-racist provision in particular.

While the predictable response to calls of this kind will be the contention that this resource simply does not exist and that additional funding cannot be made available, even a cursory audit of the existing system belies such a claim. Vast amounts of waste are generated by the austerity lens governing decisions concerning provision for disabled children. The implication often appears to be that since many of these children will not necessarily be positioned to contribute to the public coffers, when they reach adulthood, the emphasis must be on minimising the 'cost' that they can be expected to generate rather than on investing in a safe and comfortable future for them.

Quite apart from the moral argument that a society can most effectively be judged by how it treats its most vulnerable members, even a cursory fiscal review of the collapsing SEND system speaks to the urgent need for reform, and to the extent to which profiteering on the part of private providers has filled the vacuum that a short-termist focus on budget cuts has created.

This is why we posit a solution that can succeed both in cutting costs and in improving outcomes for Black autistic children and their families. We contend that the 'One Stop Shop' Wellbeing and Advocacy Hubs that we, inspired by our participants, have proposed in this book would empower local communities to build their own capacity for supporting children with additional needs.

They would co-create and deliver training for both parents and professionals and generate resources which could be repurposed and disseminated for the benefit of families across the country.

They would also function as centres of research, and as virtuous circles of transformation in which professionals and policymakers could improve their practice in conjunction with the communities that they exist to serve.

They would improve efficiency, streamline access to frontline services, and reduce the costs associated with lengthy waiting lists by providing the means to offer drop-in services and Multidisciplinary Team Meetings, even prior to an official diagnosis.

They would provide space for Black families to celebrate their autistic children, improving self-esteem, developing life skills, and subverting assumptions of deficit and failure currently projected onto those whose identities sit at the intersection between racialisation and disability.

The Wellbeing and Advocacy Hubs, though consciously tailored to meet the needs of Black families, would provide a blueprint for services and resources which could support any number of other groups. Given the structural failings consolidating disadvantage for, for example, children from socio-economically deprived backgrounds, children in the adoption and foster care systems, and children who have physical disabilities, creating a model for research, service provision, and capacity building would be a vital step toward transformation and equity across the board.

A word on further research

Within the scope of this project, we set out to identify the challenges faced by Black women in their attempts to navigate healthcare, education, and social care systems, on behalf of their autistic children. We also sought to platform these women's views on how those experiences could be improved.

The next stage of our research will entail a collaboration with the London-based organisation, Black SEN Mamas, whose founder, Marsha Martin, is currently developing a version of precisely the 'One-Stop-Shop' of anti-racist and culturally competent resources and support services for which our participants have so persuasively argued. Black SEN Mamas estimates that, across its digital platforms and in-person events, the organisation has already reached in excess of 4,000 mothers, with a great many

Black families having benefitted enormously from its burgeon-
ing advocacy activities. These include, but are not exclusive to,
funded therapies, opportunities for socialising, and access to
networks of Black professionals and practitioners from across
healthcare, education and social care. As this organisation looks
to expand the breadth and depth of such provision, we will
review, quantify, and evaluate its emancipatory impact with a
view to creating a scalable blueprint for Wellbeing and Advocacy
Hubs across the UK.

In particular, we intend to campaign for funding and support for
local, regional, and national centres which can serve the needs of
Black mothers of autistic children who are based outside London,
with an initial pilot project envisaged for South Wales, where
Claire is based. In addition, we plan to develop post-diagnostic
resources and 'toolkits' that act as a practical guide for families
navigating the period after an autism diagnosis. These resources
will centre the experiences of Black autistic children and their
caregivers, offering clear explanations of post-diagnostic processes, common needs, and suggested next steps. Drawing on
the expertise of racially minoritised practitioners, including educators, social workers, occupational therapists, speech and language therapists, music therapists, and others, these guides will
provide culturally responsive, accessible support that addresses
both the systemic gaps in care and the everyday realities faced
by Black families.

In this, and all future research, we will proudly embrace our own
positionality and vulnerability and eschew expectations that
academic credibility necessitates sterility and 'emotional distance' from the research topic or from participants. We will take

this stand mindful of, and grateful for, the words of Stacy-Ann who stated:

> I'm being interviewed by a Black woman, so that already makes me feel good. But I'm being interviewed by a Black woman who has a child that has autism, so that in itself makes me feel like I'm not going to be portrayed by someone who doesn't really understand my situation.

We will continue to develop our own agenda for building a community of resistance among those with marginalised, inter-sectional, identities, and we will foster relationships of trust and respect with other academics and organisations concerned with empowering Black women and their families.

At all times, our research will be replicable and rigorous, just as this project has been. Where others might see 'confirmation bias', we see the basic courtesy of taking Black women at their word when they share their own experiences. Where others may look to the minutiae of methodology as a way to generate 'plausible deniability' in the face of institutionalised racism, we choose a commitment to societal transformation, over an uncritical defer-ence to outmoded academic convention.

We call on fellow researchers to join us in demonstrating the extent to which current SEND provision is hampered by myopia and waste, and we would welcome a project which can provide a more detailed, fully costed, breakdown of where resources can be redirected to serve the interests of those who need them most.

Finally, to the healthcare, education, and social care profession-als – those in practice and those in training – who have engaged with this research, we have one simple plea: prioritise your humanity. At times of overwork and underfunding, it can be easy to underestimate how much difference you can make to a family in crisis. It can be tempting to abdicate this responsibility, to seek refuge in the rationalisation that 'the system' is not fit for purpose, and to take comfort in the biases and prejudices that enable you to tolerate the suffering of others. In those moments, we ask that you remember the stories of Matilda, Ayesha, Laura, Imogen, Sareeta, Brianna, Toni, Stacy-Ann, and Linda, who have willingly shared with you some of their gravest challenges and lowest moments, so that you might be inspired to advocate for othered mothers.

Remember too, Mae and Sam and the power that you have to make the world a safer place for children like them.

Recommended projects

Reflective essays and critical analysis

- Intersectionality in Practice: Write an essay analysing how intersectionality operates in the experiences of Black mothers raising autistic children. Discuss how gender, race, and disability interact to shape their realities.

- Counter-Narratives and Voice: Reflect on the importance of counter-narratives in qualitative research. How does centring the voices of marginalised communities challenge dominant narratives in education, healthcare, and social care?

- Policy Review: Choose a specific policy related to education, social care, or healthcare that impacts Black mothers of autistic children. Critically evaluate its effectiveness and propose evidence-based reforms.

Group discussions and debates

- *Medical vs. Social models of disability*: Facilitate a discussion or debate contrasting these models. Which model better serves Black mothers navigating autism support systems?

- *Cultural competency in practice*: Work in groups to create a training resource for professionals (teachers, social workers, or healthcare providers) on improving cultural competency when working with Black families of autistic children.

Case study analysis

- *Applying CRT*: Analyse a real or fictional case study using Critical Race Theory. Discuss how structural inequalities manifest in the lived experiences of the subject.

- *Multiplicity of burdens*: Analyse a real or fictional case study and examine the different types of burdens (physical, psychological, cultural, practical, and temporal). How can policies and practices be improved to alleviate these burdens?

Creative and community-based projects

- *Advocacy project*: Develop a campaign to raise awareness about the intersection of race, gender, and disability in autism support services. Include social media strategies, community engagement, and policy advocacy.

- *Autoethnography assignment*: Students write their own short autoethnographic pieces reflecting on their positionality and biases concerning race, gender, and disability.

- *Oral histories:* Conduct an interview with a parent or caregiver of an autistic child from a marginalised background. Analyse their narrative using key concepts from the book.

References

Adams, R. and Stacey, K. (2024)., Labour vows to tackle school absences and 'broken relationship' with families. *The Guardian*, Available at: www.theguardian.com/education/2024/jan/07/labour-vows-tackle-school-absences-broken-relationship-families. [Accessed 14 Oct. 2024].

Adhikari, E. D. (2023). Ethnography as a Research Methodology – A Critique. *Open Science Framework*. Available at: https://doi.org/10.35542/osf.io/t86uc [Accessed 16 Dec. 2024].

Adkins, A. (2022). The Cycle of Care: How Generational Caregiving Disproportionately Impacts Black Women. *Generations*. Available at: https://generations.asaging.org/how-generational-caregiving-impacts-black-women [Accessed 16 Dec. 2024].

Akbar, S., & Woods, K. (2020). 'Understanding Pakistani parents' experience of having a child with special educational needs and disability (SEND) in England'. *European Journal of Special Needs Education*, 35(5), 663–678. https://doi.org/10.1080/08856257.2020.1748428

American Psychiatric Association. (2013). *Diagnostic and statistical manual of mental disorders: DSM-5*. American psychiatric association.

American Psychiatric Association. (2022). *Diagnostic and statistical manual of mental disorders. Fifth Edition, Text Revision (DSM-5-TR)*, Available at: https://doi.org/10.1176/appi.books.9780890425787 [Accessed 14 Dec. 2024].

Anderson-Chavarria, M. (2021). The autism predicament: models of autism and their impact on autistic identity. *Disability and Society*, 37(8), pp. 1321–1341. Available at: www.tandfonline.com/doi/abs/10.1080/09687599.2021.1877117

Angell, A. M., Empey, A. and Zuckerman, K. E. (2018). A review of diagnosis and service disparities among children with autism from racial and ethnic minority groups in the United States. *International Review of Research in Developmental Disabilities*, 55, pp. 145–180. Available at: https://doi.org/10.1016/bs.irrdd.2018.08.003

Autry, R. (2020). Sociology's Race Problem: Urban ethnographers do harm in speaking for Black communities. *Aeon Essays*. Available at: https://aeon.co/essays/urban-ethnographers-do-harm-in-speaking-for-black-communities [Accessed 13 Dec. 2024].

Banks, A. (2024). The problem with Black Resiliency. *Duke Global Health Institute*, Available at: https://globalhealth.duke.edu/news/problem-black-resiliency [Accessed 26 Mar. 2025].

Begeer, S., El Bouk, S., Boussaid, W., Terwogt M. M. and Koot, H. M. (2009). Underdiagnosis and referral bias of autism in ethnic minorities. *Autism and Developmental Disorders*, 39(1): pp.142–148. Available at: https://doi.org/10.1007/s10803-008-0611-5

Berenguer, C., Miranda, A., Colomer, C., Baixauli, I. and Roselló, B. (2018). Contribution of theory of mind, executive functioning, and pragmatics to socialization behaviors of children with high-functioning autism. *Autism and Developmental Disorders*, 48, pp.430–441. Available at: https://doi.org/10.1007/s10 803-017-3349-0

Berghs, M., Atkin, K., Graham, H., Hatton, C., and Thomas, C. (2016). Scoping models and theories of disability, Implications for public health research of models and theories of disability: A scoping study and evidence synthesis. *NIHR Journals Library*. Available at: www.ncbi. nom.gov/books/NBK378951/

Bishop, M. (2020). "Don't tell me what to do" encountering colonialism in the academy and pushing back with Indigeneous autoethnography, *International Journal of Qualitative Studies in Education* 34(5): pp.367–378. Available at: https://doi.org/10.1080/09518398.2020.1761475

'Black Mothers Matter' Available at: https://www.blackmother smatter.org/ [Accessed 20 Mar. 2024].

Blair, I. V., Judd, C. M., Sadler, M. S. and Jenkins, C. (2002). The role of Afrocentric features in person perception: judging by features and categories. *Journal of Personality and Social Psychology*, 83(1), pp. 5–25. Available at: https://doi.org/10.1037/0022-3514.83.1.5

Bourdieu, P. (1973). *Cultural Reproduction and Social Reproduction*. Oxfordshire, UK, Routledge.

Bromley, J., Hare, D. J., Davison, K. and Emerson, E. (2004). Mothers supporting their children with autistic spectrum disorders: Social support, mental health status and satisfaction with services. *Autism*, 8(4), pp. 409–423. Available at: https://doi.org/10.1177/1362361304047224

Brown, J. E. H. (2023). The Stories We Tell or Omit: How Ethnographic (In)Attention can Obscure Structural Racism in the Anthropology of Mental Healthcare. *Medicine Anthropology Theory*, 10(1), pp.1–15. Available at: https://doi.org/10.17157/mat.10.1.6890

Brown, Z. (2021). Tweet regarding resilience. Available at: https://x.com/zandashe/status/1394805726825099279?lang=en [Accessed 13 Dec. 2024].

Bruner J. (1986). *Actual minds, possible worlds*. Cambridge, MA: Harvard University Press.

Carr, M. (2023). The Motherhood Penalty. *Henley Business School News*. Available at: www.henley.ac.uk/news/2023/the-motherh ood-penalty [Accessed 16 Dec. 2024].

Carter, P. L. (2003). "Black" cultural capital, status positioning, and schooling conflicts for low-income African American youth. *Social Problems* 50(1), 136–155. https://doi.org/10.1525/sp.2003.50.1.136

Chang H. (2013). Individual and collaborative autoethnography as method: A social scientist's perspective. In S. Holman Jones, T.

E. Adams, C. Ellis (Eds.), *Handbook of autoethnography* (pp. 107–122). Walnut Creek, CA: Left Coast Press.

Clark, D. (2024). Expenditure per prison place in England and Wales. Available at: www.statista.com/statistics/1202172/cost-per-prisoner-england-and-wales/#statisticContainer [Accessed 17 Nov. 2024].

Clauser, P., Ding, Y., Chen, E. C., Cho, S.-J., Wang, C., & Hwang, J. (2020). Parenting styles, parenting stress, and behavioral outcomes in children with autism. *School Psychology International*, 42(1), 33–56. https://doi.org/10.1177/0143034320971675

Collier, A. K., and Smith-Johnson, D. (2024). How Stress Affects Black Women and Tips for How to Manage. *Healthline*. Available at: www.healthline.com/health/stress-and-black-women#:~:text=And%20when%20stress%20is%20not,higher%20rates%20than%20white%20women [Accessed 14 Dec. 2024].

Collins, P. H. (2000). *Black Feminist Thought: Knowledge, Consciousness, and the Politics of Empowerment*. 2nd ed. New York, NY: Routledge.

Collins, P. H. (2022). *Black Feminist thought: Knowledge, consciousness, and the politics of empowerment (30th anniversary edition)*. New York, NY: Routledge.

Collins, P. H., da Silva, E. C. G., Ergun, E., Furseth, I., Bond, K. D. and Martínez-Palacios, J. (2021). Intersectionality as Critical Social Theory: Intersectionality as Critical Social Theory. *Contemporary Political Theory*, 20(3), pp.690–725. Duke University Press. Available at: https://doi.org/10.1057/s41296-021-00490-0

Cooper, H. (2020). *Critical Disability Studies and the Disabled Child: Unsettling Distinctions*. UK: Routledge.

Courea, E. (2024). Badenoch criticised for pamphlet's 'stigmatising' remarks on autism. *The Guardian*. Available at: www.theguardian.com/politics/2024/oct/14/kemi-badenoch-conservative-leadership-autism-campaign-pamphlet [Accessed 14 Dec. 2024].

Crenshaw, K. (1989). Demarginalizing the Intersection of Race and Sex: A Black Feminist Critique of Antidiscrimination Doctrine, Feminist Theory, and Antiracist Politics. *University of Chicago Legal Forum*, pp. 139–167.

Dabanah, S., Shaia, W. E., Campion, K. and Nicholas, H. M. (2018). We had to keep pushing: Caregivers' perspectives on autism screening and referral practices of Black children in Primary Care. *Intellectual Developmental Disabilities*, 56(5), pp. 321–336. Available at: https://doi.org/10.1352/1934-9556.5.321

Dabanah, S., Kim, I. and Shaia, W. E. (2021). I am so fearful for him: a mixed-methods exploration of stress among caregivers of Black children with autism. *International Journal of Developmental Disabilities*, 68(5), pp. 658–670. Available at: https://doi.org/10.1080/20473869.2020.1870418

Davis, L. J. (1995). *Enforcing Normalcy: Disability, Deafness, and the Body*. London and New York: Verso.

Davis, J. L. and Manago, B. (2016). Motherhood and associative moral stigma: The moral double bind. *Stigma and Health*, 1(2), pp. 72–86. Available at: https://doi.org/10.1037/sah0000019

Delgado, R. and Stefancic, J. (2017). *Critical Race Theory (Third Edition): An Introduction*. New York: New York University Press.

Dillon, S. (2012). Possessed by death: The neoliberal carceral state, black feminism, and the afterlife of slavery, *Radical History Review*, 112: 113–125.

Dunham, Y., Stepanova, E. V. Dotsch, R. and Todorov, A. (2015). The development of race-based perceptual categorization: skin color dominates early category judgements. *Developmental Science: 5*. Available at: https://static1.squarespace.com/static/5595b648e4b0e7f9efabeef3/t/559b0c3ce4b0167e53043a77/1436224572698/the-development-of-race-based-perceptual-categorization.pdf

Eberhardt, J. L., Goff, P. A., Purdie, V. J. and Davies, P. G. (2004). Seeing Black: race, crime, and visual processing. *Journal of*

Personality and Social Psychology, 87(6), pp. 876–893. Available at: https://doi.org/10.1037/0022-3514.87.6.87

Edwards, J. (2021). Ethical Autoethnography: Is it Possible? *International Journal of Qualitative Methods*, 20, pp. 1–6. Available at: https://doi.org/10.1177/1609406921995306

Ellis, C. (2007). Telling secrets, revealing lives: Relational ethics in research with intimate others. *Qualitative Inquiry*, 13(1), pp. 3–29. Available at: https://doi.org/10.1177/1077800406294947

Enna Global. (2022). Why is Autism Considered a Spectrum? What it Actually Looks Like. Available at: https://enna.org/why-is-autism-considered-a-spectrum-what-it-actually-looks-like/ [Accessed 3 Sep. 2024].

Ennis-Cole, D. (2019). *Seeing Autism through Parents' Feedback, Sketchnotes, Technology, and Evidence-based Practice.* Springer, Cham. Available at: https://doi.org/10.1007/978-3-030-15374-8_2

Evans, T. (2015). Street-level bureaucracy, management and the corrupted world of service. *European Journal of Social Work*, 19(5): pp.602–615. Available at: https://doi.org/10.1080/13691457.2015.1084274.

Evans-Winters, V. E. (2019). *Black Feminism in Qualitative Inquiry: A Mosaic for Writing Our Daughter's Body.* London: Routledge.

Fagg, J., and Woodhead, L. (2023). Autism diagnosis wait times hit 300 days – NHS data. [Online] BBC News. Available at: www.bbc.co.uk/news/uk-england-67713838 [Accessed on 14 Dec. 2024].

Fox, F., Aabe, N., Turner, K., Redwood, S. and Rai, D. (2017). It was like walking without knowing where I was going: A qualitative study of autism in a UK Somali migrant community. *Journal of Autism and Developmental Disorders*, 47(2), pp.305–315.

Frank, A. W. (2016). Truth telling, companionship, and witness: An agenda for narrative ethics. *Hastings Center Report*, 46(3), 17–21. https://doi.org/10.1002/hast.591

Ferguson, L. and Hollingsworth, D. (2024). Autism and Parental Blame Project Blamed Instead of Helped How parents of autistic children experience parental blame when they approach. Available at: https://10.1177/0143034320971675 [Accessed 1 Dec. 2024]

Fyre, J. (2020). On the Frontlines at Work and at Home: The Disproportionate Economic Effects of the Coronavirus Pandemic on Women of Color. Avaible at: www.americanprogress.org/article/frontlines-work-home/ [Accessed 16 Dec. 2024].

Galea, A. M., Qui, W. and Duarte-Guterman, P., (2018). Beyond Sex Differences: Short and Long-term implications of Motherhood on Women's Health. *Current Opinion in Physiology*, 6, 82–88. Available at: https://doi.org/10.1016/j.cophys.2018.06.003Get rightsand content

Gemegah, E. (2022). An intersectional approach to Black parents' experiences of autism in the UK. *PhD thesis*. University of Warwick. http://webcat.warwick.ac.uk/record=b3851679

Geronimus, A. T. (2023). *Weathering: The Extraordinary Stress of Ordinary Life on the Body in an Unjust Society*, London, UK: Virago Press.

Global Child and Maternal Health. (2024). Our Mission and Values. *Global Child and Maternal Health*. Available at: https://globalblackmaternalhealth.org/our-mission-and-values/ [Accessed 14 Oct. 2024].

Goodley, D. (2014). *Dis/ability Studies: Theorising Disablism and Ableism*. Abingdon: Routledge.

GOV. UK. (2019). Expenditure by Local Authorities and Schools on Education, Children's and Young People's Services in England. Available at: https://assets.publishing.service.gov.uk/media/5e15f75540f0b65dc85c671e/LA_and_school_expenditure_2018-19_Text.pdf [Accessed 14 Dec. 2024].

GOV. UK. (2023). DWP benefits statistics Available at: www.gov.uk/government/statistics/dwp-benefits-statistics-february-2023/dwp-benefits-statistics-february-2023#health-disability-and-care [Accessed 14 Oct. 2024].

Green, M. and Malcolm, C. (2023). Degrees of change: The promise of anti-racist assessment. *Frontiers of Sociology*, (8). Available at: https://doi.org/10.3389/fsoc.2023.972036

Grinker, R. R. (2020). Autism, "Stigma," Disability: A Shifting Historical Terrain. *Current Anthropology*, 61(S21). Available at: https://doi.org/10.1086/705748

Guy-Shetfall, B. (1995). *Words of Fire: An anthology of African American Feminist Thought*, New York, NY: The New Press.

Hagiwara, N., Kashy, D. A. and Cesario, J. (2012). The independent effects of skin tone and facial features on Whites' affective reactions to Blacks. *Journal Of Experimental Social Psychology*, 48, pp. 892–898. Available at: https://doi.org/10.1016/j.jesp.2012.02.001

Hamilton, P. (2020). *Black Mothers and Attachment Parenting: A Black Feminist Analysis of Intensive Mothering in Britain and Canada*. GB: Bristol University Press.

Hankivsky, O. and Grace, D. (2015). *Intersectionality-Based Policy Analysis Framework*. Vancouver: Institute for Intersectionality Research and Policy, Simon Fraser University.

Heer, K., Rose, J. and Larkin, M. (2012). Understanding the experience and needs of South Asian families caring for a child with learning disabilities in the United Kingdom: An experiential-contextual framework. *Disability and Society*, 27(7), pp. 949–963. Available at: https://doi.org/10.1080/09687599.2012.699276

Henshaw, P. (2023). Councils lose 96% of SEND tribunals – at a cost of £60m. *Headteacher Update*, Available at: https://www.headteacher-update.com/content/news/councils-lose-96-of-send-tribunals-at-a-cost-of-60m/ [Accessed 14 Nov. 2024].

Hernández-Saca, D. and Cannon, M. A. (2019). Interrogating dis-ability epistemologies: towards collective dis/ability intersectional emotional, affective and spiritual autoethnographies for healing, *International Journal of Qualitative Studies in Education*, 32(3), pp. 243–262. Available at: https://doi.org/10 .1080/09518398.2019.1576944

Hill, R. B. (2004). Institutional racism in child welfare. *Race and Society*, 7(1), pp. 17–33.

Holman, J. S. (2005). Autoethnography: Making the personal political. In: N. K. Denzin and Y. S. Lincoln, eds., *The Sage handbook of qualitative research (Third Edition)*, pp.763–791. London: Sage.

House of Commons Women and Equalities Committee. (2023). Black maternal health: Third Report of Session 2022–23. Available at: https://committees.parliament.uk/publications/38989/documents/191706/default/ [Accessed 14 Dec. 2024].

Hughes, D., Rodriguez, J., Smith, E. P., Johnson, D. J., Stevenson, H. C. and Spicer, P. (2006). Parents' ethnic-racial socialization practices: a review of research and directions for future study. *Dev Psychol*, 42(5), pp. 747–770. Available at: https://doi.org/10.1037/0012-1649.42.5.747. PMID: 16953684.

IPPR (Institute for Public Policy Research). (2024). Revealed: School exclusions and suspensions rise by a fifth last year, finds new report. Available at: www.ippr.org/media-office/revealed-school-exclusions-and-suspensions-rise-by-a-fifth-last-year-finds-new-report [Accessed 14 Oct. 2024].

Jegatheesan, B., Miller, P. J. and Fowler, S. A. (2010). Autism from a religious perspective: A study of parental beliefs in South Asian Muslim immigrant families. *Focus on Autism and other Developmental Disabilities*, 25(2), pp. 98–109. Available at: https://doi.org/10.1177/1088357610361344

Jegatheesan, B. and Witz, K. (2013). An ethnographic study on religion, spirituality, and maternal influence on sibling relationships in a Muslim family with a child with autism. *Review of Disability*

Studies, 9(1). Available at: https://rdsjournal.org/index.php/jour nal/article/view/68

Jemal, J. and Kenley, A. (2023). Wasting money, wasting potential: The cost of SEND tribunals. *pro Bono Economics*. Available at: www.probonoeconomics.com/Handlers/Download.ashx-?IDMF=93a69e8a-fe29-4567-b594-9ad874f1a348 [Accessed 23 Sep. 2024].

Joon, P., Kumar, A. and Parle, M. (2021). What is autism? *Pharmacological Report*, 73, pp.1255–1264. Available at: https://doi-org.libezproxy.open.ac.uk/10.1007/s43440-021-00244-0

Kapp, S. (2019). How social deficit models exacerbate the medical model: autism as case in point. *Autism Policy and Practice*, 2(1), pp. 3–28. Available at: https://openaccessautism.org/index.php/app/article/view/16

Karalis, N. T., Minematsu, A. and Bosca, N. (2023). Collective Autoethnography as a Transformative Narrative Methodology. *International Journal of Qualitative Methods*, 22, pp. 1–9. Available at: https://doi.org/10.1177/16094069231203944

Kent, H., Kirby, A., Hogarth, L., Leckie, G., Cornish, R. and Williams, H. (2023). School to prison pipelines: Associations between school exclusion, neurodisability and age of first conviction in male prisoners. *Forensic Science International: Mind and Law*, (4), pp.2666–3538. Available at: https://doi.org/10.1016/j.fsiml.2023.100123

Kildahl, A. N., Helverschou, S. B., Rysstad, A. L., Wigaard, E., Hellerud, J. M., Ludvigsen, L. B. and Howlin, P. (2021). Pathological demand avoidance in children and adolescents: A systematic review. *Autism*, 25(8): pp. 2162–2176. Available at: https://doi-org.libezproxy.open.ac.uk/10.1177/13623613211034382

King T. (2003). *The truth about stories: A Native narrative*. Toronto, Ontario, Canada: House of Anansi Press.

Kinouani, G. (2021). *Living While Black: The essential guide to overcoming racial trauma*. Great Britain: Ebury Press.

Kintzinger, R. (2021). Equity: What Model Should We Use When We Talk About Autism? *Canadian Journal of Autism Equity*, 1(1), pp. 32–39. Available at: https://doi.org/10.15173/cjae.v1i1.4982

Kleider, H. M., Cavrak, S. E., Knuycky, L. R. (2012). Looking like a criminal: stereotypical black facial features promote face source memory error. *Memory & Cognition*, 40, pp.1200–1213. Available at: https://doi.org/10.3758/s13421-012-0229-x

Knight, M., Bunch, K., Patel, R., Shakespeare, J., Kotnis, R., Kenyon, S. and Kurinczuk, J. J. eds. (2022). *MBRRACE-UK Saving Lives, Improving Mothers' Care Core report: Lessons Learned to Inform Maternity Care from the UK and Ireland Confidential Enquiries into Maternal Deaths and Morbidity 2010*. Available at: www.npeu.ox.ac.uk/assets/downlo ads/mbrrace-uk/reports/maternal-report-2022/MBRRACE-UK_Ma ternal_CORE_Report_2022_v10.pdf [Accessed 14 Dec. 2024].

Kvale, S. and Brinkmann, S. (2009). *InterViews: Learning the Craft of Qualitative Research Interviewing*. 2nd ed. Thousand Oaks, CA: Sage Publications.

Ladson-Billings, G. and Tate, W. F. (1995). Toward a critical race theory of education. *Teachers College Record*, 97(1), pp. 47–68. Available at: https://doi.org/10.1177/016146819509700104

Lai, M-C., Lombardo, M. V., Ruigrok, A. N., Chakrabarti, B., Auyeung, B. and Szatmari, P. (2016). MRC AIMS Consortium: Quantifying and exploring camouflaging in men and women with autism. *Autism*. Available at: https://doi.org/10.1177/1362361316671012

Lapadat, J. C. (2017). Ethics in Autoethnography and Collaborative Autoethnography. *Qualitative Inquiry*, 23(8), pp. 589–603. Available at: https://doi.org/10.1177/1077800417704462

LGA (Local Government Association). (2023). Children's social care placements costing £10,000-plus rise sharply in five years – new LGA analysis. *Local Government Association*. Available at: www. local.gov.uk/about/news/childrens-social-care-placements-cost ing-ps10000-plus-rise-sharply-five-years-new-lga [Accessed 14 Dec. 2024].

Liggins-Chambers, L. (2024). Shattering the Illusion of Invincibility in Black Women: Challenging "resilience" stereotypes in Black women. *Psychology Today*. Available at: www.psychologytoday.com/gb/contributors/lisa-liggins-chambers-phd [Accessed 26 Mar. 2025].

Link, B. G. and Phelan, J. C. (2001). Conceptualizing stigma. *Annual Review of Sociology*, 27, pp. 363–385. Available at: https://doi.org/10.1146/annurev.soc.27.1.363

Lipsky, M. (1980). *Street-Level Bureaucracy: Dilemmas of the Individual in Public Services*. New York, NY: Russell Sage Foundation.

Mandell, D. S., Ittenbach, R. F., Levy, S. E. and Pinto-Martin, J. A. (2007). Disparities in diagnoses received prior to a diagnosis of autism spectrum disorder. *J Autism Dev Disord*, 37(9), pp.1795–1802. Available at: https://doi.org/10.1007/s10803-006-0314-8

Martin, M. of Black SEN Mamas. (2024). @guardian newspaper has published my article!. Available at: www.instagram.com/p/C5Nm iEKlykO/?utm_source=ig_web_button_share_sheet&igsh=MzR lODBiNWFIZA== [Accessed 12 Oct. 2024].

Modirrousta, A. and Harris, Y. R. (2024). Parental strategies to promote theory of mind development in autistic children of color. *Frontiers in Psychology*, 15. Available at: www.frontiersin.org/journ als/psychology/articles/10.3389/fpsyg.2024.1347504 [Accessed 19 Mar. 2025].

Moore, A. (2020). Pathological demand avoidance: What and who are being pathologised and in whose interests? *Global Studies of Childhood*, 10(1), pp. 39–52. Available at: https://doi-org.libezpr oxy.open.ac.uk/10.1177/2043610619890070

Morgan, E. H. and Stahmer, A. C. (2020). Narratives of single, black mothers using cultural capital to access autism interventions in schools. *British Journal of Sociology of Education*, 42(1), pp. 48–65. Available at: https://doi.org/10.1080/01425692.2020.1861927 [Accessed 10 Dec. 2024].

Milton, D. (2018). Pathological Demand Avoidance (PDA) and alternative explanations: A critical overview (Conference Paper). Available at: https://kar.kent.ac.uk/67064/1/PDA%20and%20alternative%20explanations.pdf

Munroe, K., Hammond, L. and Cole. S. (2016). The experiences of African immigrant mothers living in the United Kingdom with a child diagnosed with an autism spectrum disorder: an interpretive phenomenological analysis. *Disability and Society*, 31(6), pp.798–819. Available at: https://doi.org/10.1080/09687599.2016.1200015

Nash, J. (2019). *Black Feminism Reimagined: After Intersectionality*. USA: Duke University Press.

Nazroo, J. Y., Bhui, K. S. and Rhodes, J. (2019). Where next for understanding race/ethnic inequalities in severe mental illness? Structural, interpersonal and institutional racism. *Sociology of Health & Illness*, 42(2), pp. 262–276. Available at: https://doi.org/10.1111/1467-9566.13001

Nickerson, R.S. (1998). Confirmation bias: A ubiquitous phenomenon in many guises. *Review of general psychology*, 2(2), pp.175–220.

OECD. Stat. (2020). Time use survey. Available at: https://stats.oecd.org/Index.aspx?DataSetCode=TIME_USE

Ofori, M. (2024). UK's black children 'face cultural barriers' in accessing help for autism and ADHD. *Guardian Newspaper*. Available at: https://www.theguardian.com/education/2024/mar/31/uk-black-children-cultural-barriers-accessing-help-autism-adhd [Accessed 11 Oct. 2024].

Onchee, Y., Schulze-Rath, R., Grafton, J., Hansen, K., Scholes, D., Reed, S. D. (2020). Adenomyosis incidence, prevalence and treatment: United States population-based study 2006-2015. *Am J Obstet Gynecol* 223(1):94.e1-94.e10. https://doi.org//10.1016/j.ajog.2020.01.016

Oyěwùmí, O. (1997). The Invention of Women: Making an African Sense of Western Gender Discourses. Minneapolis, USA: University of Minnesota Press.

Pellerone, M. and Bellomo, M. (2015). Racial identity and disability: the perception of the "other" in a group of Italian school teachers. *Procedia – Social and Behavioral Sciences*, 197, pp. 161–166.

Pepper, Y. (2024). Children with SEND 'at higher risk of exclusion'. *Children and Young Now*. Available at: www.cypnow.co.uk/content/news/children-with-send-at-higher-risk-of-exclusion/#:~:text=school%2Dage%20children.-,Children%20with%20SEND%20faced%20a%20higher%20exclusion%20rate%20than%20their,0.2%20for%20pupils%20without%20SEND [Accessed 17 Dec. 2024].

Peter, M. and Wheeler, R. (2022). The Black Maternity Experiences Survey: A Nationwide Study of Black Women's Experiences of Maternity Services in the United Kingdom. Available at: https://fivexmore.org/blackmereport [Accessed 13 Oct. 2024].

Peterson-Salahuddin, C. (2022). Posting back: Exploring Platformed Black Feminist Communities on Twitter and Instagram. *Social Media + Society*, 8(1). Available at: https://doi.org/10.1177/20563051211069051

Reaume, G. (2014). Understanding critical disability studies. *Canadian Medical Association Journal*, 186(16), pp.1248–1249. Available at: www.ncbi.nlm.nih.gov/pmc/articles/PMC4216267/#:~:text=Critical%20disability%20studies%20seek%20to,to%20the%20world%20around%20them

Reeve, D. (2008). *Negotiating Disability in Everyday Life: The Experience of Psycho-Emotional Disablism*. PhD Thesis. Lancaster: Lancaster University.

Riazi, K., Swain, M. G., Congly, S. E., Kaplan, G. G. and Shaheen, A. A. (2022). Race and Ethnicity in Non-Alcoholic Fatty Liver Disease (NAFLD): A Narrative Review. *Nutrients*, 14(21), p. 4556. Available at: https://doi.org/10.3390/nu14214556

Sharland, E. (2013). Where are they now? *Social Work and Social Sciences Review*, 16(2), pp. 7–19. Available at: https://doi.org/10.1921/swssr.v16i2.528

Singer, J. (1999). Why can't you be normal for once in your life? From a problem with no name to the emergence of a new category of difference. *Disability Discourse*, pp. 59–70.

Soley-Bori, M. (2023). Black women face the worst health inequalities in South London. Available at: https://www.kcl.ac.uk/news/black-women-face-the-worst-health-inequalities-in-south-london [Accessed 16 Dec. 2024].

Steen, J. (2024). Councillors alarmed by 'unbelievable' school suspension figures. *Islington Citizen*. Available at: www.islingtoncitizen.co.uk/2024/09/12/councillors-alarmed-unbelievable-school-suspension-figures/#:~:text=Suspension%20rates%20for%20secondary%20schools,suspensions%20but%20the%20%E2%80%9Cdisproportionality%E2%80%9D [Accessed 14 Oct. 2024].

Steinberg, S. B. (2017). Sharenting: Children's Privacy in the Age of Social Media. *Emory Law Journal*, 66(4), pp. 839–884, Available at: https://scholarlycommons.law.emory.edu/elj/vol66/iss4/2

Stepanova, E. V. and Strube, M. J. (2009). Making of a face: Role of facial physiognomy, skin tone, and color presentation mode in evaluations of racial typicality. *The Journal of Social Psychology*, 149(1), pp. 66–81. https://doi.org/10.3200/SOCP.149.1.66-81

Tepest, R. (2021). The Meaning of Diagnosis for Different Designations in Talking About Autism. *J Autism Dev Disord*, 51, p. 761. Available at: https://doi-org.libezproxy.open.ac.uk/10.1007/s10803-020-04584-3

Thomas, A. (2022). Autism diagnosis six years longer for girls, research finds. [Online] BBC News. Available at: www.bbc.co.uk/news/uk-wales-61553150 [Accessed 11 Dec. 2024].

Thomas, G. M. (2021). Dis-mantling stigma: Parenting disabled children in an age of 'neoliberal-ableism'. *The Sociological Review*, 69(2), pp. 451–467. Available at: https://doi-org.libezproxy.open.ac.uk/10.1177/0038026120963481 [Accessed 11 Dec. 2024].

Tolich, M. A. (2010). Critique of Current Practice: Ten Foundational Guidelines for Autoethnographers. *Qualitative Health Research*, 20(12), pp.1599–1610. Available at: https://doi.org/10.1177/1049732310376076

Toliver, S. R. (2022). *Recovering Black Storytelling in Qualitative Research: Endarkened Storywork*. Oxon, UK: Routledge.

Trade Union Congress (TUC). (2023). TUC: BME women 12 times more likely than men to be out of the labour market due to caring commitments. Available at: www.tuc.org.uk/news/tuc-bme-women-12-times-more-likely-men-be-out-labour-market-due-caring-commitments [Accessed 17 Dec. 2024].

Tyack, D. B. (1974). *The one best system: A history of American urban education*. Harvard, Cambridge: MA University Press. https://doi.org/10.2307/j.ctv136c61j

Vergès, F. (2019). A decolonial feminism, London, UK: Pluto Press.

Vivanti, G. (2020). Ask the Editor: What is the Most Appropriate Way to Talk about Individuals with a Diagnosis of Autism? *Journal of Autism and Developmental Disorders*, 50(2), pp. 691–693. https://doi.org/10.1007/s10803-019-04280-x .

Walker, M. and Wänke, M. (2017). Caring or daring? Exploring the impact of facial masculinity/femininity and gender category information on first impressions. *PLoS ONE*, 12(10), e0181306. Available at: https://doi.org/10.1371/journal.pone.0181306

Watson, I. (2025). Anxiety over welfare cuts rises among Labour MPs. *BBC News*, Available at: Anxiety over welfare cuts rises among Labour MPs – BBC News. [Accessed 26 Mar. 2024].

Wheeler, R., Agyepong, A., Benhura, C., Martin, M. and Peter M. (2024). Accessing special educational needs and disabilities (SEND) provision for Black and mixed Black heritage children: Lived experiences from parents and professionals living in South London (Executive summary). *Global Black Maternal Health*.

White, N. (2024). Pupil exclusions soar as Black Caribbean and Traveller students kicked out of school at higher rates. *Independent.* Available at: www.independent.co.uk/news/educat ion/education-news/school-exclusions-black-caribbean-travel ler-students-b2606996.html [Accessed 14 Dec. 2024].

Williams, T. (2021). Materialising tension: The laborious, woven documentation of a black, queer, crip body mind in Indira Allegra's documented disability. *CLA Journal,* 64(1), 82–99.

Wynter, S. (2002). 'A different kind of creature': Caribbean litera-ture, the Cyclops factor and the second poetics of the propter nos. In T. J. Reiss, eds., *Sisyphus and Eldorado: Magical and Other Realisms in Caribbean Literature. 2nd edn,* pp. 143–67. Trenton, NJ.

Yosso, T. J. (2005). Whose culture has capital? A critical race the-ory discussion of community cultural wealth, *Race Ethnicity and Education,* 8(1), 69–91. https://doi:10.1080/136133205200 0341006.

Yosso, T. J., Parker, L., Solórzano, D. G., & Lynn, M. (2004). Chapter 1: From Jim Crow to Affirmative Action and Back Again: A Critical Race Discussion of Racialized Rationales and Access to Higher Education. *Review of Research in Education,* 28(1), 1–25. https://doi.org/10.3102/0091732X028001001

Yu O, Schulze-Rath, R., Grafton, J., Hansen, K., Scholes, D. and Reed, SD. (2020). Adenomyosis incidence, prevalence and treatment: United States population-based study 2006–2015. *American Journal of Obstetrics & Gynecology,* 223(1), p. 94. e1-94.e10. Available at: https://doi.org/10.1016/j.ajog.2020.01.016

Index

www.ingramcontent.com/pod-product-compliance
Lightning Source LLC
Chambersburg PA
CBHW050335270326
41926CB00016B/3461